Hanif Kurei

Hanif
Kur

Hanif Kureishi
POSTCOLONIAL STORYTELLER

Kenneth C. Kaleta

 University of Texas Press, Austin

The publication of this book was assisted by a grant
from the Andrew W. Mellon Foundation

Kaleta, Kenneth C.
Hanif Kureishi : postcolonial storyteller / Kenneth C. Kaleta. —
1st University of Texas Press ed.
      p.   cm.
   Includes bibliographical references (p.) and index.
   ISBN 0-292-74332-7 (cloth : alk. paper). —ISBN 0-292-74333-5
(paper : alk. paper)
   1. Kureishi, Hanif—Criticism and interpretation.   2. Literature
and society—England—History—20th century.   3. National
characteristics, English, in literature.   4. Pluralism (Social
sciences) in literature.   5. London (England)—In literature.
6. Decolonization in literature.   7. South Asians in literature.
8. Immigrants in literature.   I. Title.
PR6061.U68Z7 1998
822'.914—dc21   97-16243

For Jane

Passage to more than India!
Are thy wings plumed indeed for such far flights?

—"Passage to India," in *Leaves of Grass* by Walt Whitman

CONTENTS

ACKNOWLEDGMENTS

This study has been accomplished with the assistance of my family, friends, colleagues, and members of the art and entertainment communities. I wish particularly to note my wife, Jane Green Kaleta; extenders Rudy and Casey; my friend Kevin Pawley; Candice McClain-Cranford, reader, and draft readers Matthew Bartley, Anthony D'Antonio, and Rosemary and William Salmon; Dean Toni Libro, colleagues, and support staff of the College of Communication and the administration, faculty, and staff of Rowan University; Edna Craffey; Mary Corliss, the New York Museum of Modern Art Film Archives; Sharon Dynak, Scribners Publishers; Amy Kaleta; Pat Richardson; Ali Hossaini, Jr.; the University of Texas Press staff, particularly copyeditor Mandy Woods; my mother, Wanda Kaleta, and my father, Charles Kaleta, Sr.; Honors Film Seminar students; and all my film students past, present, and future.

In the United Kingdom I acknowledge the generosity of Hanif Kureishi; producers Tim Bevan, Kevin Loader, and Chris Curling; actor Steven Mackintosh; director Roger Michell; Pippa Best at Zephyr Films; Mike Laye and Jacques Prayer; Vicki Challinor and the rest of the staff of the British Film Institute; Bobbie Mitchell in the BBC stills library; Leila Fahri at Condé Nast Publications; Juliette Dow and everyone else at Working Title Films; the staffs of the BBC Television Centre, the Mountbatten Hotel, and the Neal's Yard Desktop Publishing Studio; Luke Vinten at Faber and Faber; Ian Gollin at the *London Review of Books*; and the Royal Garden Hotel Business Centre.

Thank you.

introduction

LIQUID WINDOWS
Kureishi as Storyteller

Specific elements in narrative are recognized as "English": an English mystery, an English thriller, an English comedy. "Englishness" is an identifiable storytelling sensibility. Hanif Kureishi has inherited this rich literary tradition. And Kureishi is a "proper Englishman. Almost."

Exploration and the British Empire's resultant expansion around the world carried English literature far from London to Africa, Asia, Australia, and North America. Because of the British Empire, the untranslated literary works of English-language writers have enjoyed a uniquely worldwide readership. Today, although the sun has set on Great Britain's political empire, the influence on the rest of the world of the nineteenth century's colonial export of English-language writing remains significant.

England's literature is now uniquely part of other cultures in addition to that of Great Britain. In the United States, the study of English is now synonymous with the study of literature. In much of Canada, Australia, and India, too, a knowledge of English literature is regarded as essential to a general education. Certainly, the works of William Shakespeare, Percy Bysshe Shelley, and Charles Dickens—to name but a few in English literature—are now—in their original language—part of the world's artistic treasury.

This global familiarity with the writers of Great Britain has made their literary tradition a foundation of most of the English-speaking world's literatures. It has made English literature part of other cultural traditions, its literary tradition reflecting both the individuality and the nationalism of the culture that produces it.

But if English customs were imposed in the colonies, colonial cultures were also introduced into England. London, capital of a small, homogeneous island nation with the western world's most studied storytelling tradition, was the hub of the British Empire—a worldwide geographical network. Through the centuries of the empire, marriage and menu, government and economics, novels and afternoon tea all intertwined colonial cultures with England's in the capital city. It is noteworthy that the historical expansion of the empire is looking glass today to the mid-twentieth-century implosion of commonwealth immigration in London. Thus yesterday's colonials are now an indispensable part of contemporary London society.

South-bank London neighborhoods, for example, are inhabited by Indian families who have never seen Bombay's Marine Drive, but who instead travel the M25 fording the Thames. In London's East End, streets once linked most strongly with Jack the Ripper, the Elephant Man, the vicious Kray twins, and other legends of British history (and of the movies) are now more evocative of a bazaar in Karachi. A maze of stalls from which to select wedding saris neighbors the fish-and-chip shops along Brick Road, a main road in one of the heavily Asian-dominated boroughs. Nearby, Patrick Keiller's movie *London* is advertised on the window of a trendy Bengali take-away restaurant next door to a tired theater featuring a spectacular Hindu movie musical.

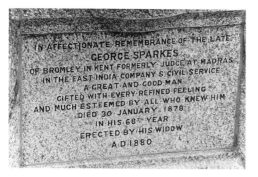

Fig. 1. Thames marker. This tablet, by the riverside in Chelsea, notes the historical role of Londoners in colonial politics. Like Hanif Kureishi, George Sparkes, the empire builder cited, was born in the London suburb of Bromley. (Photo by author.)

It is undeniable that the green isle that is forever Shakespeare's England now also belongs to Hanif Kureishi. In Kureishi's case, first, and perhaps most importantly, his writing evidences the English sensibility, the English eccentricity, and the English regard for words. It displays the English sense of humor. He incorporates the English duality of national pride and political suspicion. His writing is founded on the English awareness of class distinctions that underscores his social commentary. These traditional elements underlie Kureishi's loving stories of London society. But although Kureishi acknowledges that his writing reveals a strong national identification, he demands a new definition of his nationalism:

I think English literature has changed enormously in the last ten years, because of writers from my background—myself, Salman Rushdie, Ben Okri, Timothy Mo. You know, there are many, many of us, all with these strange names and some kind of colonial background. But we are part of English literature . . . writing about England and all that that implies. Whatever I've written about, it's all been about England in some way, even if the characters are Asian or they're from Pakistan or whatever. I've always written about England, usually London. And that's very English. Also the comic tradition, I think, is probably English, the mixture of seriousness and humor. Most of the pop music and the interest in pop music's a very English thing. Everything I write is soaked in Englishness, I suppose.[1]

At the root of his English storytelling, therefore, Hanif Kureishi suggests that the dogma of nationalism is in conflict with the reality of today's multicultural England. He demands that we accept the inherent contradictions of a pluralistic society within England. Contemporary English society is a paradox of overlapping communities, and told from his Anglo-Asian perspective, his stories proclaim that as individuals reinvent their identities, so too must nations.

His characters illuminate the irony of the parallel realities that make up the fabric of the cosmopolitan, pluralistic society he knows. What is going on and how it is perceived by different characters in his stories illustrate his insistence that society overlaps in similarities and differences and in the perceptions of its members. His outsider/insider point of view becomes, consequently, a crucial element both in and of his work.

To appreciate Kureishi as a storyteller, it is necessary to view his writing both in its traditional context and within contemporary experiences. His fiction relies on his readers' recognition of both the conventions of literary history and the philosophy and politics of today's dynamic urban society. His cosmopolitan characters see who they are and dream who they want to be. Kureishi writes that if one is to redefine identity, one must redefine, expose, and, finally, confront nationalism. Kureishi's stories, therefore, illuminate a distinctive new national identity.

Aware of his individualism, Kureishi is an observer of society, involved yet separate. Distanced by color, culture, and race, he is also separated by his art. Kureishi traces the formation of his perspective of society back to the days when, as a child living in the South London borough of Bromley, he would look out his window at London life. In his early essay *The Rainbow Sign*, the author remembers himself as "a boy in a bedroom in a suburb, who had the King's Road constantly on his mind and who changed the pictures on his wall from week to week, was unhappy, and separated . . . as by a thick glass wall against which he could only press his face."[2] Now it is Kureishi himself who creates the pictures on the walls, while his storytelling has made him an integral part of that world on the other side of the glass. Yet it is the fact that he continues to see our world through glass barriers, these so-called liquid windows, that most obviously distinguishes Kureishi's point of view. According to an article in a national newspaper about him, he is "a curious cultural icon: exotic from Bromley, successfully scathing about the cult of success, a man of integrity who had betrayed the Asian community, an Asian who could write with charity about the National Front."[3]

The term "liquid windows" recalls the way in which, in a certain light, windows not only frame the scene viewed on the other side of the pane, they also reflect the viewer; that is, a mirror image of the viewer sometimes commingles with the vista in the glass. By the same token, then, Kureishi's storytelling is illustrative and reflective of the author; that is, Kureishi perceives society from the distinct vantage point of his cultural hybridity and, as importantly, through the distanced perspective of his artistry. Thus "liquid windows" not only describes his point of view, it is also a trope that illuminates the dynamics of Kureishi's fictional universe.

Glass and liquidity are essential elements of Kureishi's stories themselves. Although sometimes transparent, social and cultural divisions remain. As with life on either side of glass windows, racial, economic, class, gender, political, and religious separations define distinct communities in his stories. The communities change; the divisions are fluid. He divides and then divides and changes again in his dynamic, liquid storytelling.

Ironically, it is an apparent inconsistency in his perspective—namely, this fluid mutability—that continues to provide him with an appreciation of the humanity in all of his characters. Hybridity generates his stories and propels his characters in search of their identities. His outsider/insider point of view is integral to and consistent with his aesthetic. It results in the universality of his work. He is, according to a British newspaper article, an Anglo-Asian artist whose "opposing cultures [lay] him open to abuse from both. . . . Kureishi changes course easily. Yet he remains the same, a trend spotter not trend setter. . . he is like a boulder in the stream of cultural and political change: awkward and obstructive, in the way and here to stay."[4]

In three sections, the first and third in England, the second in Pakistan, *The Rainbow Sign* portrays the ambiguities of identity as defined by color, culture, immigration, and exile, the convoluted issues that remain central throughout Kureishi's writing to date. This persuasive essay begins with autobiographical information but concludes with a call to recognize a dynamic society unhindered by dated gender, racial, and national stereotypes. Kureishi's first-person point of view establishes the essay's immediacy, and he candidly acknowledges that he had secured the balm of distance from his memories by originally writing the essay in the third person.

The essay recalls a boy in the London suburbs, a racial misfit among British and Asians alike, at home in neither England nor Pakistan, romantically attached to his roots, resentfully attached to his country of residence, tied culturally to both. Autobiographical episodes illustrate his frank introspection. Kureishi relates hearing wealthy Pakistanis in Pakistan rationalize racism by damning their own peasant class as inherently inferior because of their poverty. The author counters that peasant immigrants are not the only objects of racism in the west, because "racists didn't ask whether you had a chauffeur."[5] The prejudice and class distinctions behind the linguistic nuances of being talked down to as a "Paki" or addressed as a Pakistani in England are ironically brought home to Kureishi as he travels in another country. An Asian author coming home to a Pakistan that he has never seen before, Kureishi does not feel at home in the country of his family. He is as uncomfortable eluding border guards as a Pakistani in Pakistan as he was as a British schoolboy having to measure his sophisticated family against classroom slides of

Pakistani peasants. Finally, it is when he travels to his motherland that the author realizes the ironic overlap of national identities in his life in contemporary London. Rather than finding himself at home there, he writes, "In Pakistan, England just wouldn't go away."[6]

The Rainbow Sign also records another autobiographical experience that was pivotal to Kureishi's storytelling. The adolescent Kureishi had been stunned by Eldridge Cleaver's attack on the American novelist James Baldwin, and Kureishi writes: "How strange it was to me, this worthless abuse of a writer who could enter the minds and skins of both black and white."[7] Kureishi confronts his refusal to romanticize good guy and bad guy races. He determines that if a writer subscribes to championing only what is different in any of a society's communities, storytelling is limited as the literature of a subculture.

Fundamentally, in Kureishi, it is the hybridity of the author's point of view that conveys the individuality in all of us. He refuses to intrude into his storytelling by classifying his characters in terms of how they act out his philosophy. His fictional characters are as contradictory—remarkable and repulsive, hopeful and devastating—as people are in reality. Hanif Kureishi does not invent character types, he creates a cast of individuals.

Today, separate if overlapping communities are mixed into one nation, regardless of the lack of bonding into any redefined national identity. There are no easy divisions in Kureishi's writing, in which non-exclusive groups may one time divide by culture, another time metamorphose by race, split according to gender the next time, and still another time divide by class or generation. In Kureishi's fiction, characters unable to let go of the traditions of the past attempt to live in present-day London. The impoverished, tattered, and uneducated white street punks in *My Beautiful Laundrette*, for example, still live off the heady, long-lost days of the British Empire, grafting British public school traditions onto the conservative economics of Thatcherism. The Asian Rafi in *Sammy and Rosie Get Laid* slips between the cracks in today's political rhetoric, while his son spouts pseudo-liberal jargon as he surveys the riot-torn streets of racist London. At college, *The Black Album*'s Anglo-Asian Shahid confronts his father's dreams for him and the religious traditions of his past, pitting consumerism against fundamentalism.

Amalgamation cannot address any of theses characters' needs; it merely satiates some dated sense of nationalism.

Now a celebrated author, the grown-up Kureishi is no longer excluded by thick glass barriers from the glamor of London. He is an integral part of it. Today, Hanif Kureishi can by no means be marginalized by a racial, national, or professional identity. "Critics have written that I'm caught between two cultures. I'm not," he says. "I'm British; I've made it in England." His is a success story by any standard—traditional or popular—of Western society—even by his own assessment. Film critic David Nicholson has written of Kureishi: "Writing is, at best, vicarious, and if Kureishi was really a victim, an outsider, then his vision could never accommodate such wealth of humour, diversity of character, or level-headed intelligence."[8] And his storytelling illuminates the fact that the hybridity of his insider/outsider point of view is unique; it remains his artistic vantage point.

Kureishi thus determines that, like the hybridity he attained through his experience, the hybridity he defines in his writing is new and unrecognized. He proclaims a new national identity:

I'm British, as I wrote in *The Rainbow Sign*. Just like Karim in the *Buddha*. But being British is a new thing now. It involves people with names like Kureishi or Ishiguro or Rushdie, where it didn't before. And we're all British too. . . . But most of the critics in England don't understand that. So there isn't any understanding of Britain being a multicultural place. They think that I'm, let's say, a regional writer or writing in a sort of subgenre. They think writers like [me] are on the edges. We are still marginalized culturally. . . . They don't see that the world is now hybrid.

The critics don't understand that, but the hyphenated Anglo-Asian author does.

In today's mass-communication empire, international cinema, media, and music forge a new identity. Thus *The Black Album*'s Shahid wears a black leather jacket to express his style, his Jimmy Dean rebel-without-a-cause look in itself a global symbol of pop-culture machismo and youthful rebellion; Shahid is desperate to get tickets to a Prince concert. In *London Kills Me*, main character Clint Eastwood's garish red cowboy boots not only provide a costume for his street hustling in

Notting Hill Gate, they emulate his movie-star namesake's cinematic persona. With the right footwear, Clint metamorphoses from urban cowpoke into movie-folk bistro waiter.

Style is individual and style is superficial. Therefore, style is indicative of the contradictions of conformity in our society. Characters ironically assert their individuality by complying with the conventions set down by a celebrity, a designer, or a recognized group. However, contemporary style no longer only emulates the fashions of the rich or the celebrated. Style today is often rooted in emulating the clothing of the urban disenfranchised. Style is increasingly street-generated and street-conscious. The street has become not only a thoroughfare but a way of life from cruising to homelessness. Thus, fashions now selectively imitate the radical, marginal class; that is, they "trickle up" onto the music charts and the haute-couture runway, and they also "trickle up" into middle-class conventions. Outrageous fashion makes the conventional look—and feel—radical.

Kureishi thus employs dressing up to carry some significant social commentary. Style illuminates not only the need and search for new identities, but also the pretense of assuming them. That is, in Kureishi, fashion sometimes reveals the societal identity of the characters, while at other times it reveals that characters confuse attaining that identity with copying its costuming.

Musical trends have particular importance in and to Kureishi's stories. Song titles, musical groups, and genres of rock music pervade the fiction. Music is consistently mentioned as a cultural and historical occurrence, and readers recognize Kureishi's musical references. His stories, according to Gilbert Adair in an article in the *New Statesman*, include a "soundtrack, so to speak, [that] is threaded through with rock standards which function as the instantaneously legible signifiers of [the] period."[9] But music in Kureishi is often more than a mere trip down rock's memory lane. Music becomes imagistic: Kureishi employs it to invite the readers' input and suggest a different, more personal interpretation of the stories. Kureishi's ties to music serve as more than a device to trigger memory or invite input. His prose style is itself musical. His stories run with the rhythm of rock, sexy and throbbing, hopeful and melancholy, simulating the pulsating beat of the music of their time. Drugs and fame and seduction and manipulation whirl around

The Buddha of Suburbia's Karim Amir as he makes his way—and is continually "made"—in London. And like the music of his time, this first novel is idealistic, rote, bored, degrading, anarchistic, and, ultimately, a love song, a lyric to youth.

In conversation, Kureishi acknowledges that music is part of his life and of his writing:

Music was an integral part of my life, growing up in the sixties. Also, it was—it was culture, man, those kids in mop wigs. The Beatles as a whole. They were fun. They were making art. They were like twenty-one, twenty-two. And they were free, making money. That influenced me, you know what I mean? That made me think, oh, I can do that. I don't have to be a bank manager. I'll make money. I'll be a writer. . . . if you grow up in the suburbs, you either usually get married quite young and you have a family and have a job and get a house. Or you try and make a break and run away and get away, which a lot of kids in the sixties and seventies obviously were doing. It just seemed natural to me then that you would just go and crash around in sleeping bags and eventually something would happen.

Today's London is what "happened": its depiction demands storytelling with hybrid plots and themes because Kureishi's contemporary world is a contradictory, hyphenated society. Like music and fashion styles, empire and colonialism, individualism and assimilation, freedom and exile are now often inverted. Thus, depicting this dynamic world in fiction also includes paradoxes in structure and point of view. As looking through a window can, in a certain light, both reveal the view and reflect the viewer, so Kureishi creates a universe that both reveals his world and reflects him.

Henry James likened writing to opening a window onto the world, the storyteller recording his or her world as though it were passing before a window. But Kureishi is not in James's sense a literary realist. Instead, he presents the world cinematically. It is noteworthy that although he is also an editor, essayist, playwright, short-story writer, and novelist, he made his reputation as a storyteller in the international cinema. Kureishi writes a flood of images, montages, close-ups, fades, and technicolor sequences. Kureishi's prose has a frantic pace, a contemporary literary rhythm, evoking the fast cross-editing of the movies.

As the author acknowledges, his writing is strongly rooted in English traditions: His interest in class is from the English tradition; his comic style has predecessors in English writing. But because of the English-language bridge between Great Britain and the United States, and also because of America's role in pop culture, Kureishi's writing indicates ties to American culture as well. His racial comedy recalls the stories of Mark Twain. His musical prose echoes F. Scott Fitzgerald's style. His sexual stories flaunt the earlier hilarious prose investigations of Philip Roth.

Moreover, transatlantic references in his storytelling are not only to American writers, but more obviously to trends and fashions, from Calvin Klein underwear to Elvis and from McDonald's to blue jeans. Much of contemporary pop culture has American roots. And the most American of these, which Kureishi also incorporates, is Hollywood cinema. Although his fiction includes American film references, in his storytelling movies become more than just symbols of American pop culture: American cinema is central to Kureishi's point of view.

Kureishi first sought a niche writing for the London stage, but found that a theatrical point of view did not suit his storytelling: Kureishi envisions not for the proscenium arch, but rather through the hand-held camera. Kureishi sees his stories in movement, and to this day, his writing remains stylistically cinematic—whether he is writing screenplays or prose.

His themes are cinema-influenced as well, with his characters living out—or against—the Hollywood-movie dream of finding that "someplace better." Some cinema classics not only reflect the archetypal yearning for that idyllic Elsewhere, but themselves have defined it. Author Salman Rushdie suggests that the 1939 Victor Fleming film *The Wizard of Oz* is

unarguably a film about the joys of going away, of leaving the greyness and entering the colour, of making a new life in the "place where there isn't any trouble." *Over The Rainbow* is, or ought to be, the anthem of all the world's migrants, all those who go in search of the place where "the dreams that you dare to dream really do come true." It is a celebration of Escape, a grand paean to the Uprooted Self, a hymn—the hymn—to Elsewhere.[10]

Fig. 2. *The Wizard of Oz*. Dorothy Gale's 1939 cinematic trip down the yellow brick road is now an international icon. (Photo copyright ©1974, Metro-Goldwyn-Mayer, Inc.)

Thus this century's dream of Elsewhere, whether depicted on film or in sound or prose, is now both presented and perceived cinematically. The motion-picture medium has become the passport to a global community—that of the moviegoing audiences around the world, the citizens of the world of films. Film director Jean Renoir summed this up when he declared, "the environment which has made me what I am is the cinema. I am a citizen of the world of films."[11]

As cinema enters its second century, whether it is good or bad for culture remains in question; but that cinema is integral to who we are is indisputable. Even if we are not all viewers of motion pictures, certainly we are all *aware* of them. Quite simply, the motion picture is no longer only a way to tell stories, it increasingly shapes our storytelling. And

Kureishi's point of view as a filmmaker is pivotal throughout his story-telling.

Kureishi exposes the ironies in our fin-de-siècle global community. Abandoning the divisions of the nineteenth century, society has lost none of that century's prejudices while questioning all of its definitions. It is no longer a world of east and west. The third world is no longer the colonial inferior to imperial powers. Our world is not limited by the western Judeo-Christian ethics which bound earlier centuries as surely as it ignored previous national boundaries and altered yesterday's maps. But mass media continues merely to foster cultural, racial, and national community just as the dark of the first movie theaters fostered artificial community for its early immigrant audiences. And as diverse immigrants throughout the world have become increasingly influenced by the cinema, increasing conflicts worldwide suggest that the American "Dream Factory" has produced only electric kinship among—and within—nations where visas, prejudices, and philosophies impede the formation of any other community.

From its beginnings about one hundred years ago, the motion picture, the twentieth century's collaborative art form, promised its audiences "such stuff as dreams are made on." Movies realized illusion. Cinema was able to offer a universal depiction of the world's social, cultural, and national dreams for the first time in history. The studio system producing motion pictures was known as the Dream Factory, and the Dream Factory was an immigrant phenomenon.

Early film entrepreneurs were European immigrants who, as the new century dawned, had left the familiar behind and headed to the golden coast of California and what they hoped would be a shimmering road to success in their adopted country. First audiences, too, were immigrants to the emerging new world, people who had forsaken their pasts, homes, and birthrights to seek a dream. Watching motion pictures bonded these new citizens into a moviegoing community.

American filmmakers created a romanticized world with their cameras, about which they invited world audiences to dream—and, consequently, to dream also of the idealized world where they had found their dream—namely, Hollywood. Movies became the new world's most important export, promoting, even advertising, the mythical streets paved with gold and the other side of the rainbow to an expanding world audience. Thus movies projected values and ethics that powered and shaped the twentieth century's immigrant dream, both reflecting and defining it.

Audiences fantasized while watching the beautiful people live out their dreams on—and off—the silver screen. Movie tycoons created names, biographies, wardrobes, marriages, and families—whole new identities for actors thus transformed into "personalities." Gossip columnists, themselves newsworthy, were media alchemists who turned celebrities into stars. The packaging of celebrities and the glamour of their lifestyle were integral to the Dream Factory and kept world attention focused on the place where movies were made—Hollywood, which thus became the undisputed headquarters of this twentieth-century dream industry. Not only were the movies made there, the people who made them lived their dreamy lives there. The movie industry's campaign to promote the dreamer as the dream made Hollywood into everybody's Elsewhere.

The invention of the motion picture heralded the electric age, just as the mass-communications industry generated by technological and electronic advance defines the century at its close. Film financing is now global, production casts and crews are international, and films have worldwide TV and theatrical distribution. In a windowless tent in the Guatemalan village of Chichicastenango the night before market in the *zócalo*, Mayan peasants watch Quentin Tarantino's *Pulp Fiction*, having made the weekly trek to the village from their isolated mountain farms. Ang Lee's *Sense and Sensibility* plays on a VCR in an east LA storefront, the British-made film's social and economic messages competing with looters shattering the windows.

Previous storytelling had never been so easy or so accessible—nor was it ever so powerful—as it became via the motion-picture image. The movie audience's dream is literally focused through the lens of the camera—revealed through the window of the camera lens. The conduit of storytelling through cinema has become integral both to artistic creation and to artistic perception, and it is noteworthy that today, storytellers are among the filmgoing audience. Mass communication has made the moving picture into the most powerful global influence of this or any other time. For all it promised to do so, however, ultimately the Hollywood Dream Factory couldn't possibly, in reality, make its audiences' dreams come true.

Hanif Kureishi's stories follow the immigrant beyond the closing credits and confront the incendiary results of the dream's failure. The twentieth century opened with emigrés pursuing this cinematic dream — the quest to find some place better exploded into the largest mass exodus from the grip of an old world into the hope of a new order. But today, no journey across an ocean can replace the crumbling old world with a promising new one. Those pursuing the dream in underdeveloped nations spill their blood to find freedom and strain to find food, while others in developed nations struggle with unemployment and hide from violence and crime. Hoards of refugees flee from "ethnic cleansing" and waves of street people fight to set up communities on the edges of today's defined societies. They seem to come from everywhere and be heading nowhere. The dream of some place better still burns, but it is a dream unfulfilled.

Too many immigrants have never attained their dreams after moving to the new promised lands. Utopias suffer from overpopulation, pollution, economic recession, unemployment, discrimination, and violent crime. Even among those who do realize their dream, many immigrants question the price paid for having done so. They refuse to forsake their identities; they struggle both with old conflicts and with revisionism within their traditions. They dream of assimilation, and they demand acceptance.

Kureishi's immigrants struggle with reality: with political hypocrisy, racial and ethnic prejudice, and economic failure. Their journey often challenges not only national borders but also economic barriers. *My Beautiful Laundrette*'s white Johnny, and Omar, too, Clint of *London Kills Me*, *The Buddha of Suburbia*'s Changez, and *The Black Album*'s Chad—all dream of escaping the streets to find a land of opportunity. The quest of today is often not a transatlantic or transcontinental odyssey, but instead is a journey around the corner from urban squalor and poverty to the comfort of lower-middle-class neighborhoods. It is an immigration of class.

Immigrant dreamers have continued changing as the world has changed, and mere passage to some new geographical location, there-

Fig. 3. In *London Kills Me,* a film filled with Oz imagery, Clint (Justin Chadwick) and Sylvie (Emer McCourt) travel a yellow brick road of their own as they work the London streets. (Still photo courtesy of Jacques Prayer.)

fore, can no longer satisfy today's immigrant dreamers. Finding a better Elsewhere is not so straightforward a journey as it once was; today, it involves more than finding streets paved with gold down which to travel. Consequently, modern-day immigrants undertake trips down a yellow brick road that leads beyond Dorothy and Toto's Oz to some psychological destination on an internalized map.

As the twentieth century ends, global communication has linked the world electronically. The earth is imaged as a coherent unit on a satellite picture from space, while conversely its myriad races, religions, and sects demand recognition of their individualism. Immigrants now not only come from more distant nations, cultures a world apart from each other now exist on opposite corners of a city intersection. Assimilation and identity grow more problematic. Worldwide, political, social, even personal quests become the stories told every day, but these quests — and their retelling — only serve to further fragment populations into new communities. Multiple cultures coexist, although they may appear to commingle.

Hanif Kureishi defines today's hostile melting pot–turned–boiling pan. His is the urban world of street people and street crime, a world of gangs and family, of love and prejudice. His plots include drug dealing, entrepreneurism, sex exploration, and violence. He portrays both whites and Asians in a "warts-and-all," yet affectionate, depiction. His works are concerned with expanding issues, and he is experimenting in new genres to carry his themes.

His stories relate the multicultural incidents of a world redefining itself racially, economically, and artistically. Aware of the past and un-flinching in his assessment of the present, Kureishi writes stories that present the universal truths underlying the idiosyncratic activities of his unconventional characters. His prescient point of view gets Kureishi into trouble with critics. The sense of humor evident in his storytelling is most provocative for today's global society. It is humor born of melancholy, the defensive retort of an idealist. His bold presentation of racism stings; political correctness, revisionism, and flagrant prejudice affront and coexist in his ironic stories. "When somebody says, 'fuck off home, Paki,' you have to laugh," he explains. "The fucking irony—you drown in it." He chronicles the overlap of poverty and wealth, of power and oppression, of custom and dream to illustrate his unique perspective of today's dreamers, immigrants in a new world.

Kureishi asserts that "the immigrant is the characteristic figure of the twentieth century."[12] Moreover, his characteristic immigrant figure is new, taking a place in the world, with both hope and resentment. This is the significant evolution in his dreamers: they resent that the price paid for attaining the dream is the forfeiture of their history, and they resent even more that it is a price that is often paid without any gain. Unable to achieve their dreams, they fail even to find assimilation. "Elsewhere" had promised the fulfillment of their dreams, but had only delivered exile and alienation.

Just as European immigrants had surrendered their names to officials at Ellis Island, so the earlier Anglo-Asian dreamers embraced assimilation into London life at any price. Kureishi's fiction benchmarks today's break from these attitudes. In conversation, he explains: "In those days, . . . there wasn't the same thing about having your own identity that there is now. Now we want to have our own culture, find our own background. Even in the sixties I think the idea was that you should become as English or as American as you could if you were an immigrant. You would strip yourself of the past, of your identity." Kureishi sees the dreamers' demands as having evolved during the last decades of the twentieth century. "In the sixties the idea was to fit in here. Then through the seventies and eighties there was a sense of holding on to your own culture, whatever that was." He continues by expressing the paradoxical resentments of today's dreamers: "Then in the nineties there's also a sense that by holding on to their own culture here, people here are getting left behind."

The contradictions and problems of reshaping identity overlap in differing cultures; the evolution of the dream of Elsewhere that underlies them remains, and remains unfulfilled. Portraying the tension inherent in this retooled immigrant dreamer's quest is fundamental to Kureishi's themes. His pairing of "immigration and exile" exposes the contradictions that he sees intermingled in multicultural acceptance and assimilation.

Kureishi views the world through liquid windows. Divisions are transparent. Dreams are images framed on the silver screen. Perceptions reflect and are themselves reflections because his translucent windows are also looking glasses. Because of his hybridity, Kureishi realizes that contradictions are inevitable from every perspective. "But I don't care," his first novel's narrator qualifies, "Englishman I am (though not proud of it) from the South London suburbs and going somewhere."[13] He records our mutability and realizes its inevitable rhythm. Living is, after all, he writes, kinetic. Kureishi writes with humor about today's disparity and diversity, and neither romanticizes nor propagandizes present-day incongruities.

one
FROM BROMLEY TO BARON'S COURT
Plays, Early Prose, and English Tradition

Hanif Kureishi was born in a South London suburb on 5 December 1954 to a Pakistani father and a British mother. He was the first of two children, with a sister four years younger. Growing up in his birthplace of Bromley, Kureishi inherited his father's love of reading, saw movies at the local theater, had a paper route, and was an avid fan of cricket and English football. He went on to attend Bromley Tech, the same school David Bowie and Billy Idol attended, in the early seventies. In those years after the Beatles phenomenon, he was rock-music conscious, his musical influences including the Beatles and the Rolling Stones, together with the "Philly" sound of black rhythm and blues from the United States.

While he experienced a typical English childhood, Kureishi's cultural background was uncommon. Although English, he did not grow up within the Church of England tradition; although Pakistani, he did not grow up within the Muslim tradition. He does not speak Urdu. His father, who attended the same Catholic public school in Bombay as Salman Rushdie, called himself Pakistani although he had never lived in Pakistan, having emigrated to London from India when the rest of his family moved from India to Pakistan. The elder Kureishi was employed as a civil servant in England but, as his son remembers, although never published, his father, a journalist before immigrating, always remained a writer. Kureishi recalls:

My dad had been a journalist, and there were many journalists in my family in Pakistan. My dad wanted me to be a writer. He was a novelist himself; I mean, he wrote novels which were not published, so he encouraged me to write. He told me that being a writer was the best job you could have. That's what he wanted me to be, and I wanted to be that, too. I kind of didn't have any choice.

When I was fourteen or fifteen, I remember being at school and making up my mind to be a writer. This was a very unusual thing in a school like that. It was lower middle class. Most of the kids would be in insurance or maybe working in a shop or bank. They wouldn't be doctors or lawyers.

When I knew I was going to be a writer, it completely changed my life because it made the present unimportant. Whatever was happening to me, the racism, the drag of being in such a violent school, were made unimportant because I lived in the future, which was sitting in an apartment in New York being interviewed by you.

Kureishi has extensively related his adolescent experiences growing up in the racially charged seventies and this experience has played a significant part in his fiction as well. Although his comic style is biting, ribald, and machine-gun rapid, it was born of frustration. In a 1990 newspaper interview, he cited his fight against despair as his motive for writing: "When people insult you, when friends of yours become skinheads and go out Paki-bashing and you don't have anyone to talk to about your feelings and you're far too nervous to confront your friends directly, you have to express yourself somehow."[1]

His response to the racism was always intensified by his mixed racial background: as an Anglo-Pakistani, he is after all Asian, and he is after all a Londoner, born and bred. He uses laughter to handle the racism he sees around him. Therefore in his fiction hilarious incidents—particularly those flaunting sex, graphic language, and drugs—are sensational. But his humor carries the frightening truths and disheartening themes of today's most pressing social issues. "They are heavy," Kureishi acknowledges. "[The Black Album] is heavy. It's about fundamentalism, censorship, and book burning." But he continues, explaining his comic style, "I want to make it funny. The stuff I do is funny because the world is funny, the world as I see it. Funny. That's how I see things. I don't think, oh, I will make this a bit funny; I just want to make it palatable."

Kureishi's attraction to a cosmopolitan lifestyle led him to read philosophy at King's College in London. Amusing, attractive, and brilliant, the young writer easily moved into London's arty crowd. He began his

Fig. 4. The fountain in London's Sloane Square, home also to the politically aware Royal Court Theatre, where Kureishi apprenticed. (Photo by author.)

writing career in London as a playwright. However, he had to maintain a number of jobs in the theater to support his struggle to establish his playwriting career. Colleagues already recognized in the young writer the paradox that underlies his style. According to an article in the *Observer* in 1993, "David Gothart, who started the Riverside Theatre in the late Seventies and employed Kureishi, then an impoverished writer, to type scripts . . . [remembers] 'When Hanif seems to care least is when he cares most. He finds a joke in everything, and is often surprised to find agony in his own work.'"[2]

Kureishi spent a great deal of time as a jack-of-all-trades at the Royal Court Theatre in London's Sloane Square. His unpublished first play, *Soaking the Heat*, which ran forty-five minutes, earned a Sunday-night reading at the Royal Court in 1979. The young playwright was on his way. It was an exciting experience for the young Kureishi. Early the following year, Kureishi's first full-length play, *The King and Me*, debuted on 9 January 1980 at the Soho Poly Theatre.

The play depicts an impoverished married couple and pop icon Elvis Presley as the elements of a delusionary triangle. Noting the racial mix of the playwright and his outsider status, theater critics at first placed the production in the English tradition of socially conscious literature. But as quickly, they went on to distinguish Kureishi from other contemporary socially conscious dramatists: "Mr. Kureishi is too good a storyteller to invite moralizing, but his play follows Barrie Keeffe's Soho Poly shows as another first-hand report from the bottom of the social heap," wrote one reviewer. "The difference is that, where British specialists in this field are apt to give up their characters for lost, Mr. Kureishi ends by showing that there are other escapes from the social trap than dreams. We have acquired a good new playwright."[3]

Generally well received, Kureishi's first play was particularly praised for its characterization, which " . . . showed his capacity to write about working-class Britains without the least trace of ethnic bias."[4]

The fact that both members of the play's married couple were Presley fans was also seen as humanizing them, not merely as caricaturing them. Yet by placing Kureishi's characters beyond the "socially conscious category," the critics are instead labeling those characters' dreams—a bit murky in this first play—with socially conscious terminology.

In the English tradition, theater has always been a forum for criticizing the social and political failures of London life. In 1980 England was in the conservative Thatcher era; self-reliance was the thing. Social programs and assistance were the object of budgetary cuts. Although the play's characters may have been bottom of the heap, the play revolved around a "royal" personage—a familiar Kureishi figure, Elvis Presley, the King of Rock 'n' Roll. A commentary on pop culture from its title to the final curtain, the play is saturated with irony. But as the young playwright had not yet found his voice, the play faltered in expressing the new dreams and attitudes of its characters.

It is noteworthy that critical reaction to Kureishi's earliest writing identified his individualism. The individualist has always been a romantic figure among English writers, and remains so with Kureishi. Fundamentally, Kureishi is a social liberal at odds with the doctrines of political conservatism throughout his writing. However, during that conservative time, Kureishi's individualism was misconstrued as earnest social pragmatism.

The labeling was based more on the fledgling author's lack of focus than on a critical unfamiliarity with the newness of his ideas or on the audience's current political leanings. Tentativeness in the writing prompted the misdirected criticism. In retrospect, *The King and Me* can be seen to have been the work of a young writer: although in the context of later writing, the play does suggest that the characters attempt to escape—they lose themselves in the pop-culture delusions of Elvis, rock lyrics, and fast money fixes—they appear static because their dreams remain unfocused in the writing.

Moreover, the writing seems limited by the stage. Drama as a forum is a literary construct that did not lend itself to Kureishi's aesthetics, techniques, and interests as fully as the novel and the cinema would later prove to do. Thus he would only clearly define his hybrid, cinematic dream in his screenwriting and novels. Nonetheless, the young author did more successfully focus this new dream in his later plays as he became a more experienced playwright.

Kureishi became a clearer writer in his next play—*The Mother Country*, produced in 1980 at the Riverside Studios in the "Plays Umbrella" series. This second play, staged within the same year, built his reputation. Reviews again stressed Kureishi's background and the similar Anglo-Asian racial mix of the main character. *The Mother Country* introduced a character who recurs in his fiction—an immigrant portrayed by Saeed Jaffrey, who would play a similar Kureishi character on the screen—Uncle Nasser in *My Beautiful Laundrette*. The Anglo-Asian protagonist and the use of David Bowie recordings in *The Mother Country* also foregrounded some of the writer's continuing interests and moods: The sarcasm and resentment of his tone were becoming more evident.

The second play generated more critical interest, but its failure to convey the author's underlying anger to its Hammersmith audience was noted. This shortcoming was blamed on Kureishi's autobiographical attachment to his subject, resulting in, according to one critic, "the airlessness and lack of focus that often afflict a writer when the material is to [*sic*] close for comfort."[5] He had not yet perfected the emotional distance that is considered part of the English temperament and that has been an aesthetic principle in British tradition since William Wordsworth's *Preface to the Lyrical Ballads* at the close of the eighteenth century.

The play's ironic tone was identified by the same critic as a distracting inconsistency in an already disorganized play. "Particularly in its early scenes," he wrote, "the play is rich in bitter ironies."[6] But the play just trails off, and the author's ironic tone is not sustained. The tone is there, but in its early stages it lacks consistent focus and sends out mixed signals. The lack of a dramatic climax, essential for the stage, further confuses the piece. As the reviews of his later plays suggested, even when he handled tone better, as he did in those later works, Kureishi's tone, like his structure, is not best conveyed in stage productions.

Criticism isolates a fundamental stylistic element of the young author's writing—namely, violence, which is an integral—but unvisualized—storytelling element. Although suggested off-stage, the pivotal violence in *The Mother Country* was recognized by critics as theatrically weak. Without staging this violence the play lacks a theatrical climax. The criticism identifies parameters that stage production puts on Kureishi's writing that would not be as constrictive to his writing for the screen, and which would become insignificant in his later fiction.

Kureishi acknowledges that although a number of his stories include—even revolve around—violent incidents, he is not interested in portraying violence. Nonetheless, he continues including violence in his stories without featuring the violent incidents. Violence is a part of contemporary experience and his stories mirror our violent times. Moreover, some of these contemporary violent incidents are simply too broad for staging. Violence, like the terroristic book-burning in *The Black Album* and the racist police brutality and urban rioting in *My Son the Fanatic*, is better described in words or envisioned by the larger scope of the motion picture than staged. This is simply a matter of the portayal of violence being better suited to the properties of the page or the camera than to those of the theater.

London theater critics illuminated the fact that a problem in Kureishi's plays is rooted in the fundamental differences between playwriting and other storytelling. That there is an appreciable difference in writing for these forums is of significance in relation to Kureishi's stories, for Kureishi does not see his stories as stage plays.

Outskirts, Kureishi's third staged play, opened on 28 April 1981 at the Royal Shakespeare Workhouse in London. This more demanding play balances two narratives, one taking place in 1969 and the other in 1981, relating an uneasy friendship with hints of sexual tension. The play is introduced as "a play in twelve scenes set over twelve years." This was Kureishi's most experimental stage writing, and is his most inherently stage-written play; that is, *Outskirts* is an example of writing specifically for theatrical stage production. "I think *Outskirts* is a good play; I know it is a true play. I like the way it is done on a tiny scale," Kureishi offered fifteen years later. Today, if not entirely pleased with his plays, he recognizes that his playwriting was a formative element in the development of his style and evolutionary in terms of his point of view. He sees the stage as having been his training ground, providing his ideas with a forum.

Of its detractors in 1981, some critics found the play too arty and abstruse. "Lugubriously familiar, *Outskirts's* images are obvious hand-me-downs from Eliot and Beckett,"[7] wrote one reviewer who, despite his negative comments, also saw Kureishi's techniques in the play as appropriate to his experimentation: "I readily concede that the play has a lived-through intensity and that the mannerist dialogue splendidly counterpoints the subject," he also declared.[8] *Outskirts* was also awarded the George Devine Drama Award in 1981. The critical controversy helped sell tickets—Kureishi had become a fringe writer attracting considerable press. This play continues to generate critical interest.

Borderline opened on 2 November 1981 at the Royal Court Theatre. Again generating critical interest, the play provided Kureishi with his first major popular success. "*Borderline*, a study of the Asian community in Britain, is the best thing by Hanif Kureishi that I have seen," wrote the *Sunday Times* reviewer, who went on to describe it as having "some accurate characterization, funny dialogue and supple political analysis."[9] In writing *Borderline*, Kureishi had come to understand the dynamics of the stage and, more importantly, had learned to portray his themes in terms appropriate to the theatrical parameters. And, as in British literary tradition, he had achieved a following and an audience for his writing. The play placed him at the top of his theatrical career.

His distinctive point of view had evolved through his stage writing. Reviews of his fourth staged play recognized that he had defined an area of interest. "*Borderline* is a portrait of a community under threat. Running through it is the fear of violence and intolerance that will compress all its subtle distinctions into one stark antithesis," wrote the *Times Literary Supplement* reviewer. "Kureishi describes himself as a beige liberal. His picture of the diverse and contradictory values of the immigrant community is a fine example of the possibilities of investigative theater."[10]

Searching for his voice for the stage, Kureishi found praise. It was critically recognized that he did not merely present dogmatic social commentary; rather, he portrayed individual human issues that have universal resonance. In the play's introduction, he cited lines from *Medea* that reveal an enduring interest in the immigrant experience—"You have navigated with raging soul far from the paternal home, passing beyond the sea's double rocks, and you now inhabit a foreign land." One critic quoted lines of dialogue from this fourth play as evidence of the playwright's own growing literary objectivity toward his created characters: "'I believe it's possible to be honest and accurate about other people's experience,' [the character] declares, in words which clearly indicate Kureishi's own convictions," the critic noted.[11] Another critic agreed that "where [Borderline] comes marvelously to life is in its treatment of the individual characters irrespective of any public issues they represent." But again, this otherwise positive review opened by chastising Kureishi for lacking authorial objectivity because this spokesperson for liberal causes had "his heart definitely in the right place to please white liberals."[12]

Although the response to Kureishi's playwriting remains positive overall, attempts like these to categorize his storytelling by race are not unusual. Critical descriptions of his treatment of issues of race in reviews of the play—whether he is seen as outraged and/or as patronizing in his attitude toward racism—evolve from critical analysis of the play into personal inquiry regarding its author's stand on issues of race. The contradictory liberal-to-leftist, upmarket-to-marginal labeling found in Borderline's reviews represents yet another attempt by critics to categorize him racially; such attempts have dogged him throughout his career. Categorizing Kureishi as the Asian voice crying out in white London or as the speaker for white sensibilities in a dusky body has been imposed upon his work in much the same way that it has been imposed upon him. Kureishi is an author. His hybridity separates him from any subgenre labeling as obviously as the universality of his storytelling distinguishes him from subgenre storytelling.

Another critical barb at the plays also proves important in the context of Kureishi's continuing work. Critical discontent with his dialogue continues to hamper acceptance of his stories on film. The brilliance of his dialogue in representing the language of immigrants, the uneducated, and street society is questioned as well by some critics of his prose. The theatrical criticism had identified another important paradoxical stylistic element: Kureishi's heightened dialogue. The Royal Court's Max Stafford-Clarke puts this telling duality into words: "Hanif is serious and glib: that is his charm and his weakness."[13]

Kureishi was now a respected, recognized London playwright. Regardless of the critical success of his plays, or perhaps because of it, with

Borderline he began to tire of stage writing. For a writer who sought challenges, the stage had become too familiar a forum. He recognized the difference between the dynamics of writing for the stage and the aesthetics of his writing style; although researching the plays had interested him, the incidents and language seemed to him to have been grafted onto the produced play. Looking for a new mode of expression, the young playwright, who has always liked to juggle projects, worked on a prose story at the same time that his next play was in production. The three-page draft he began at that time was to be the watershed work of his career.

Birds of Passage, Kureishi's last produced play, debuted at the Hampstead Theatre the following autumn, opening on 15 September 1983. It tells the story of a white South London family's home being taken over by a Pakistani student. The play's treatment of racial relations and generational differences among immigrants is a central issue in much of Kureishi's writing. Reviews placed this play squarely in the tradition of stage comedies, "in a style as English as a soggy weekend."[14]

Although the play's debt to traditional theater was noted, Kureishi again experimented with both language and style. But by his last play, this distinctive style had been critically acknowledged. Thus the counterpointing of language with action in *Birds of Passage* was now clearly recognized as a stylistic technique—not a shortcoming. "There is a tension between the anti-naturalist writing and the style of presentation," wrote reviewer James Fenton for the *Sunday Times*. Negative reviews found that his experimentation with this device clouded understanding of his play, making the production more stagy than realistic, and Fenton's review continued, "I found it difficult to see why Mr. Kureishi had written it this way."[15]

Positive critical response, paradoxically, identified the same elements that the play's detractors had identified—but welcomed them as innovative techniques employed to make the play's themes universal. The playwright had acknowledged his last play's debt to Anton Chekhov, a favorite author. A critic noted the similarity, writing, "I am not going to press any comparison with *The Cherry Orchard*, except to say that with Kureishi as with Chekhov you cannot tell where (if anywhere) the author's sympathies lie. Apart from the general excellence of its dialogue, the play's great strength is that it tells a true tale offering equal comfort to Asian activists and Little Englanders."[16] Whether they found it praiseworthy or unacceptable, however, the critics were in agreement about the fact that Kureishi's aesthetics had evolved into a discernible style.

Kureishi's playwriting fits into a niche in English theater. Just as Aphra Behn and Ben Jonson criticized social hypocrisy as it was reflected in the social customs of their eras, so too does Kureishi in his stage plays. In this way his writing is part of a tradition that reaches back to *Bartholomew Fair*. The sniping between characters in *Birds of Passage* is as lethal, too, as the witty drawing-room exchanges that later characterized Sir Arthur Pinero's Victorian social dramas. Also like Pinero, Kureishi's plays scrutinize his city's daily comings and goings. In their satirization, his drama also resembles the nineteenth-century plays of Oscar Wilde. Class distinctions separate *Borderline* characters as surely as if they too had been either raised by an aristocrat or abandoned in a valise as were Wilde's characters in *The Importance of Being Ernest*. Again, like Wilde, Kureishi often writes with unconventional, underlying sexual tensions. The social divide that separates Kureishi's verbal battles between the classes recalls as well the writing of Sir Noel Coward. As such, *The King and Me* is a successor to Coward's groundbreaking *Design for Living*, the penthouse, white satin bias-cut gowns, and martini stirring of the thirties' trio being replaced by Kureishi with a council flat, white trash, and Elvis-impersonation competitions.

Coward, too, shocked his audiences by including drug use and pushing conventional sexual and gender attitudes beyond the repressive expectations of contemporary society. He used humor as his method of presentation. His lines are heightened theatrical exchanges. His plays used sexual liaisons to shatter the myriad societal roles among his characters. His work was also heavily influenced by the fact that Britain is a country with a class system, a system not so far removed from India's ancient caste system, or from that of the street society of which Hanif Kureishi writes today. Coward's plays ensured the continuation of the tradition of the English social commentary into the first half of the twentieth century, and it is this unbroken tradition that Kureishi, too, has continued as he has investigated, through his drama, contemporary London society as the century closes.

"He's lower class. He won't come in without being asked," Asian Omar says of a white street tough in Kureishi's first screenplay, *My Beau-*

tiful Laundrette, qualifying, "unless he's doing a burglary."[17] Omar's is the kind of statement that echoes Coward's language. Ironic and understated, it at first appears to be comic—and it is funny; but the lines of dialogue also contain numerous other implications. Not only do they ridicule the British class system, they mirror the pretensions of high society's hypocrisy and the code of the lower class as well. Stinging social commentary is made through verbal wit.

Kureishi's plays not only have a place in this English comic theater tradition, they also have context in the avant-garde theater. From the two separate time spans of *Outskirts* to the experimentation with clipped language in *Birds of Passage*, Kureishi continues a stage tradition of challenging dramatic conventions. As critics recognized, these plays have ties to the revolutionary plays of Samuel Beckett and T. S. Eliot. Themes are often politically relevant and intense, while the staging is artistic and intellectual with a reliance on stylistic devices. Most important, just as the avant garde's breaking with its theatrical history demands an understanding by both author and audience of dramatic traditions, in order for them to appreciate the ways in which the play is unconventional and innovative, so Kureishi's writing demands a knowledge of English literary traditions in order to understand his deviation from them, as well as his affirmation and celebration of them.

Joe Orton's irreverent plays set in sixties London are the most proximate ancestor in English playwriting of Kureishi's London plays. Orton's plays exhibit pacing that propels farce toward frenzy. Things happen at a rapid clip, spilling on, off, and around the stage while the facile language rushes the dialogue forward with its own energy at the same breathless speed. The dialogue is filthy, funny, and biting.

Orton's *What the Butler Saw* is a hilarious romp through British politics and marital and social hypocrisy, while *Loot* investigates the comic possibilities of crime. *Entertaining Mr. Sloane* is gender aware, laughing at sexual roles, sexual appetites, and sexual power; the graphic nature of the lines assaults the audience. The lodger in *Birds of Passage* is not unlike Sloane himself in the upheaval he inspires. Critics had noted the connection in Kureishi's plays to Orton, one of them writing, "It's the kind of Ortonesque epigram that gives a fluency and polish to this picture of the underprivileged."[18] More importantly, Kureishi himself recognizes his connection to Orton. "Of course I've read Orton; I like Orton, he's quite funny," he acknowledges. "I might see tracing my aphoristic, heightened dialogue to my reading of Orton."

Orton foreshadowed Kureishi, too, in his use of celebrity. Joe Orton himself was one of the first media personalities, an observer of and a player in his London scene. Having written plays, Orton then attempted a novel and experimented with writing a screenplay for the Beatles and is himself the subject of Stephen Frears's film *Prick Up Your Ears*. Orton's writing exploded beyond the theatrical community to the pop culture of sixties London. Orton's London scene occurred just before the decade in which Kureishi became part of the London crowd. Orton's theater writing resonates into the following decade, the historical seventies in which Kureishi wrote his plays and in which he sets his fictional stage world in *The Buddha of Suburbia*.

The importance of Kureishi's stage work is undeniable. London theater audiences were the first to recognize Kureishi's new voice, and theater critics as quickly provided him with a place in English theatrical tradition. With his social consciousness, he continues a line of British playwrights from Richard Sheridan and his brutal wit to John Osborne and his brutal anger. Kureishi has worked directly with classic works of this theatrical tradition. His version of Brecht's *Mother Courage* was produced at Britain's Royal National Theatre in 1993 and toured into 1994. In that same year, Kureishi considered writing a new version of Ibsen's *Pillars of the Community*, also for production at the Royal National Theatre.

Thus, although Kureishi has not remained primarily a dramatist for the stage, he does remain connected to the English dramatic tradition. Most importantly, because he started out writing for the dynamics of the stage, he was able to learn how to focus his writing. Playwriting gave Kureishi confidence and practice as well as a reputation. Small-budgeted stage productions allowed him to experiment with his methods of storytelling. Such experimentation would prove an impossible luxury in the expensive process of filmmaking. Today, Kureishi assesses his plays in the following way:

Their significance is in finding [my style] and also in finding my forum . . . because I never felt comfortable in the forum of the theater. The demands of the theater are a space, four or five bodies, and do whatever you want. That doesn't interest me in the way it interests other writers. It isn't like writing a novel. It didn't suit me. If I had stayed in the theater, I wouldn't have really developed as a writer. What I found is that I prefer writing for film and writing novels to writing for the theater.

Kureishi's plays illuminate the development of a young writer's aesthetics. He developed his storytelling skills and techniques during—and to an extent because of—his playwriting. The boys in *Outskirts* foreshadow Omar and Johnny in *My Beautiful Laundrette*; other stage characters foreshadow Ted and Jean in *The Buddha of Suburbia*. His themes and style have their roots in and evolve from his stage experiences. Most important to Kureishi's development, learning to focus his stage writing necessarily taught him what simply does not work for him. Specifically, the young author found the voice for his fiction—that of cinematic storyteller—as a result of the limitations he experienced in writing for the theater.

Some criticism of Kureishi's plays had specifically targeted the dialogue as too literary, too "arty." Criticism of dialogue in his films and his prose echoes these charges. "Heightened dialogue" continues to be a target of critics, and his dialogue, albeit most often considered interesting and amusing, is sometimes labeled flawed due to mannerist affectation, sensationalism, and excessive didacticism.

Undeniably, Shakespearean stage characters literally interrupt battles or preface their suicides with gushes of gorgeous poetry, obviously speaking better than ambitious soldiers or fourteen-year-old lovers do. Instead of identifying how he continues in that dramatic tradition, critics of Kureishi conclude that his stage dialogue is unsuccessful. Reading his plays today affirms that the author's heightened language is a stylistic modernization of heightened theatrical dialogue, whose tradition spans hundreds of years.

Finally, as Kureishi acknowledges in his introduction to a 1992 reprint of his plays,[19] it is from his playwriting that he learned how much of storytelling's power lies in the unsaid: "Language could point to where language could not go." This explains his attraction to cinematic expression. In Kureishi's filmwriting, the absence of dialogue does not mean the absence of sound. And, of course, in his cinematic novels, use of the first person and exposition enhance the prose language no longer limited by the stage. Thus Kureishi used the theater to formulate how he would use sound, sound effects, silence, and music in his developing cinematic aesthetic.

In an essay relating his memories of writing his first play when he was eighteen, he describes his passage from auditorium ice-cream seller to writer in residence at the Royal Court Theatre. Specifically, he records his reworking of theatrical autobiography into fiction as he does when he details Karim's West End experiences in *The Buddha of Suburbia*. He suggests as well how fictional stage characters of this period would recur as characters in his later storytelling for the movies and in novels. Consequently, when Kureishi relates Evelyn Waugh's envy of author Anthony Powell for having used the same characters in several works, he does so in order to outline his artistic rationale for this recycling process. Thus Kureishi reveals that autobiographical translations are not the only materials he brings from his theater work. An accomplished essayist, Kureishi here also illuminates his artistic passage from playwright to cinematic storyteller.

Another use to which Kureishi puts his essay writing is also illustrated in this introductory essay to his plays. Kureishi is doing more than recollecting a changing theatrical era when he remembers that "like other vestiges of the sixties, the fringe became self-indulgent." Ostensibly an aside to address changes in fringe theater from his days in the experimental London theater scene, the statement suggests more—in pointing an accusing finger at the excess in fashion and music, hinting at the popularization of recreational drug use, chronicling the disintegration of the Beatles' London as the pop center of the world, and, finally, alluding to the excesses of self-indulgence that followed the idealistic sixties in British politics and economics, Kureishi writes this essay as a traditional social critic.

Kureishi concludes the essay by stating why he next sought the challenges of movie and novel writing:

Since then I haven't attempted another play. This is partly a matter of form rather than choice. I stopped being able to find a tone or style to accommodate my voice or themes. I didn't feel comfortable writing plays anymore: I didn't know what sort of plays they should be; and the challenges of that doubt didn't stimulate me. It was strange, because for at least ten years all I wanted to do was write plays, and I took it for granted that a life in the theater was the life for me.

Kureishi's essay writing provides another tie to English literary traditions. He has written essays throughout his career. In early essays such as "The Rainbow Sign" and "Some Time with Stephen: A Diary"[20] he details his creative process. "The Road Exactly," an essay written to be published with the *My Son the Fanatic* screenplay in 1997, is a defense of storytelling and an indictment of the Fundamentalist intolerance of literature. "This creativity, the making of something which didn't exist before," Kureishi writes, "is a human affirmation of another kind, and a necessary and important form of self-examination. Without it, our humanity is diminished." In "Eight Arms to Hold You" he again assumes the role of social critic through an assessment of music. This essay, published with the screenplay of *London Kills Me*, brilliantly conveys post-Beatles British pop culture. Kureishi has also had essays published in periodicals. In one, "Erotic Politicians and Mullahs," Kureishi differentiates between race and class.[21] The essay confronts racial prejudice as English class bias. His scathing "Bradford,"[22] revealing how the poor and illiterate of Pakistan are the immigrants known in Britain, is a brutal indictment of racial prejudice, poverty, and bigotry in industrial England. Here the hybrid political essayist exhibits ties to the Asian-born English writer George Orwell as he boldly describes a separatist society on the dole and out of hope. In "Wild Women, Wild Men,"[23] Kureishi investigates sexual power in the struggle of a band of prostitutes determined to humiliate their male oppressors. His social commentaries are a call to action in the tradition of English political essays.

As they are in Kureishi's fiction, racial bigotry and class struggles experienced by England's urban poor are important subjects in his essays. Kureishi has written explanatory essays to accompany each of his four published screenplays, as well as an essay to introduce his reprinted collected plays. (Neither Kureishi's play *The Mother Country* nor his theatrical version of *Mother Courage* is yet published.) In addition, he penned a second essay as the introduction to the published essay and script sequence in his *London Kills Me* text. His nonfiction essays, which address historical, artistic, political, and social issues, continue an English literary tradition of arguing problems to a solution rather than fictionalizing them into a narrative.

Kureishi has written essays to address what he sees as political and social ills. He has investigated aesthetics and criticism. And he has used the personal essay to give voice to his personal impressions. The topics of his essays range from a theoretical explanation of his writing to an autobiographical record of his experiences. Thus he writes essays for various purposes: in one, he explains how he creates characters, and in another he records how he felt about visiting Los Angeles when he attended the Oscar ceremonies as a nominee for his screenplay of *My Beautiful Laundrette*. Music, so important in his storytelling, also plays a significant role in his nonfiction. As a contemporary cultural influence on Kureishi's times, music is the subject of some of his essays, while in others he considers music's influence on his writing.

Kureishi's proves to be a most traditional use of essay writing. He wrote "London's Killing Off Its Filmmakers,"[24] for example, as a published response to the critical disapproval of his writing and directing *London Kills Me*. In it, he analyzes British cinema in order to illuminate his personal displeasure with the negative criticism of his film. His own practical problems with distribution and commercial filmmaking become, in this essay, a theoretical model for the problems of British filmmaking. Kureishi expands "Finishing the Job,"[25] an essay analyzing reaction to the *fatwa* on Salman Rushdie and his *Satanic Verses*, into an indictment of Margaret Thatcher and the Conservative Party, demonstrating another traditional use of the essay genre, in that he is writing to state an argument and express his personal philosophy.

While in his fiction he separates the described story from himself as its creator, in his essays he argues his point of view—which, seen in this literary context, is a traditional English, satiric perspective. It is obvious that he incorporates comic extremes in his storytelling, which thus includes new, contemporary material from terrorism to dildos and from street drugs to tag-team masturbation. But his satiric point of view, if contemporary, is not new. And the bite in his point of view is easily understood in reading his essays. Kureishi finds everyone equally worthy—and also equally worthy of ridicule—but he does not find prejudice, cruelty, or stupidity defensible. This is the same comic sensibility that elevates Jonathan Swift beyond political abuse to political satire.

Undeniably irreverent, Kureishi's perspective is based on a traditional English blending of political freedom and cultural identity. Kureishi knows he is free to express himself and is proud of that freedom. Accepting that freedom as a given, he spares no one. His point of view resents and respects; thus it satirizes English successes as well as English failings. This is the tradition of English satire. Writing in many genres, Kureishi remains a traditionalist.

From its beginnings in England, the novel, that populist prose genre, has been a vehicle for comic storytelling. Immensely popular among the voracious British reading audience, the comic English novel as social commentary is an integral part of the tradition of English writing. Although also a playwright and essayist, and later a scenarist and short-story writer, Kureishi finds himself most comfortable composing in this most English of genres—the novel. "I would rather write novels. That's the forum that I like the most," he has admitted. "It interests me the most, actually. It is the flexible forum. I find it hard writing for the theater, and the cinema's got other problems. . . . I'd rather write books."

Initiation novels, perhaps the most long-lasting type of novel, treat the process of maturation. In them, the protagonist, an adolescent, is exposed to the hypocrisy and cruelty of adult society. These protagonists are made aware that they must take their place in that society—their conformity to its rules is necessary—and they are made aware, too, of their own mortality.

In Henry Fielding's *Joseph Andrews* (1742), among the earliest of novels, the title character is exposed to the hypocrisy of aristocratic society. He starts his climb up society's ladder in promiscuous service in eighteenth-century Britain. *Tom Jones* (1749), too, beds much of English society in search of his identity. The classic novel's setting is a green landscape in bucolic England where every wench is willing, and willing over and again. Hungrily devouring the women he meets, Fielding's Tom stops just before adding his mother to his sexual conquests.

In twentieth-century British initiation novels, issues of history appear increasingly significant. Although a more somber tone colors Evelyn Waugh's *Brideshead Revisited* (1944), for example, at core in this wartime initiation story, Charles Ryder grows up, goes to war, and goes to seed. The war against oppression is fought not on London streets but on European battlefields. Nonetheless, Charles Ryder's melancholy initiation into a new wartime Britain foreshadows Karim's passage almost fifty years later from a schoolboy with a crush on Charlie Hero to a disillusioned groupie in the new global rock society.

Out of his league at Brideshead thinking he can marry Sebastian's sister, Charles is out of his head too, dallying in the lush school holidays there with Sebastian, blind to the fact that continuing their intimacy as adults in hypocritical British society is simply impossible. In the adolescent passion of their school days, Charles and Sebastian are intimate, but the adult Charles can never really move into Sebastian's aristocratic class: the two can share an equality only as boys. Ironically, as school chums, the only hindrance to their intimacy is Sebastian's injured leg. As boys they are really free, free from the conventions and responsibilities of adult society.

When the middle-aged Charles Ryder returns to Brideshead during the war, he may look free once more from class divisions in his army uniform, a great social equalizer. But it is only costume, not convention, that has changed. By then, Sebastian, having fared best as a teddy bear–carrying Oxford eccentric, has already foundered in the reality of growing up. Charles, too, has found reality inescapable as he has reached maturity. At the story's conclusion, Sebastian is a ruined man and Charles, in his own words of disillusionment, is left "homeless; childless, middle-aged, and loveless,"[26] resigned to the knowledge that he has forfeited everything—including his bittersweet memories of promise, passion, and Sebastian. Charles, too, is lost.

English initiation literature has a melancholy strain. The social satire is brittle, sometimes cold and hard. Even comic portrayals appear tempered by a national cruel streak, as it were. The comic composite is actually rooted in the authors' awareness of the disillusionment of living. British social commentary characteristically recognizes the social bottom line. Sex, family, and politics are seen without romanticizing. Jane Austen saw that girls entered marriage as an economic institution; Thomas Hughes saw that schoolboys get caned and buggered. Thus, not the tragedy of Greece but a specific—if bitter—comic English tradition is now found, too—if in a more outrageous way—in Kureishi's novels.

With their raw look at contemporary street life, Kureishi's novels continue the tradition of the English initiation novel. Integrity is still tested in a hypocritical society. Humor is broad and coarse in *The Bud-*

dha of Suburbia as in Fielding, while in his second novel, *The Black Album*, Kureishi, like Waugh, takes a different voice. It is our society that has created—and that continues to widen—the extremes. First, Kureishi tells an outrageous, comic initiation story of Karim Amir's growing up in seventies London. Next, the contradictions of multiculturalism are exposed in Shahid's initiation through the religio-racist, postcolonial turmoil of the next decade. Like his forerunners, Kureishi writes about growing up in London. Like his times, Kureishi's novels are comic as well as sad, cruel, and contradictory.

In Kureishi's writing, melancholy is inherent to the way in which he perceives his outlandish novels. While a dynamic mixture of comedy and melancholy is part of the English tradition, Kureishi's melancholy flares up with a blunt fatalism. This mixture of hilarity and melancholy is not new; what Kureishi has contributed to the evolution of this initiation storytelling, however, is a depiction of today's overt clash of extremes, the particular "Englishness" of his hybrid despair.

Kureishi endows characters and stories with hybridity. *The Buddha of Suburbia*'s Karim Amir most obviously fits the description of "a proper Englishman—almost," insisting as he does on a qualification just as he proclaims himself undeniably English. He further adds, "(though not proud of it)," again qualifying his assertion. These convolutions can be traced to Kureishi's formative writing for the theater, in which the meshing in his comic storytelling reveals the hybridity of Kureishi's insider-outsider point of view. "But while the disjunction between style and content is fascinating," wrote a London theater critic, "what does trouble me is Mr. Kureishi's naked despair."[27] In a later review, a critic of Kureishi's first novel cites this same hybridity as being visionary of today's multiracial society, claiming, "*The Buddha of Suburbia* is an utterly, unselfconsciously multiracial artefact. Karim himself, sexy, dusky, and game for anything, is the offspring of a racially mixed marriage, and what lends his story its consistent energy and ebullience is the fact that none of the races in Kureishi's beige-y spectrum is accorded narrative supremacy over any other. Here, at least, from surface to psyche, the equality is absolute."[28]

The Buddha of Suburbia, therefore, is a classic contemporary initiation novel. In it, Kureishi accepts the reality of racism and of climbing today's racial slippery slope. He describes the contemporary, pluralistic

London scene through conventional storytelling devices: characterization, pacing, tone, theme, and point of view. During the last two centuries British literature has been peopled with protagonists who must relinquish youth's innocence; with the exception of the hero in J. M. Barrie's *Peter Pan* who flies off still a boy, these characters have learned that to function in their society, they must play by its hypocritical rules. And like these traditional characters, ultimately Kureishi's main character does as he must: he grows up. Thus, in a review of *The Buddha of Suburbia*, critic Ian Buruma places Kureishi's initiation novels firmly in the English tradition:

> But the theme is essentially the same as the one that has exercised the minds of English novelists, and indeed the English people, for what seems like forever: the long and arduous climb up the slippery slope of society. In short, getting on.[29]

English literature has already seen the main characters of novels evolve as, and because, English society changes. Kureishi flaunts a new national identity. Proclaiming that postcolonial immigration and mass communication have altered homogeneous English demographics, this insider-outsider confronts contemporary hybridity.

At the root of Kureishi's novels are traditional storytelling elements—but they are in motion. As the writer moves among the storytelling forms, the overlap of contradictions and connections not only in themes, but in these forms, is revealed. The twentieth-century art form, cinema, increasingly influential in our perspective, has been significant in the evolution of Kureishi's point of view. But Kureishi's novels come out of a tradition that began with Fielding and that links Kureishi's Karim Amir with Wilde's Dorian Gray (to whom conventions are also boring and commitments, like aging, are hell). And like Waugh's Charles Ryder, *The Black Album*'s Shahid Hasan exhibits the traditional English literary characterization of the youthful confusion, vanity, foolishness, and promiscuity of social initiation.

As did those English writers before him, Kureishi pushes the English literary tradition a step forward. In writing novels and essays, as well as in his writing for the London stage, Kureishi does not invent new forms; rather, he writes from a distinctive perspective. A 1993 article in the *Guardian* described his stories as "invok[ing] the 'glorious, scabrous, picaresque, savage, sentimental tradition that stretches from Chaucer to dirty postcards on Brighton Pier.'"[30] Whereas earlier protagonists in the English tradition sought their family names, true love, or fortune, his seek a fix, a South Kensington swipe, or tickets to a Prince concert. We clearly hear Kureishi's voice, and as clearly must identify it, but the literary sleights of hand Kureishi performs are well-grounded and much practiced in British storytelling.

Today the Royal Court Theatre is still a politically aware house for British theater and controversial lectures and presentations. Kureishi uses the building in the montage scene in *Sammy and Rosie Get Laid.* The West End theater scene in the late seventies that Kureishi knew becomes an element, too, in *The Buddha of Suburbia.* Moreover, he recognizes the role that his earliest writing has played in his development as a storyteller. Kureishi reminisces:

I wrote plays because in the sixties and seventies, when I was growing up, the theater was a hot thing in England. We didn't really have a cinema. Coppola and Woody Allen were in the States in the seventies, you know, but we didn't have any cinema in our country, really. It was the emergence of the cinematical stage. The alternative theater was great; it was really cooking, and it was about music and sex and class. There were plenty of theaters all over London. And you got to meet actresses. But the work didn't really suit me. I don't like writing plays.

By Margaret Thatcher's eighties London theater was changing; the days of "really cooking" on the stage were coming to an end. Yet Kureishi's stint in the theater proved essential to his evolution as a writer and continues a tradition of working in the theater as a training ground for writers and actors in Britain.

Through working in the theater, Kureishi became familiar with its traditions and conventions. The West End provided him with a first showcase for his ideas and gave him collaborative writing experience. He not only exchanged ideas with other artists, he came to understand the workings of drama and dramatic language. He learned, too, about audience expectations and gained provocative material. Thus this early theatrical experience was important, for it was through playwriting that Kureishi became more aware of the traditional English genres that he could work within—as well as those that he could do without.

two
FILMS WITH FREARS
My Beautiful Laundrette &
Sammy and Rosie Get Laid

Kureishi was not content writing

for the stage. To use storytelling to relate today's experiences, he turned to writing for motion pictures. Altering the presentation of the immigrant dream from Hollywood's depiction of finding streets paved with gold, he insisted that contemporary cinema must reflect social and political reality. He confronted contradictory demands of a universal depiction of the myriad dreams within today's society, arguing instead that today's new dreamers must be depicted in a cinema created especially for them. Kureishi writes:

There is an international cinema, of movie stars, big budgets, and fat executives. That is a given. But the world is a far more interesting place than Hollywood would have us believe. To reflect that, we need a more localized and specific cinema that will take risks, not in its finances but in its ideas. It may be more difficult than the international entertainments, more eccentric, but it will be more individual; it will be small in its scale but not necessarily in its resonance. It will ask questions and not play for the usual responses.

We need this; we need a cinema that is both critical and intelligent, sensuous and celebratory, reflecting the diversity and contradictions of our lives. It could exist; it is waiting to happen, except for the fools standing in its way."[1]

Increasingly Kureishi enjoyed the experience of researching his stories on the streets of London. And, as often, he became disenchanted with the constraints of writing for the theater. It was too elitist and restricting. He had become a young playwright with a reputation, but he wanted something else. The opportunity presented itself in a classic scenario, glamorous and glittering enough to be a screenplay itself. The author remembers:

Channel 4 asked me to write a film for them and I was broke. I wanted to do a film. I came with a story which I wanted to tell. A story about a neo-Nazi and a gay Paki running a laundrette. I wanted to tell that story. I couldn't do it like an Eric Rohmer film. It just couldn't be like his film; it had to be one of my own style, a forum for my ideas.

I thought I should break [in] with television, because I'd never make any fucking money working with the theater. Unless I was Harold Pinter. So I thought I would have a go, try and do something with the cinema. Just because it wasn't the cinema anyway, it was television. Remember British television was really good in the seventies and eighties. And it was kind of a rage.

Kureishi abandoned his three-page draft of a prose story about opening a laundrette and worked rapidly on writing the story instead for the camera; after five drafts, he completed the film script during his second trip to Pakistan. *My Beautiful Laundrette* was shot in London on 16-mm film in six weeks during the bleak months of February and March in 1985. Budgeted at less than $850,000, the film teamed Kureishi with producer Tim Bevan, director Stephen Frears, and actor Daniel Day-Lewis.

First shown at the Edinburgh Film Festival, "the celebrated *My Beautiful Laundrette* . . . turned out as one of Britain's most commercially and critically successful films of 1986."[2] Its festival success and the avalanche of critical praise when it was internationally distributed on 35-mm film were evidence that Kureishi had authored a story of far more significance than simple television fare. From its festival debut, critics proclaimed that the young writer had put his hand on the pulse of the new Britain. According to one enthusiastic reviewer,

The surprise hit in all this was *My Beautiful Laundrette* directed for TV by Stephen Frears. Hanif Kureishi's brilliant script details the love affair of Johnny, a white, working class youth with former National Front connections and Omar, a South London Asian torn between the aspirations of his impoverished socialist father and the get-rich-quick philosophy of his unscrupulous uncle. Made with economy and a notable sensitivity to the complexities of a multi-racial society shot through with colonial attitudes, the film combines comedy and fantasy to effect: pleasurable, provocative and disturbing, one of the highlights of the British film year.[3]

My Beautiful Laundrette was the first film produced by video producer Tim Bevan and the first starring film role for actor Daniel Day-Lewis. It was Kureishi's first screenplay. Stephen Frears had previously worked in television and directed two theatrically released films. The film's critical triumph had a considerable personal impact on its creative team. Tim Bevan remembers that "our lives changed, literally, that night when the film was screened. It was the beginning of Dan's stardom, as it were. It was the beginning of Working Title, in that here was a film that was a big hit. It established Stephen as a major filmmaking talent. Hanif's first movie was a success."[4] Earning an Oscar nomination for best screenplay of 1985, *My Beautiful Laundrette* boosted Kureishi's international reputation. Looking back ten years later, the author also acknowledges another benefit of the television film that launched his movie career:

Well, in the mid-eighties there was a lot happening, wasn't there? Channel 4 started commissioning films from people, Derek Jarman, Stephen Frears and Neil Jordan. It was happening.

It was also happening because of the war between the politics of the left of the seventies that we all came out of and the new ideological right of the eighties. And there was, at the same time, the money to make films. That created the cinema for a short time. It was quite vigorous. It's now gone.

It was very attractive to me to go into television—to write the film *My Beautiful Laundrette* because I really reached a wide audience. This had never happened to me before, and I thought would never happen to me working in the theater. The theater audience is so limited. I mean, if you write a play with Asian characters in it, they are not going to do it in France.

Film is a populist medium, and TV production adds to a film story's aura of immediacy and approachability. Although not first shown on TV, *My Beautiful Laundrette* was conceived and shot for the TV screen, making it seem a less distanced and elitist work of art than one made specifically for the cinema, and more a personal narrative to be easily viewed in the privacy of the home. Thus this immediacy makes his story a more powerful assault on class, racial, sexual, and economic issues.

Television was—and remains—an important part of film production in Britain. As had been the case with many of the most promising British films of the eighties and nineties, Stephen Frears's *My Beautiful Laundrette* was produced for Channel 4's *Film on Four* series. Among other films either shown or partially financed by *Film on Four* are Neil Jordan's *Angel*, Peter Greenaway's *The Draughtsman's Contract*, Jerzy Skolimowski's *Moonlighting*, Pascal Ortega's *Bad Hats*, Barney Platts-Mills's *Hero*, and Peter Duffel's *Experience Preferred but Not Essential*. Channel 4's rival, the BBC, has continued the ties between innovative filmmaking and television broadcast in the UK, with Michael Lindsay Hogg's *Object of Beauty* (1991), Mike Newall's *Enchanted April* (1991), and Anthony Minghella's *Truly, Madly, Deeply* (1992). Kureishi's first novel, *The Buddha of Suburbia*, was screened by the BBC in 1993 as Roger Michell's four-episode television production.

My Beautiful Laundrette was an extraordinary and young-spirited production. It was as unencumbered by the prejudices of a previous generation's thinking as it was unattached to the conventional process of making a movie. Producer Tim Bevan assessed the experience as follows:

I had an office at that point which I ran my music videos out of, which was about as big as this room. I remember there were only three phones in there, but ten people on that side producing music videos so that we could all eat, and then on this side the whole of the *Laundrette* preproduction. It was complete chaos. Stephen just used to sit in the corner a lot . . .

The great thing about *Laundrette* was that no one knew exactly the proper way to do it. It was completely undercrewed, it was completely underfunded, it was completely, you know, . . . The construction team was two people who both were on the set. We'd just grab extras off the street.[5]

One of the most visible choices made in film production is in the casting, and in this respect this first Kureishi/Frears production proved interesting. *My Beautiful Laundrette*'s cast included, as Papa, preeminent Indian actor Roshan Seth, whose stage work at the National Theatre Kureishi had admired; over the next ten years, indeed, Kureishi continued to work with him. The part of Papa's brother, Nasser, was

Fig. 5. Pakistani entrepreneur Omar (Gordon Warnecke) and his white, working-class lover, Johnny (Daniel Day-Lewis), challenge ethnic, gender, and class conventions in *My Beautiful Laundrette*. (Still photo courtesy of Mike Laye.)

written to be played by Saeed Jaffrey, who had previously played a similar uncle in a Kureishi stage play, *The Mother Country*. Rita Wolf, who plays Tania, was also a veteran of Kureishi's West End stage production *Borderline*, and she in turn introduced Kureishi and Frears to Gordon Warnecke, who played Omar. Critics acclaimed the performances, one of them lauding the cast as "marvelous."[6]

The part of Johnny, the gay neo-Nazi of the National Front, is pivotal to the film. The casting choice, Daniel Day-Lewis, was praised by the *New York Times* for a performance "that has both extraordinary flash and emotional substance."[7] Another American critic found that Day-Lewis's performance "gives the film an imaginative, seductive spark,"[8] while a British review predicted him to have "clearly . . . far to go."[9] Now a matinee idol and superstar, Day-Lewis gave a strong performance in this early role, making the complicated character both compelling and sympathetic. The list of actors initially considered for that role, however, reads like a *Who's Who* of British contemporary cinema. Kureishi remembers the field of excellent actors:

I will tell you about that. The thing is, we were not really looking for stars. Then you could sort [of] have had anyone. For Johnny's part we just saw all of the young men of that age who were around in London at that time. And it was a very rich time for people.

Gary Oldman was around. He had just worked with Stephen [Frears]. Tim Roth was around. He'd worked for Stephen. Ken Branagh was around to play the part. And Dan came in. Stunningly charismatic. We thought he was by far the most glamorous.

Producer Bevan remembers the decision to cast Day-Lewis and recognizes its significance to *My Beautiful Laundrette*'s immense popularity and appeal. Bevan determined that Day-Lewis was right for the part on their first meeting, when the "persistent" actor appeared with his "very odd . . . Frankenstein" stage haircut at Frears's house. As was its practice, the production team next had Day-Lewis read with Gordon Warnecke, cast as Omar. "When you find a star, magic things happen to the picture. . . . And that also occurred with Daniel on *Laundrette*," remembers Bevan. "If this magic creeps into it, the audience, beyond finding the movie itself, thinks they've found somebody. That is a very exciting thing to behold."[10] Critics would later recognize the importance of Day-Lewis's casting; his appeal to audiences would prove magnetic.

My Beautiful Laundrette's reviews are raves. Moreover, unusually for a screenwriter, the reviewers frequently identify Kureishi's writing specifically. According to one London critic, the film "marks the TV debut of a young Asian, Hanif Kureishi, whose script is largely responsible for the film's success." She concludes her praise, "there is no doubt on this evidence that Hanif Kureishi is an exciting new voice in British television."[11]

The writing is noted as particularly effective and is lauded for its humanity and, at its core, the honest depiction of contemporary politics. "*Laundrette* is political in the best sense; its politics are imbedded in its humanity," claimed another reviewer. "The screenplay, by 29-year-old Hanif Kureishi, grinds no ideological axes in its loving and ironic examination of Pakistanis caught between cultures."[12] The successful collaboration of Frears and Kureishi in portraying a controversial political situation is isolated again as the root of the film's strength. "It's an enormous pleasure to see a movie that's really about something, and that doesn't lay down any syrupy coating to make the subject go down easily. (It's down before you notice it)," proclaimed yet another critic. "Frears and Kureishi take a pile of risks in this movie, and take them in stride."[13]

The collaboration of director and writer is extraordinarily successful. Bevan notes that although film is an inherently collaborative art, what Frears and Kureishi had working together was something special. "I believe that all of the best films are collaboration," he asserts, continuing, "I've worked in many different ways. I've worked for some very fine talented directors, writers and all the rest of it. And I've worked on some very arty pictures. I don't ultimately believe in that auteur theory of filmmaking. I believe that the best films come out of collaboration. At the deep, you know the Hanif-Stephen relationship is a very strong one."[14]

Although Kureishi had already attained awarded status as a writer in residence at London's Royal Court Theatre, *My Beautiful Laundrette* brought world celebrity to him. This reputation has proven to be a mixed blessing. As with his plays, Kureishi's autobiographical connection to his screenplay was the subject of much speculation. Kureishi himself had yet to learn how to deal with critical and popular expectations, and he condemned the continuing racial accusation of having sold out his Asian heritage by not projecting consistently positive Asian characters in his writing. "I don't know how the Asian community will deal with it," he admitted when discussing his Asian characters and *My Beautiful Laundrette*'s success. "They think that I'm perpetually throwing shit at them anyway. They'll think that this is the last straw: now he's showing us as drug dealers, sodomites and mad landlords. . . ."[15]

Kureishi further tauntingly claimed that he intended to create not only a political film, but an antidote to "dourness and didacticism [which would cause] mass erections."[16] Newspaper pieces publicizing *My Beautiful Laundrette,* therefore, not only trace critical response to the author's film-writing creation, but chronicle Kureishi's creation of his incendiary persona. During the year following the release of *My Beautiful Laundrette*, Hanif Kureishi became a personality. Interviewed throughout the world, he came to recognize that stirring up controversy was an inevitable result of his achievement of celebrity status. Kureishi now undermines the film's hoopla with the witty disclaimer that "writing films isn't an occupation for grown-up people."

Does Kureishi take a devilish pleasure in shocking his audience, in eliciting shock for shock's sake? Following another critical outcry, this time engendered by Kureishi's television adaptation of *The Buddha of Suburbia*, producer Kevin Loader remembers going to the Whitbread Awards with him:

Hanif has always taken a rather mischievous glee in how dirty this [adaptation] was going to be—and I remember going to the Whitbread Awards with him when *The Buddha* won the Whitbread Award for best novel in 1990. We were at the ceremony after lunch when the winner was announced. Hanif was taking great glee even then, going around saying, "Oh, yes. It is going to be the dirtiest thing ever seen on television." So he was playing it up from a very early state.[17]

By the time he wrote his second novel, his experiences with film critics had taught him how better to respond with humor without inviting the press to manipulate the meaning of his remarks. Both his social attitudes and his role were evolving. Today, Kureishi chooses to make his points *in*, not *about*, his writing. Yet had he not played the enfant terrible in the previous decade's newsprint, Kureishi would not have gained his current position with the press. Thus, in the nineties, Kureishi concludes, "I'm more interested in writing well than in making dramatic statements now. I mean in the eighties people like me who came out of the seventies were appalled. Then I thought it was important to make a statement. Now I think the most important thing is to make a statement through my writing, not through talking to newspapers."

But in retrospect, even his colorful remarks at the debut of *My Beautiful Laundrette* were already more than mere ranting or posturing. His use of provocative and/or outrageous language in interviews was a calculated method of demanding attention for his ideas. His persona thus mirrors his prose. "With this return to faith," began the flamboyant author about his refusal to be branded an Anglo-Asian writer in a Marcia Pally interview in 1986, "we're moving back almost to a medieval state . . . Prejudice is also the pursuit of certainty. It's an easy way of explaining the world's various wrongs. You see one group as ineradicably corrupt and lacking the humanity that you yourself have." Extrapolating from the inflammatory wording, it can be seen that Kureishi was clearly voicing his conviction that he speaks not for a subgenre but as a British author. "You don't have to examine the political or economic reasons for exploitation," Kureishi continued in this same interview. "Men say women are stupid or that their sexual organs will devour them. Women argue that all men are essentially rapists or that the source of sexism is the penis. Whites say blacks are stupid or worthless; blacks counter that white men are devils. So no one has to look at why people become the way they are or notice that people resist their training and change."[18]

In addition to being quite humorous in this interview, the author was thus able to focus on critical hang-ups with race, sex, and gender in a further jab of social irony. Called to task by the Asian community for creating a "vile" story, Kureishi used his sense of humor in the interview as a means of confronting the criticism and exposing its racist and homophobic underpinnings: "The last time I was in New York, 300 men from the Pakistan Action Committee demonstrated every Sunday outside the theater where My Beautiful Laundrette was showing. The placards read, 'this film is the product of a vile and perverted mind.' Of course none of them had seen the film. They were disturbed by the homosexuality, and because they felt the film was a Zionist plot—the director is Jewish—to disrupt relations between the US and Pakistan. There are no Pakistani homosexuals, they say."[19]

Underplaying his defense of the homosexual love story, Kureishi concluded by amusingly targeting a favorite U.S. film theme, the male buddy story, with the irreverent remark, "Laundrette is like [Butch] Cassidy with kissing."[20] A one-liner suitable for quoting, the flip humor was employed by Kureishi to carry a biting observation, a device he has continued to use throughout his career.

This easy punchline would later be widened in context to provide a provocative cultural and aesthetic insight. In a published account of his trip to the United States to promote My Beautiful Laundrette, Kureishi perceptively identifies an American cultural attitude: "We wonder why the film has done well in the US. It's partly, I think, because of its theme of success at any price; and partly because the puritan and prurient theme of two outcast boys (outcast from society and having escaped the world of women), clinging together in passionate blood-brotherhood is a dream of American literature and film from *Huckleberry Finn* to the work of Walt Whitman and on to *Butch Cassidy and the Sundance Kid*."[21] Even this early in his career, Kureishi was savvy enough to manipulate the controversy sparked by his story of the streets.

Although Kureishi has continued to be interested in the same themes throughout his career in film and prose writing, critics in 1987, as well as the screenwriter himself, quickly distinguished between the dynamics of his first and second films with Frears. One critic wrote, "*Laundrette* was a fractious house party; *Sammy & Rosie* is a Black Mass block party and everyone is invited to attend at his own risk."[22] And although there remain some recognizable ties, such as the films' creative teams, Kureishi makes the distinction that "*Laundrette* was written—not from my own experience—but written from within my own life [whereas] . . . *Sammy and Rosie* is a much more polemical film. It is a film about its day, strikes on factories, and rioting."

Also like *My Beautiful Laundrette, Sammy and Rosie Get Laid* (1987), Kureishi's second screenplay, was directed by Stephen Frears and produced by Tim Bevan; the production and financing of this film were both innovative and interesting; and the collaboration provided a happy working experience. But this second collaboration also had its differences. Bevan remembers how many things were different this second time:

Because of the success of *My Beautiful Laundrette,* when it came to *Sammy and Rosie* what we decided to do was shoot the film on 35 millimeter [film] but we still wanted to keep it cheap because we wanted to retain control. Also we realized it was a risqué story and that we were on the edge of things basically as to whether and how it would be received. So we got everyone to participate, to sort of work for scale, but be a participant in the profitability of the picture. Unfortunately, it never showed profit, that film, so it's a sad story. And also, it did cost a lot more than *Laundrette* . . . —all of a sudden there's ten people doing what one person did on the last movie. And that was very much the state of affairs of *Sammy and Rosie.*[23]

Additionally, this second film, although it remains for the collaborators a positive experience, met with less enthusiastic, more mixed reviews than had *My Beautiful Laundrette*.

Kureishi documented the complicated production history of *Sammy and Rosie Get Laid* in his diary published with the screenplay. As he did with *My Beautiful Laundrette*, Kureishi rehearsed actors, made script changes with Frears, and other times determined not to change the text during the shooting. According to a 1988 article in the *Hollywood Reporter*, "Kureishi acknowledges Frears's influence on his two stories. 'I'm a very lazy person. What's so good about working with someone else is that you can reflect on your work. You yourself would not be critical enough.'"[24] The Kureishi/Frears pairing had again proved productive.

Kureishi recognizes not only the aesthetic possibilities that opened up to him in his collaborating again with Frears, but also the other advantages to him of this collaboration: "I thought that there were some really good things in [*Sammy and Rosie Get Laid*], some fantastically good things in it, many of them had to do with the way Stephen directed it . . . In a way the *Laundrette* on film is really, I suppose, a record of what I'd written in a way that *Sammy and Rosie* isn't. Stephen took it beyond the script."

Here he suggests that the screenplay exhibits flaws in focus, although these writing problems were addressed during production in collaboration with the director. The author agrees today that the story could have been given a clearer perspective by tightening the screenplay. He also recognizes that an assessment of a film gains or loses according to the changing moods of whoever is assessing. "What I doubt sometimes is the focus of my writing," he says. "But I think it's probably a more interesting film than it was given credit [for] at the time. And sometimes it's easy to be too hard on oneself about one's own work rather than looking for things in a piece that are interesting. Maybe I'd been too hard on it, but one is the last person to be able to judge one's own work really."

That the film lacks focus is a fair criticism. The intriguing title, for example, is not fully realized. Aside from the obviously irreverent sexual slang, it also suggests a more involved interplay of semantic connotations. Sammy's name, for instance, is a common racial slur, a shortened form of "little black Sambo," while Rosie's name conjures up the "perfect English Rose." Thus their coupling and the title's play on the slang term "getting laid" as having sex and/or being used have fascinating, dual, and ambiguous postcolonial ramifications.

Ambiguous in name allusions, the two lead characters also lacked certainty in terms of their characterization. The casting of the title roles did not provide the characters the necessary magnetism. Ayub Khan Din as Sammy does not hold his own against Rosie. And as Rosie, Frances Barber is a bit too glamorous for Kureishi's social worker. The story sometimes concedes to the visual requirements of the movie. For example, although Rosie's merry widow jumps off the screen, it seems inappropriate to the character. At other times, the story abruptly abandons a narrative episode to start another one or simply to flow in tangents. Kureishi acknowledges the need for tightening the writing's frenzied spin. His admission suggests, too, that the film's focus is blurred because it is a more innovative attempt than *My Beautiful Laundrette* and, even if better realized, is simply more difficult to understand. Regardless of its success, therefore, an awareness of the innovative focus of this film is a prerequisite to appreciating Kureishi's script.

The second pairing of Kureishi and Frears was cited by some critics as one of the reasons for the misfire of *Sammy and Rosie Get Laid*; in this second partnership, Kureishi's point of view is labeled as overbearing, one reviewer complaining that "this time the writer dominates, and the film is off balance. It's literate to an almost looney degree. Everyone speaks his mind—or Kureishi's mind."[25]

This loss of balance in storytelling may stem from the attempt at more innovative collaboration in this production. The success of *My Beautiful Laundrette* had bonded together a company of young artists, technicians, and other professionals, many of whom both contributed their talents to and bought into the financing of this second film. "Continuing the philosophy of extending the *Laundrette* spirit, all members of the crew were offered profit participation points," explained film writer Graham Broadstreet in an article in *Screen International* about the making of the later film. "Each, without exception, accepted. *Sammy and Rosie* was now genuinely a product of all those involved, with everyone participating in its potential success. The commitment was intense."[26] Distribution of this second Kureishi/Frears film was similar to distribution of *My Beautiful Laundrette*. Despite the possibility of TV presentation, this second film had a theatrical release—and not in Britain first, but in the United States, as producer Bevan preferred. But unlike *My Beautiful Laundrette*, which had been a "sleeper," distributed after it had received acclaim following its showing at the Edinburgh Festival and then rising to become an international critical triumph, the second film debuted to higher critical expectations and to greatly reduced box-office momentum.

Sammy and Rosie Get Laid's cast consisted of a more established ensemble of actors than that of *My Beautiful Laundrette* and included noted actress Claire Bloom, stage actress Frances Barber, and rock star Roland Gift. But although the film was graced with a star-studded cast mixed in race and generation, the casting itself engendered criticism, with one casting choice in particular proving quite controversial. The casting of Asian film star Shashi Kapoor as Rafi, a bloodied tyrant, caused members of London's Asian community to bristle. As well as being attacked by offended special-interest groups, the production was also seen as unsatisfactory by many film critics.

This dissatisfaction is especially pronounced in relation to the screenwriter's politics, the film's political messages criticized as being, if ironic, leaden and confused, at the core, too blatant. "Politics weakens Mr. Kureishi's touch—as was apparent in his didactic and dismal second film, *Sammy and Rosie Get Laid*," complained the *Economist* in a 1990 article.[27] Labeled didactic by some, other critics found the politics superficial. "*Sammy and Rosie* appears to be Kureishi's attempt to demonstrate that the artist can be a political force, but the flickering little fires—they go on burning in the windows of the dark houses—are mystical, decorative," declared one writer in 1987.[28] Such criticism, however, actually disregards one of the script's most interesting elements—namely, the mix of intensity and superficiality in its politics.

The *Sammy and Rosie Get Laid* screenplay portrays themes that remain central throughout Kureishi's writing. This film and *My Beautiful Laundrette* have been termed "two of the most original, ambitious, and complex films about eighties English society."[29] In them, Kureishi portrays extremes in the urban political situation. His cityscape aptly envisions the contradictory savagery and sophistication of the inner city. Violence and sensitivity are depicted as the strange bedfellows of gentrified liberalism. According to film writer Richard Corliss, "*Sammy & Rosie* is Screenwriter Hanif Kureishi's double vision of London as the

Fig. 6. Political refugee Rafi (Shashi Kapoor) strolls the streets of his beloved London in *Sammy and Rosie Get Laid*. (Photo courtesy of Working Title Films, Ltd.)

hip place to be and the last place on the postimperial earth."[30] At the film's release, however, this double vision was criticized as a lack of focus and Kureishi's artistic grafting onto the film of paradoxical, political elements was seen as contributing to a lack of thematic clarity and cohesion in the film.

Ironically the tensions that resulted from what was faulted as a lack of focus in the writing have been lauded as creative filmmaking, even in negative reviews of the film. Kureishi and Frears were credited for having created a surreal motion picture, in which images of the oxymoronic politics of urban life abound. Urban demolition is underscored in the film with speeches by Margaret Thatcher, strains of T. S. Eliot, and choral singing; a photographer takes a posed photo of riot violence for a coffee-table book. According to a 1987 article in the *New Republic* magazine, "the surreal effect is of a string of Francis Bacon paintings viewed while listening to ultramod William Blake songs of London."[31]

Often criticism failed to recognize that the surreal pictures, sound-track, and script created a distinctive focus. The fragmented story line demanded an episodic mode of presentation and this is, indeed, the power of Kureishi's *Sammy and Rosie Get Laid:* contradictory shards are incorporated into the story through Kureishi's mode of storytelling to convey his themes of contemporary political and cultural paradox. Thus the use of cross-editing, soundtrack, and everything from gimmick to Gandhi portrays elements of the film story without aspiring to shape them into the author's political tract.

In *Sammy and Rosie Get Laid,* what characters say and the structure of the film have a symbiotic relationship that becomes the film's cinematic foundation. That is, Kureishi's aesthetic creates the tension in structure essential to Frears's filmmaking. Frears's structure, criticized as undeveloped, is, rather, inherently unresolved and ironic. And Kureishi's plot, criticized as disjointed, overloaded, and pretentious, is in actuality conjoined, multiple, and episodic.

Seen as distanced and lacking humanity, the script, like the shots, is a hodgepodge. This is, however, where it achieves its impact, too—that is, not through blending, but through fragmenting. Irony is put to hilarious use. Sometimes the clever wording of disillusionment stings. Other times the language borders on being coy. Often meanings collide. This is the result of the Kureishi/Frears collaboration in this film as much as it was in *My Beautiful Laundrette.* Critic Leonard Quart concludes:

It's [Kureishi's] belief in a life of spontaneity—free of guilt and crass self-interest—which the films set in opposition to all that is respectable, repressive and calculating in society. Frears's directorial style reinforces this vision by making use of split screen, rapid, rhythmic cross cutting, shock cuts (e.g., cutting from the police killing a middle-aged black woman to the bare, tattooed behind of a nubile woman photographer), swish pans, tracking with a hand-held camera, overlapping dialogue, vivid color (a use of bright light and red filters)—a barrage of visual and aural fireworks to help disrupt our sense of order and affirm a life lived without conventional constraints.[32]

Rafi succinctly transfers the film's surreal juxtaposition of visual and political messages into literal message when he puts the urban riots into words, on a postcard he sends back to Pakistan: "Streets on fire—

wish you were here." This is how "the ultramod" Kureishi sings about London.

Many critics have complained that Kureishi's lack of identification with any of the large cast of characters leaves both his story unresolved and the audience uninvolved. "The film is constantly cross-cutting between characters, events, and scene-setting images. As each character is overwhelmed to a greater or lesser degree by contradictory impulses, so is the film,"[33] wrote one critic. However, other critics have praised the effect of Kureishi's distance from and lack of sympathy for his many characters. Political despot Rafi, for example, is characterized by Richard Corliss as having "no more or less sympathy than any other character in this exuberant egalitarian stew of a movie." Corliss continues, "Once the empire has died, taking with it the old notions of great men who shape destinies and insignificant men who suffer like extras in an antediluvian epic, every motive is up for grabs. And what do we find in the empire's night ashes? Punks and ghosts and madmen dancing in the carnage or singing a Motown medley as all the survivors copulate on Armageddon Eve. In *Sammy & Rosie*'s cultural revolution, the radicals strike not poses but sexual sparks. They give a lovely light."[34]

The story is contradictory. The characters emerge during a London riot triggered by a police murder of a black woman; but the violence leads to convolutions that frustrate any attempt at a simple summary of the plot. One critic, for example, abandoned any attempt at "synopsis because it implies smooth, continuous narrative," explaining,

The texture of *Sammy and Rosie* is quite different. It is a bursting aggregate of counterpoints—the plaiting of six lives, those of Sammy, Rosie, Rafi, Alice, a silky black man called Danny whom Rosie beds in his caravan, and an American photographer called Anna whom Sammy beds in her studio. Two lesbians, one of them Pakistani and the other black, are also prominent. The film's scheme is to keep all these lives going forward at the same time, as far as possible, along with the general life of the inner city. Music, other than that from the musicians on screen, is another counterpoint. After an opening shot of urban squalor, we hear, under the credits, an Edwardian waltz. Under the bulldozing eviction of the squatters, choristers sing a 19th-century hymn.[35]

Most audiences are unfamiliar with the Anglo-Indian political situations detailed in the film—subcontinental politics do not get anywhere near the same media coverage that domestic events receive, nor are they portrayed with the same sentiment evidenced in coverage of the politics of other third-world regions. So *Sammy and Rosie Get Laid*'s explosive pacing warrants another look. The density and convolutions of the film—like the politics portrayed—are noncumulative and tentative. The quagmire of complex political issues is handily reflected in the whirl with which complicated incidents are depicted in Kureishi's script. Regardless of the seriousness of the political situation or the earnestness of Kureishi's political convictions, this does not become a political advertisement. *Sammy and Rosie Get Laid* is above all an exhilarating story and an exhilarating film, sometimes mesmerizing and often hilarious.

Films produced since *Sammy and Rosie Get Laid* have continued to expand audience expectations, and less commercial themes and marginal points of view have been employed more frequently. Motion pictures with unresolved narratives and the occurrence of film-conscious techniques have become more familiar. Additionally, *Sammy and Rosie Get Laid* itself has become more understandable in the nineties, as looting, firebombing, and domestic terrorism have become almost routine occurrences. These outrageous nonsequiturs are no longer merely surreal plot incidents dreamed up by Kureishi; they are the daily events of contemporary electronic news reporting.

An understanding of Kureishi's film story demands recognition of the distinction not between his intentions and previous ones, but between today's world and previous societies. Like traditional political authors, he writes for and from his world. His characters involve themselves in political, legal, moral, and sexual situations as they speak, act, and operate without his editorial comment on their actions. Farce and misery are juxtaposed. Music is an inherent element of reality. The urban world is stimulating and brutal, beautiful and violent. Kureishi's story does not romanticize a world for the audience to recognize; instead, it splashes the contradictory real world across the screen. Thus his characters function on screen as the audience must function in today's world.

Kureishi is unwilling to lapse into using stereotypes, whether defined by yesterday's prejudices or by today's politically correct jargon. His characters are on the move and complicated, and resist reduction to common denominators of race, ethnicity, gender, or economics. Just as this makes his characterizations interesting and without stereotype, so it also makes them more confusing and harder to identify with. As film writer Vincent Canby commented in a 1987 article in the *New York Times,* "The movie doesn't exactly lack for characters, incidents and ideas which is both its problem and its fascination."[36]

The most inventive sequence in *Sammy and Rosie Get Laid* is a triple split screen of three couples having sex. The writer recognizes that the scene is integral to his story. "The fuck sandwich was in my script," he explained. "I saw it and the way it worked. That was the center of the film, the fuck sandwich, and I wrote around it." Kureishi continued that he also heard the scene as it played, although he made some practical alterations in his musical choices on film. "I wanted it to be 'Sexual Healing' but we couldn't get the rights for 'Sexual Healing,'" he said. "It would have been great if we had done that, especially with the fucking, you know, but we couldn't get the rights. So we had to use another soul song, and we used 'My Girl.'"

Certainly Kureishi and Frears recognized the anticlimax of the scenes following this explosive montage. But it is precisely because it neither ends the film nor concludes the story that the segment is a stunning sequence. *Sammy and Rosie Get Laid* had gone through an extensive editing process, and placing the scene at the film's end would have altered its context, suggesting a sense of closure to a plot that the writer has made clear must remain unresolved. Cinematically, therefore, peaking the story here and returning to incidents of film plot was not only innovative filmmaking and mimetic imaging, it was honest storytelling.

A review in the *New York Times* described the scene as follows:

About three quarters of the way through *Sammy and Rosie Get Laid,* there's a particularly rich, riotously busy montage, a succession of shots of urban decay, exuberant West Indian street singers and three separate shots of lovers who alternately reminisce and argue while, at the end of a long London night, they make their circuitous routes to bed. The tempo of the editing increases. Suddenly, the screen splits—horizontally—and we see each of the three couples, layered, more or less, one pair atop another, simultaneously but in separate images, as they achieve transitory satisfaction. That's about all they can hope for.[37]

Sammy and Rosie Get Laid is a film that must be seen more than once and that must be scrutinized in terms of its individual elements, not merely in its entirety. The startling triple split-screen montage, for example, tells a story in movement. The Kureishi/Frears segment incorporates elements of contemporary color and sound. The sandwiched lovers, diverse in age and race, and the rock-and-roll music, both ironic and familiar in its throbbing commentary, practically break through the screen. Unleashed by a shot of the syncopated street musicians preceding it, the segment flaunts itself—then implodes back into the film.

Critics, however, were generally unimpressed by the artificiality and didactic imbalance in the film's writing. Unlike the reviews of *My Beautiful Laundrette*, those of the second Kureishi/Frears film were mixed. Bevan suggests that "as the best films always come out of collaboration, the best films of this sort always come out of some form of autobiographical honesty as well. I think that there's truth from Hanif's life in *Laundrette*. There wasn't that truth in *Sammy and Rosie*, and the audience felt that."[38]

Although ordinarily praised for its glitter and strength, Kureishi's dialogue in this film was often experienced as unreal, overpowering his story's realistic actions. Most of the negative criticism centered on his artificial language. One reviewer both praised and criticized the dialogue in the same passage, claiming: "The talk is usually literate and witty (a rarity in most contemporary films) and ranges from Sammy's homage to London, to Rosie's lesson with concomitant demonstration of the different types of kissing. At times, however, Kureishi becomes too enamored with his own eloquence and wit, and the characters just take off on interminable soliloquies."[39] But his film characters speak not as yuppies and buppies (the black, upwardly mobile segment) speak, but rather as they think they speak. Kureishi employs a writer's license to perfect their verbal exchanges. As English stage characters speak perfected dialogue, so Kureishi extends that theatricality to his movie dialogue.

Yet international film critics dismissed the theatrical precedents, along with Kureishi's playwriting experience, and categorized Kureishi's clever language as a genetic English language hang-up. Pauline Kael, in a 1987 article for *The New Yorker*, encapsulated this criticism: "But

Fig. 7. Rosie (Frances Barber) uses husband Sammy (Ayub Khan Din) as an audiovisual aid to demonstrate her treatise on kissing in *Sammy and Rosie Get Laid*. (Photo courtesy of British Film Institute.)

the film suffers from the curse of the British: verbal facility, a terrible empty brilliance. I don't ever recall hearing so many failed epigrams in one movie."[40] However, fictional characters traditionally handle situations with more panache than we do in our daily routines. If, as some critics suggest, Kureishi's dialogue does not echo slice-of-life conversation, it does nonetheless find root in theater as he creates a language for the screen.

Whereas the dialogue of *Sammy and Rosie Get Laid* is, of course, funny, in reality cosmopolitan chatter is merely maddening—how the people Kureishi satirizes love to hear themselves talk! It may be the case in the film that, as Pauline Kael observes, "nobody ever gropes for a word or stumbles over a phrase; everybody is linguistically confident and ready to go."[41] Nonetheless, in its send-up of today's trendy social intercourse, the self-conscious conversation penned by Kureishi brilliantly hits its mark. It is the meter and delivery of Kureishi's lines as dialogue, however, not their replication of conversation, that carries their truth. One only needs to listen to the people in Kureishi's stories to appreciate this—how they love to hear themselves talk, too! Posturing and posing, these characters spend little time listening as they prepare their next quip. Kureishi's aesthetic underscores his dialogue with silences, sound effects, and musical commentary—he creates a soundtrack that tells his story. Appropriate to the collaborative and multi-genre creation of sound in film, Kureishi's language evolves as screen dialogue. Sound design and editing of the sound for film further charges his dialogue with its cinematic energy. Thus his dialogue and the music become cinematic sound created to move, in a nonstop linguistic, melodic, aural avalanche. "*Sammy & Rosie* is never dull," one critic confirms. "Indeed it shrinks from the ordinary as it does from decorum, balance or coherence. Kureishi and director Stephen Frears, who two years ago collaborated on the low-budget *My Beautiful Laundrette*, have no time for the dramatic verities. They're breathless with all the hot news inside them."[42]

Positive critical response to this second film went hand-in-hand with the fault-finding criticism; with Kureishi himself being controversial by choice and growing in reputation, unanimously favorable reception of his work by now had become increasingly unlikely. The negativity of the critical reaction to *Sammy and Rosie Get Laid* also foreshadowed the brutality of the critical response that would assault Kureishi's next film. And when critics distinguished between the writing and the direction rather than viewing the writer and the director as a team, they exposed another interesting paradox, for this critical separation ironically further illuminated Kureishi's creative gains in the collaborative process of filmmaking just as it prompted him to seek more control over his next projects.

A survey of the reviews of the Kureishi/Frears films also enables the introduction of an important, additional critical perspective to be identified. Although critics continued to note Kureishi's hyphenated identity and his position as an enfant terrible, critical expectations of him

Fig. 8. In the aftermath of a racist murder and urban rioting, London police flank Danny (Roland Gift) and Rosie (Frances Barber), a racially mixed pair of adulterers, in *Sammy and Rosie Get Laid*. (Photo courtesy of British Film Institute.)

expanded with his projects. Scholarly articles relating Kureishi to more elevated themes and literary techniques began to appear. For example, Kureishi's *Sammy and Rosie Get Laid* script was discussed as a film sibling of Eliot's poetic masterpiece "The Wasteland." Eliot's lines are identified as the graffiti on a dissolute caravan, the occurrence of another vision-impaired observer is cited, and possible redemption from the sterile landscape is seen as being ambiguously hinted at in the conclusion. "Clearly, Kureishi means us to see this as the urban desert," concludes a scholarly article. "With the lines of poetry, he establishes it specifically as Eliot's."[43]

When asked directly if his script allusions to T. S. Eliot in *Sammy and Rosie Get Laid* were intentional, Kureishi negated his use of Eliot while he reaffirmed his film writing's place among literary genres:

I think sometimes I did [allude to classic literature] for fun, but I don't find it that interesting to do. I realize that most people have never read those fucking books anyway. So there's no real fun in making arcane references. I like to tell stories simply and straightforwardly. I read a story before I came [to the States] by Isaac Bashevis Singer. He is one of my favorite writers. His stories are so simple as they are told. And yet, they speak about important things.

The critical rationale placing Kureishi's screenwriting within the British literary tradition is significant. The assessment of his screenplays as comprising an academic subject illustrates a critical recognition that writing for film is a specific genre of writing. As Kureishi clarifies, his screenplays are not filmmaking, "they are telling a story, creating character, plot, ideas: storytelling. They are writing for the cinema."

Scholarly criticism, therefore, both positive and negative, benchmarks Kureishi's appellation as a cinematic storyteller. Kureishi's screenplays affirm that his intention, in his screenwriting as in his other writing, is to tell instructive and entertaining stories; that is, his aim is to create literature.

Popular critical expectations of Kureishi's power as a storyteller had risen significantly by the time of his second film script. "But it's past question that he writes for the screen with a hot proprietary sense that is arresting," declared one critic. Kureishi's style has evolved in the collaborative process of filmmaking. He has found the forum for his stories—namely, screenwriting, which is appropriate to his evolving point of view. "'The screen belongs to me,' [Kureishi] seems to say, 'this is where I work—as I please.' He has his own quizzical, humorous, poignant view of injustice and despair."[44]

Already a respected playwright, Kureishi had thus acquired a second reputation—that of film writer. After his first two film scripts met with praise, he went on to write a third screenplay—but tabled it. He turned away from celebrity as a screenwriter, as he had done from his success writing plays, and pursued instead a new writing challenge—that of composing his first novel.

AUTHOR
The Buddha of Suburbia

A writer continually faces a range of aesthetic choices. There are myriad technical complications as drafts and revisions become a story. With three distinct manuscript drafts in existence, Hanif Kureishi's first novel, *The Buddha of Suburbia*, provides a detailed record of Kureishi's writing process. As the author, Kureishi determined his mode of exposition and structure, finding the rhetoric to frame his themes.

Characteristically for a first novel, *The Buddha of Suburbia* has a discernible autobiographical source. It appeared first as a six-page short story published in *Harper's*.[1] Also written in the first person from Karim Amir's point of view, the short story relates similar incidents to those that open the novel. The plot, which begins with Karim's father, Haroon, coming home from work one evening, follows the events of Haroon's first public appearance as the Buddha. Events in the short story include Haroon's sexual tryst in the Beckenham garden and that of his son in the attic. The story ends with the young narrator returning home later that night with his nauseous father and, realizing his father's failures, promising his disgusted mother that he will never get married.

Although the novel includes most of the same-named Amir family characters who appear in the short story, Kureishi substitutes a brother named Allie for the short story's grandmother sporting Auntie Jean's blue hair. Although they have different names, the short story's Cheryl Cooper and her son Paul are similar characters to the novel's Eva and Charlie Kay (stage name: Charlie Hero). Kureishi's short-story style is as dense as his style in the novel, crammed with allusions, descriptions, proper names, brands, and one-liners. Consequently, the seeds of the plot, tone, and style of his novel are quite identifiable in the short story that preceded it.

But the novel as published was not the next step in the process. Three early drafts of the novel show that Kureishi first made significant tonal changes in his story, including giving it a new title, before he again veered closer to his published short story. They offer evidence of his search to find his novel through a series of revisions before bringing it back to its short-story roots.

The novel's first draft, dated 27 December 1987, was typed on the backs of letters, junk mail, and flyers. Revisions were made throughout in longhand. Generally, longhand corrections to the manuscript will be considered in this chapter only if they went on to become part of a later draft. However, the title revision, in longhand, from *The Streets of My Heart* to *The Streets of the Heart*, was, the author remembers, "more a second thought than a change."

The title of a novel is significant; indeed, this particular novelist "keeps a running list of about a hundred of them." The novel's first title does not hint at the story's social commentary or Asian culture; personal, sounding like a memoir, it is more journal-like and less satiric than is the final, published title.

The two earlier titles reflect Kureishi's focus in this novel of adolescent experiences, and they make the paths of the human heart and the grid map of the city synonymous, an emotional A to Z.

Using the personal pronoun first, with "my heart," Kureishi then switched to the indefinite article, "the," in his first novel's title. This change proves telling throughout the draft. In fact, ironically, this first draft with the change to a more romantic-sounding title represents the most objective version of the novel.

Comparing the texts of the drafts is analytically productive. A study of the opening paragraphs of each draft is therefore included here to elucidate Kureishi's evolving aesthetic (see Appendix). The first draft opens:

It was the most exciting time there could have been, perhaps because everything was in flux. Movement and change and the new were in everything. It was also a gullible age and people were looking for something to believe in, to worship, to follow—someone to tell them how to live and not be unhappy. Yes, if there was one thing that characterised the age, it was people's determination not to be unhappy, though as a family we were unhappy in our own way. But that particular unhappiness wasn't to last, though I didn't know it.

The novel's opening paragraph is written in the first person. Sentences vary in length, with 70 monosyllabic words in the 96-word, five-sentence paragraph. Although almost one-third of the words are verbs, parts of verbs, or verbals, the verbs used in the main are without force, and include ten conjugations of "to be"—more than the total of all the other verbs used in the paragraph. These verbs affirm existence rather than denote actions. "Was" is the most frequently used and its tense denotes existence that is already in the past.

Other verbs, too, are weakened as actions. They are often either compounded as verbals, used with auxiliary "to be" verbs, distanced as infinitive imperatives, or negated not as action but as a convoluted reversal of actions. The action "characterised," for example, is subordinated by its syntax. The verbal "looking" introduces the sentence containing most of the active verbs in the paragraph. Not only do the infinitive forms weaken the action force of these verbs, their syntax further reduces it. These verbs are used in a series of infinitives: "to believe . . . to worship . . . to follow . . . to tell . . . to live," culminating in a negative infinitive, "not to be unhappy." Stressed already by its negation and its placement last in the series, "not to be unhappy" is immediately repeated for emphasis, then later affirmed not as the one thing the "family" does or is, but as the one thing the family was—"we were unhappy."

The condition of unhappiness is mentioned four times in the paragraph, isolating Kureishi's most telling stylistic. Although he is usually considered a visual author, his wording is actually more imagistic. He is concerned here with "unhappiness," "determination," and "excitement." "People" are looking for "something," "someone," and "everything." He writes of a "time," an "age" that is in "flux" with the "new," "movement" and "change." The prose evidences a reliance on abstract words rather than concrete descriptors.

Speaking in the first person, the narrator is neither described nor named. His relationship to the story is unknown. There is no suggestion of race as a theme. There is no introduction of the novel's suburban setting. The paragraph is expository without the comic tone of the final manuscript. Any personal reference is left until the close of the paragraph. And from the first sentence, this draft is about the times. The paragraph sounds a bit like the opening paragraph of Dickens's *Tale of Two Cities*, in fact, echoing its best-of-times/worst-of-times paradoxical setup.

In the second draft, Kureishi's working title and date remain the same, but the text is cleaner. Most of the longhand changes on the first draft have here been incorporated as revisions and there are now far fewer handwritten corrections.

The second draft's first paragraph is expanded to almost the length of the published version. Analysis of this paragraph reveals that Kureishi is still in the process of "finding his novel." It reads:

Things were usually gloomy in our family, I don't know why. But it all started to change on a long summer's evening in South London when my father hurried home from work not in a gloomy mood. I was seventeen. I could smell the train in him as he put his briefcase away behind the front door and took off his raincoat, chucking it over the bottom of the banisters. He kissed my brother and my mother and me with great enthusiasm, as if we had recently been rescued from an earthquake. He was still unaware that Mum didn't like to be touched. He handed her a greasy packet of kebabs and chapatis. Then, instead of flopping into his chair and watching the television news and waiting for Mum to bring him his kebabs and red chilies, he went into their bedroom, which was downstairs next to the living room, and quickly stripped to his vest and underpants.

This opening paragraph has more personal punch. It is still sharp, with 110 of its 158 words consisting of monosyllables, and the eight sentences are again varied in length. But this time, without padding his paragraph with additional adverbs and adjectives, Kureishi has included specific and colorful modifiers like "red" and "greasy." The paragraph is heavy with concrete nouns; "underpants," "kebabs," and "South London" are definite and vivid depictors.

The ratio of verbs is not as high as in the first draft, but Kureishi has drastically reduced the proportion of "to be" verbs. Moreover, the active verbs now outnumber the verbs of being—these verbs are vibrant, some almost onomatopoeic: "chucking," "flopping," "watching," "stripped," "kissed," "rescued," "hurried," and "touched" envision a lively set of actions, making the paragraph more active and definite.

This opening is also more personal. From its first sentence it is about a family—not about their times. And the unexplained "gloom" of their past already begins to recede in the course of this paragraph. The relationship of the narrator to the story he is telling is also now suggested: He lives with his mother, father, and brother. They have a daily routine. After the narrator blurts out that he is "seventeen," it becomes understandable why he thinks that fatherly "enthusiasm" is better saved for after an "earthquake." The succinct wording has identified the point of view. The prose now has a sense of humor and a lighter tone.

The suburb is named and life in it is introduced. Dad makes a trip on the train with his "briefcase" and "raincoat" often enough to have, as a daily commuter, that "smell" of the "train" on him. Some racial or ethnic diversity is nonchalantly suggested by the narrator's familiarity with the exotic take-away (i.e. take-out) food—chapatis and red chilies.

Kureishi characterizes the marriage of Mum and the narrator's father in an equally nonchalant way. Dad usually flops in a chair to watch TV while waiting for his wife to serve him dinner. Mum doesn't "like to be touched." Yet what most characterizes the parents is the recognition by Mum that her husband "was still unaware" of her aversion to being touched. Their characterization rests in this small, seemingly extraneous line. While the story glides by, Kureishi's exposition begins to sneak up on the reader: Dad is insensitive to his wife; Mum is shy and unable to assert herself.

Unlike the first draft's interest in a particular time, this draft concentrates on the family. It makes the narrator more individual. It reads as he talks: the words convey his feelings about the events, about the others, and about himself. Kureishi is beginning to focus in the paragraph not only on the story he wants to tell, but on the way he wants to tell it.

The author returns to the original short story's title, *The Buddha of Suburbia*, in the third draft, dated 17 July 1989. The novel's title change indicates that Kureishi has found his story—of London's Anglo-Asian hybrid, rather than of the city. There are very few longhand revisions on this final manuscript. In the first paragraph, in fact, only one sentence was inserted in pen before the text was published. Kureishi's final manuscript begins:

My name is Karim Amir and I am an Englishman born and bred, almost. I am often considered to be a funny kind of Englishman, a new breed as it were, having emerged from two old histories. But I don't care—Englishman I am (though not proud of it), from the South London suburbs and going somewhere. Perhaps it was the odd mixture of continents and blood, of here and there, of belonging and not, that made me restless and easily bored. Or perhaps it was being brought up in the suburbs that did it. Anyway why search the inner room when it's enough to say that I was looking for trouble, any kind of movement, action and sexual interest I could find, because things were so gloomy, so slow and heavy, in our family. Quite frankly, it was all getting me down and I was ready for anything.

The vagueness of the previous drafts has been diminished and the novel now reads with a rhythm that propels the story forward. The paragraph's seven sentences are still varied in length—in fact, the range of length has increased. This draft also contains a high proportion of monosyllabic words—103 of the paragraph's total word count of 153. Kureishi further decreases reliance on hazy "to be" verb forms, while he returns to, and increases his use of, verbs that denote state of being rather than action: "born," "bored," "bred," and "emerged." If both the second and third drafts are more definite in this respect, there is more focus in the third draft, away from the sing-songy colloquialisms of the earlier draft and toward words more appropriate to Kureishi's theme. Furthermore, there is now a more balanced use of past and present tenses, to distinguish what the times were then from who Karim was then and who he is now.

Other alterations also tighten the prose and better focus it. First, the changes made to the narrator—his age is resolved, and so is his name—change the voice of the paragraph. Not only is Karim's mixed nationality and race presented, his cultural mixture of pride and resentment is also now clearly stated. Confusion defines—and must continue to define—his attitude. That irrevocable posture is clear right at the novel's start, and the possibility of resolve is immediately dismissed when Karim flatly admits he is English, like it or not—"[an] Englishman I am (though not proud of it)."

The novel is set in the suburbs of London, but the wording establishes a world within its own world, a pattern of pieces that simply does not fit in this setting. And it is reinforced in the narrator's observations—from the first sentence, in which he describes himself, so exotically named, as "a proper Englishman . . . almost"—to his musings on his dual history, from continents to suburban neighborhoods. The contradictions in content and form are reasserted by the novel's call to action in the opening paragraph's last sentence: A bored teenager, bored even by being bored, we are assured, Karim is now "ready for anything."

The prose gains impact in its immediate concentration on the novel's themes—initiation, identity, the outsider looking in, and racial conflict. All of these issues are introduced in this first paragraph. The narrator is in search of anything, must get out of the suburbs, and is of mixed breed racially. His situation—and thus his attitude—is already evident.

A story told in asides is introduced and the use of certain techniques immediately establishes the novel's style. The reader is aware from this first paragraph that *The Buddha of Suburbia* is a novel of social comedy written in a style relying on extrapolation. That is, from the outset the comedic conflicts of Karim's society are lambasted, while the dense descriptions are subtly undercut by Kureishi's sarcastic message. One word—"almost," modifying Karim's self-imposed Gilbert and Sullivan–like identity as a "proper Englishman"—says it all. The parenthetical aside "(though not proud of it)" reinforces the novel's inherent contradictions in theme, in opposition to the rhythmic blending of these seemingly contradictory messages. By employing this stylistic device, Kureishi gives the novel its distinctive voice.

For the published novel, the author inserted an additional sentence—"I don't know why"—into the manuscript's first paragraph, before the last sentence. This sentence changes the ratio of verbs in the prose and alters the number of abstract words, concrete modifiers, and monosyllables. But much more significantly, it supports duality and better focuses the finished paragraph as an introduction to the novel's universe.

Kureishi tells his story through a narrator's point of view—but as immediately, the author also provides the reader with an objective view of the incidents. Humor is integral to both Karim's story and Kureishi's truth; contradiction becomes inherent in the novel as well.

Groundwork continues to be laid in these opening paragraphs in the final draft. Establishing that Karim, up for anything, is telling the story, Kureishi underscores his narrator's confusion by pairing ennui and wonder in his adolescent point of view.

The incident of Karim watching Haroon standing upside down stripped to his underwear returns to the original short-story version of the incident in the final draft. The description of Haroon's headstand—his literal inversion in the final draft—is paradoxical in tone. It ridicules the suburban and the enlightened: it embraces and lashes out at stereotypes of suburbia, race, and family.

Here stands Dad, whom Karim loves, admires, and finds quite embarrassing. The description of Haroon and his headstand gains meaning from the reader's experience—that is, it becomes an image: Talk about seeing your father naked! Karim's topsy-turvy progenitor is as fully characterized as he is bluntly physically described.

Kureishi characterizes him in a pithy way. Haroon is justly proud of his physique, and the reader, made to see Haroon, and made to see Haroon as Karim sees him, begins to read as well what Haroon is like: proud, haughty, pompous—perhaps a bit ridiculous. The paragraph also characterizes Karim. The son finds his father embarrassing and foolish—what boy of seventeen does not?

Haroon is everything Karim rejects about growing up. The author further characterizes the relationship between father and son by using the narration as ironic commentary on plot and characters. Thus, in a typical throwaway aside, musically worded, Karim expresses his awareness of his dad's attitude, and perhaps also of his creator's—"he easily became sarcastic, Dad." The father flaunts a son's every fear of growing old.

Kureishi's wording juxtaposes critical observations with respectful ones. The balanced language suggests not only Karim's ambiguous feelings for his dad but already hints at the racial conflicts within Karim's hyphenated identity.

Rhetoric underlies the opening paragraphs and interrupts itself. Words, too, connote paradoxical images in this Anglo-Asian narrative. Incidents are both ordinary and preposterous. The structure fragments images as it reflects the thesis. Actions are boring and exciting, just as Karim is both bored and excited with his future. Long sentences are juxtaposed with shorter ones. Meaning is often conveyed in the subordinated phrases rather than in the main clauses. The paragraphs continue back and forth between the vulgar and the ascetic, the comic and the serious, weighty social issues and the ridiculous, even the sentimental and the ribald.

In a novel's opening paragraphs, a reader would neither know nor want to know all that is to happen. Yet particularly in this often outrageous novel, the reader needs to feel as the story evolves that everything, however unexpected, is still very much in its place. Through exposition and tone, Kureishi has already set the novel in motion in the opening paragraphs. Although they give the reader no idea of plot or climax, by the novel's end the reader will be satisfied not only that the conclusion is true, but that it is inevitable. Kureishi achieves this because the humanity of his characterizations, the precision in his style, and the focus on his themes are strongly established in these opening paragraphs.

Hilarious as an introduction to Karim's family, the passage is also a strong exposition. It introduces the novel's issues immediately. Pervaded with bursts of satire and a stream of activities, it creates a sense of anticipation for the coming story. Fortunately, since it conveys the sense that anything can happen in the novel, Karim proclaims in equally open-ended language in this opening passage that, confused and bored, he is "ready for anything."

Kureishi's episodic novel merges content and style. Throughout the novel, familiar music provides a "soundtrack," and the use of literary conventions supports Kureishi's myriad outlandish comic sequences. Throughout the novel, too, street names and rock stars and restaurants are familiar, as are longings and secrets and memories. If iconicity is the meaning-producing interaction between form and content, the novel is iconic. Kureishi's words are a network of images that convey further meanings through their sounds and context. Thus his description is imagery demanding the input of the reader's experiences. Meaning in his novel is what rhetoricians call "emotional *gestalt*" — that is, the meaning of the novel is a process, not merely a product.

Exposition recurs, building without completion, like the narrator's contradictory boredom and anticipation. The images themselves are unfinished. Reality in description is expressed both in simple declarative sentences and in exaggerated sequences. Words collide and merge, giving each other meaning and lack of meaning in context. Themes such as racism and suburbanism collide and merge too, as do images of Haroon's asceticism and his dangling privates.

Rhetorically, the passage suggests Longinus's *On the Sublime*, a model of content arrangement. The disorganization and confusion of language and structure in this passage suggest a highly emotional state. Adding the seventeen-year-old vantage point admitted by the narrator and setting his story in the undefined seventies, Kureishi introduces his novel's meaning as its form.

This style of composition to reinforce content is found throughout the text. Kureishi uses words as sounds and as signification to create linguistic and thematic cohesion throughout his novel. His literary style carries his themes to his final paragraph, completing his piece in much the same way that a classical coda completes a symphony. A novel of style, its language is like music.

Still heady from Haroon's acrobatics, the novel spills into the next sequence. Likewise, still heady from Carnaby Street's recent run as the center of the civilized world, Karim's London spills into the next decade. Both do so musically.

The author employs costuming for the same effects. As with other decades, the seventies is most easily satirized by targeting its clothes—and in that respect, seventies fashion is a gold mine—the Cuban heels, the flared trousers, the headbands. No longer restricted to just an avant-garde few, the psychedelic look of the sixties exploded into the shopping malls in Kureishi's seventies, and free spirits stretched fashion to its limits. Like seventies fashions, the novel is garish and colorful, flamboyant and ridiculous.

Kureishi uses fashion relentlessly throughout *The Buddha of Suburbia*, from early on when, as just the right finishing touch in the short story, Karim wears "grandmother's fur coat, strapping a belt around my stomach. I was right up to date."[2] Critics have recognized the author's use of costuming as a device, and the story's inclusion of Karim's intimate toilette has been noted as underscoring the naivete and youthfulness of his times. "I enjoyed its raunchily giggle-inducing similes," an otherwise-negative review of the novel concedes, "(Karim, dolling up for some decorous debauchery in Hampstead, describes his talc-powdered testicles as being 'as fragrantly dusted and tasty as Turkish Delight')."[3]

Fig. 9. The South Kensington Station is Karim's new London tube stop as he follows the road to his dreams in *The Buddha of Suburbia*. (Photo by author.)

Karim Amir grows up in a world not unlike that of Hanif Kureishi, who, during his adolescence, watched the London world from suburban Bromley, whose school pop stars attended; the similarities continue into later life, with Kureishi making himself part of the London scene and being involved in the seventies theatrical world, becoming a writer-in-residence at a West End theater, and achieving celebrity with the writing of the television script of *My Beautiful Laundrette*.

Like Kureishi, Karim is the son of an Anglo-Asian family in the suburbs. More into music than school, he is involved with a pop-star school chum and becomes immersed in experimental theater. He has brushes with the political and social revolutionaries of the seventies London art scene. At the novel's conclusion, he goes to work in television soap opera, hoping to become a star.

And so the autobiographical connections between Kureishi and Karim, between fact and fiction, become irresistible. The book is recognized by most critics as personal to Kureishi. In criticism of the novel, this tie prompts interest in issues of race and racism. Noting that "like his fictional protagonist, Mr. Kureishi is the child of an Indian father and an English mother," one critic declared that "the book's portrait of English racism is autobiographical enough."[4]

In mentioning Kureishi's mixed racial identity, critics have referred, too, to his school days, during which he suffered "Paki bashing" in Bromley, and to the novel's racism in the suburbs. There has been frequent name-dropping of Kureishi's schoolmate Billy Broad, who became Billy Idol, and of *The Buddha of Suburbia*'s Charlie Kay, who becomes Charlie Hero, seen as a second-string David Bowie. Since Bowie also attended Kureishi's Bromley school, the fact that he composed the title song and incidental music for the television version of Kureishi's novel further amplifies this tie of the story to Kureishi's autobiography. The relationship of Kureishi's civil-servant father to Karim's father, Haroon, has also been noted by critics, as has the similarity between Kureishi's years at the Royal Court Theatre and Karim's theatrical career in London. "His book has occasioned something of a guessing game back home," concludes the *New York Times* critic who coined the party game, "Pin-the-Londoner on the fictional *Buddha* character."[5]

Colleagues, too, have made the connection between autobiography and fiction. "I think the book captured that feeling of being in London in the seventies very well and actually in the suburbs of London, which is where Hanif comes from," assessed Kevin Loader, the producer of the TV adaptation of the novel and, like Kureishi, from the suburbs. "As Hanif writes, we did feel very conscious growing up in the seventies that there wasn't anything."[6]

Yet it is Kureishi's creation of fiction that separates the novel from memoir. And *The Buddha of Suburbia* is a created universe. Material may be drawn from history or laden with autobiography, but fundamentally the book is Kureishi's creation of the seventies London of Karim Amir, not the adolescent world of Kureishi's seventies retold. Deletions, alterations, and inventions of the author—not the record of autobiographical occurrences—are the novel.

This distinction is clearest in the creation of a main character who is only superficially like the ambitious adolescent author. "Karim, his adolescent narrator, is the author's most appealing creation," wrote one critic. "It's his voice that makes the novel's anarchy coherent, propelling the plot with authority and verve."[7] Certainly narrator Karim speaks with the storyteller's voice, but Karim is conceived by his literary creator not as his young alter ego but rather as an aimless boy of the suburbs. According to Kureishi himself,

There's one difference, one main difference between me and that guy in *The Buddha,* which is that when I was young, from the age of fourteen, I fully knew that I wanted to be a writer. And so I had a great sense of purpose and direction in my life all through those years. I was very strong-willed: get out of the suburbs—be a writer—be educated—make something of yourself. The boy in *The Buddha* is much more of a drifter. He has that side of me which is opportunistic and up for anything, but he doesn't have, and never can have—I didn't give him—the fucking discipline that I have, the sense of purpose that I have. That's the main difference.

It is Kureishi's creation of this opportunist that frames the novel's chronicle of the seventies, expanding his novel's incidents for universal identification. The character bridges the gap between his own personal story and that universal identification by adding identifiable elements for readers beyond setting and plot incidents. So, too, the novel functions to fashion the decade in such a way as to bring it to literary—not documentary—life.

Kureishi customarily delves more deeply into his themes by reinvestigating similar characters in different projects. The character of Flounder in "With Your Tongue down My Throat," his short story published in 1990, comes to mind here. Not only is the bumbling Flounder like the later immigrant bridegroom character Changez in *The Buddha of Suburbia,* he too is nicknamed Bubbles. The Flounder's sexual escapades at a Pakistani beach house also resemble the family stories that Changez will later serialize for Jamila. The author explains:

I recycle a lot of material . . . because I realize that they're good ideas, but I didn't really get hold of them yet. I deepen them. I didn't really get hold of them, so I keep rewriting. I wrote the boy in *Mother Country;* he's a pop star. And I wrote a pop star in *Charlie Hero.* And there's another guy in *Mother Country* who gets obsessed with Buddhism in India. You can see that these are characters I developed more fully later on. I realize they are good ideas for me, fertile ideas, but I didn't yet do them properly. That's why I keep writing in a way, to try to get hold of this thing that is always eluding me.

In his journals Kureishi records daily events, observations, and "bits of detail" to support his fiction with precise accuracy. The diaries provide a window into his methods of composition. He has published entries from his journal *Working with Stephen* to accompany his screenplay of *Sammy and Rosie Get Laid*.[8] While writing *The Buddha of Suburbia*, Kureishi again kept a diary. He used it to map out his characters, fleshing out their backgrounds to provide a context for their actions in his story:

I did [keep an unpublished journal] with the *Buddha*. So I can look back and say this is the day when I knew the character must come to England. Of course, I always knew this guy was coming to England, but I didn't know when. He could do this; he is going to do that—he could be like this; he is like that. Then I know. And on the next day I write, "today Changez comes to London."

I tend to think about one character at a time. Then I get fed up with him and I move him a little bit. And then I move the next one. I push that one forward and then I run over there and push that one forward, and I run back here again. It's like an army. The whole fucking thing has got to move forward at the same time.

The diaries suggest how true experience is translated into his fiction. While major autobiographical experiences such as his theatrical apprenticeship in the West End, as well as painful incidents of bigotry, have previously been considered, tiny autobiographical details, too, have found themselves reinvented for his fiction. A remark made at a party in Pakistan about primitive conditions there is recorded in an early diary, but finds its way into Uncle Nasser's dialogue in *My Beautiful Laundrette*. In an entry in a later diary published with *Sammy and Rosie Get Laid*, Kureishi notes an experience of watching a fan pass a note to Talking Heads band member David Byrne while Kureishi and he were eating at London's Gate Diner. The incident is later metamorphosed by Kureishi into a plot incident for Charlie Hero and Karim's New York visit in *The Buddha of Suburbia*.

Thus while Kureishi acknowledges the story's ties to his autobiography, he only incorporates historical detail as literary technique. This technique enhances the realism of the novel's setting but emphasizes that the novel's reality—albeit detailed, evocative, and precise—is the storyteller's fiction.

Kureishi elected to write the novel in the first person, thus making

Fig. 10. The Albert Bridge, one of a number of bridges spanning the Thames as it flows through London, separating the suburbs from the cosmopolitan world north of the river. Kureishi was able to bridge this distance, too—as was Karim Amir, the main character in his first novel, *The Buddha of Suburbia*. (Photo by author.)

the story appear a more personal narrative. Details of and attention to the era of the seventies give the novel the further trappings of the historical novel. Thus, according to one reviewer, "Autobiographical or not, the London section *reads* like bits of personal narrative, casual and episodic."[9] But the historical seventies are told from a literary point of view, from an author's perspective; that is, Karim is not Kureishi, but, rather, the invented voice that the storyteller has selected to tell his story.

The story's narrator, Karim, is an innocent disillusioned by society. While it is difficult to imagine Karim as innocent—he has sex with everything in sight, his own hand when he isn't holding dope and there isn't a household pet available—Karim is, nonetheless, in that tradition of young characters who move unscathed through a series of literary exploits in their search for answers to idealistic questions: What is life? Why are people so cruel? Where is real love? And identity? Honesty? Social justice? Moving from set to set in front of a group of mantra-singing backup, daydream believers, Karim Amir is a disco-busting Candide.

Seventeen years of age as the novel opens, the novel's narrator thinks he is "ready for anything." Karim knows he can find the best of all possible worlds somewhere, anywhere, outside the suburbs. At the age of twenty in the novel's second part, he moves to London. Karim does not seek the transcendental philosophy of his father, although Haroon's preaching is music to the rest of the world. All Karim needs is love, as the Beatles sang; it's easy. And love, sex, drugs, travel, deceit, pain, and success cram Karim's days and nights in the city. He must also avoid youth's nemesis: boredom. "Nothing, not even society's decay and possible demise, is more atrocious to these characters than a moment without excitement," wrote one reviewer.[10] Launched from the suburbs, Karim becomes a man of experience in London; "happy and miserable at the same time" at the novel's close, he "thinks" both of what a mess everything has been, and that "it wouldn't always be that way."

The Buddha of Suburbia continues the tradition in the English novel that emphasizes antisocial elements, sexual excess, and adolescent rebellion as rites of initiation. And Kureishi acknowledges his place in this tradition and reaffirms the prominence of his distinctive point of view in an explanation that, like his mercurial sense of humor, relishes the profane and the impish. "Kureishi sees himself working in a very English tradition of comic realism," wrote James Saynor in a 1993 article in the *Observer*, in which he goes on to quote Kureishi: "'Looking back on the novel—though I might not like to admit it—I was influenced more by books like *Lucky Jim* and early Evelyn Waugh than I was by *On the Road*. You know funny books about boys growing up and getting into scrapes.'"[11] In seventies London Karim is surrounded on all sides by hypocrisy: sexual, political, artistic, and, more particular to Kureishi's initiation story, racial. "Like V. S. Naipaul [Kureishi] has a gift for locating the hypocrisies that inform relationships between the white and nonwhite worlds, and absolutely no misgivings about exposing those hypocrisies on both sides," claimed an article in the *New York Times* in 1990.[12]

Kureishi's story of initiation has a place as a British genre novel. As explained in chapter 1, initiation stories treat the process of maturation as experienced by the initially adolescent main character. There is a tradition of initiation novels in the States as well. Because of its racial themes, Mark Twain's *The Adventures of Huckleberry Finn* (1884) comes easily to mind as a forerunner of Kureishi's novel, Huck being brought face to face with ugly reality in his every foray into hypocritical Mississippi River society. In a later American novel, J. D. Salinger's *The Catcher in the Rye* (1945), Holden Caulfield too finds society as rigid an institution as both the school from which he has been expelled and the mental institution to which he has been committed. A more recent novel of sexual experimentation, Philip Roth's *Portnoy's Complaint* (1969), like

The Buddha of Suburbia, is a hyperbolic diary of adolescent penis personification. In the end Huck becomes the rebel society brands him, Holden accepts life in a controlled environment, and Portnoy bows to the sexual guilt, conventions, and paranoia of becoming an adult. These other protagonists, like Karim, accept being cast in a role, albeit not as an Asian soap-opera character.

A contemporary stylistic device ties Kureishi to American prose more closely than does his place in initiation literature. A comparison between F. Scott Fitzgerald and Kureishi may at first provoke some sly laughter: First, as has been discussed earlier, Hanif Kureishi is an English author from the English literary tradition, while Fitzgerald is quintessentially American in his subject matter, from his stories of East Coast socialites on Long Island and jaded expatriates on the Riviera to those of immigrant West Coast entrepreneurs in Hollywood. The graphic Hanif Kureishi writes not only of essentially British incidents and nationalism, but of incendiary racial revolution, scratchy skin rashes, Pakistani despots, and the South Kensington swipe; F. Scott Fitzgerald, on the other hand, writes of starched white linen, gloves in dance class, yellow roadsters, and women who wear bathing suits and strands of pearls.

But like Kureishi, Fitzgerald is interested in youth and its initiation throughout much of his fiction, including his masterpiece novel, *The Great Gatsby* (1925). Like *The Buddha of Suburbia*, this novel bears autobiographical investigation and is also rooted in an earlier short-story version—Fitzgerald's "Absolution" (1924). In the latter story, a Catholic priest hears a farm boy confess himself too good to have been born of his parents. This adolescent character, like *Gatsby*'s narrator, Nick Carraway, wanders from the stability of the Midwest into the genre novel's East Coast decadent world of the superficial rich as an observer. Dreaming of entering the high-power game of stocks and bonds, Nick becomes instead the broker in the affair between his glamorous neighbor Gatsby and his wealthy married cousin, Daisy Buchanan. Lured by strains of popular music playing across the lawns, as well as by the cars, the flamboyance, and the celebrities of the roaring twenties, Nick becomes involved with white trash, deceit, and murder. At the story's end, Nick rejects everything around him on New York's Long Island and abandons the glitter.

Karim Amir has everything before him as his story begins in suburban London fifty years later: He is an innocent; he is young; he defines his race by skin tone, not by political color; he finds his dreams interesting; and he actually experiences his adolescent fantasies. Karim is a narrator who literally "fucks anyone."

Karim matures. When he interrupts experiencing with thinking, all is lost: he feels the politics of color; he knows the role-playing of gender, the power play of sex; he practices the pretensions of art; and, moreover, he suspects that, like everybody else he knows, he doesn't really give a damn about any of it. As the book ends, Karim has become a character who figuratively fucks everybody. Now he is a man ready for the hypocrisies of society. The fragmented times have hardened Kureishi's Karim Amir from an aimless opportunist into an ageless cynic.

Different national identities underlie each man's fictions. But in the same way that the nationalism in each clearly separates them, so both the importance of nationalism and the importance of place and time are bonds formed by the stylistic prose of these two works: both Fitzgerald and Kureishi meticulously re-create their eras.

Fitzgerald's prose heroes do not find contentment in money, sex, or alcohol. Still romantically attached to their days at school, they tear through the Valley of the Ashes to promiscuous excess and empty glamour on Dick Diver's Riviera or in Gatsby's Manhattan: Fitzgerald's characters epitomize that generation's frustration after the Great War in attempting to understand its changing identity—that of a "lost generation" on a spree. Kureishi's specific rendering of a time and generation half a century later and across an ocean echoes the frustrations of the young. One critic of Kureishi's novel determines that

There is a mythical quality to Kureishi's South London suburbs; they are both a hell to escape from into the exciting anarchy of the city, and a source of eternal comfort and inspiration . . . The shadow of Bromley hangs over Kureishi's work in the way Eton hung over the work of Cyril Connolly. School and suburbs seem to be gilded prisons from which there is no ultimate escape, not on the Riviera, or in the deserts of Arabia, or in Manhattan, or even in Notting Hill Gate.[13]

Kureishi's contemporary prose characters cannot find escape in drugs, Charlie Hero's pants, or religion. His novels trace the redefinition of a generation's identity.

Any analysis of *The Buddha of Suburbia* as a novel, therefore, must include investigation of the story's element most frequently cited in criticism of the novel—namely, setting. Setting is crucial to novels of initiation. To take as examples Fitzgerald's Amory Blaine at Princeton, Thomas Hughes's Tom Brown at Rugby, and Twain's Huck Finn on the Mississippi River, it is clear that detailing a specific setting with realistic detail is necessary to make the young protagonist's battle against the confinement and conventions of the novel's particular setting identifiable as a microcosm for all adolescent entry into society.

Kureishi's use of seventies London as his novel's setting for Karim's initiation has spurred a stampede of seventies reinvestigation in both popular and scholarly response. Kureishi is recognized for having given the seventies a face, and his novel is seen as visualizing a historical era. In its painstakingly accurate recreation of the seventies, *The Buddha of Suburbia* appears as the seamless chronicle of an age. What Fitzgerald did for the twenties, for example, seems to be what Kureishi does for the heretofore nebulous seventies. Parties, trends, popular music, and fashion pervade both authors' descriptions. Fitzgerald and Kureishi both replicate how a time looked to illuminate how a time felt. Thus experimentation, confusion, and finding an identity challenge their characters. Each author chronicles youth, perhaps even defining his generation.

These envisioned settings feed the nostalgia of our contemporary search for a simpler past. But Kureishi's use of time in his return to the seventies is distinct from Fitzgerald's chronicles of the Jazz Age. Kureishi uses time in his story not as a contemporary setting but as a literary device. Fitzgerald wrote of the twenties from the twenties, while in *The Buddha of Suburbia* Kureishi returns to the early years of the seventies almost twenty years later, and knows the years that follow the decade he portrays in his novel. Writing his story from this chronological distance, he is able to realize Gatsby's quest, voiced when he cries "incredulously, 'Can't repeat the past? . . . Why of course you can.'"[14]

At best, the inexact science of defining history by epochs is based on nothing but hindsight. Most often the years marking an era are not synonymous with the decade named for it. Decades may be labeled from zero to nine, but ideas and trends overlap. Evidence of trends, styles, and cultural attitudes that predate the ten-year period linger on into it;

and characteristics of that decade continue to have an effect after a decade concludes.

In Kureishi's novel the frenzy of the psychedelic sixties and their fragmenting into Sergeant Pepper's drug-induced hallucinations spur the *doo-da* seventies. That is, those aimless years in which the author was growing up in the London suburbs are given a face in his story. Revolution is their inheritance, not their battle cry. The seventies inherited the new world order of the young. In the sixties, "doing your own thing" had been boldly laid on the table; in the seventies, finding oneself and empowering oneself, doing what felt good, was what everyone was doing.

The jaded attitudes left over from the bad trip of the sixties are already in place in Kureishi's seventies; innocence has plainly been lost. With no strong middle-class ethic surviving the sixties, attacking it in the seventies simply became less attractive. With the unconventional suddenly the conventional in this decade, the seventies exploded into a mass hysteria of individualism and self-expression. The energy of this new order flashed as an abortive punk rebellion before merely fizzling into collective money-harvesting by the decade's close. As American filmmaker Richard Linklater remembers the decade, "It wasn't [a] simpler, less confused time. The people who lived through the 70s know it kind of sucked."[15]

But Kureishi writes of the seventies having lived—and thought—through them. In his novel, anticipation fills the air—sometimes holding promise, sometimes full of anxiety. A brooding sense of melancholy and nostalgia, too, underlies Kureishi's happening fictional setting. As to how and why this is the case, it is so because Kureishi and his readers know what his characters don't: they know that the novel is gliding toward Thatcherism; that punk music would fade fast; that tragic rocker Janis Joplin's agony would later turn up as a Bette Midler musical film, *The Rose* (1979).

The Buddha of Suburbia electrifies the social momentum reflected in pop music, which is why music is essential to Kureishi and to his novel. "In [the Beatles] there was no sign of the long, slow accumulation of security and status, the year-after-year movement towards satisfaction, that we were expected to ask of life," wrote Kureishi himself in

Eight Arms to Hold You. "Without conscience, duty or concern for the future, everything about the Beatles spoke of enjoyment, abandon and attention to the needs of self."[16] The Beatles' celebrity had become global in the sixties, as had their notoriety; by the seventies no longer a musical group but an icon headed for pop-culture myth, they frame the decade's music. Musically, they preceded the decade—1964 was the year in which Beatlemania went global, with the American invasion; historically, however, they closed the decade, John Lennon being assassinated in 1980 in front of the Dakota apartment complex in New York. In Kureishi's novel, music defines the decade in between these two landmarks in Beatles musical history. The producer of the TV version of the novel, Kevin Loader, offers:

We knew we were in the disenfranchised decade. People told you how awful the seventies were because you didn't have anything that went on in the sixties. Teenagers in the sixties had the Stones; they had the Beatles. We had the tail end of the Stones. And the Beatles had broken up.[17]

Kureishi's seventies, therefore, is an age in which the social conservatism of the eighties had its roots while sixties idealism wilted. Music had attacked yesterday's prejudices and predicted the new dawn. Old morals and taboos annihilated, the age of Aquarius loomed.

This philosophy was popularly embraced in the seventies—usually without thought, and certainly without a fight. Sixties theorizing with its academic rationale had become the popular lifestyle of the seventies. Hindsight identifies the seventies as the decade in which the rock-message lyrics of the sixties became slogans. One critic found that Kureishi's story reads like "what might be called a novel but is rather a constant, furious, streaming 1970s circle-jerk that takes in Pakistanis, Indians, Englishmen and Americans as well."[18] To phrase it in lyrics of the time, Kureishi's decade no longer questioned "all the lonely people, where do they all come from"; instead, it glorified "all the young dudes." Thus in the story's fictional seventies, everyone is "with it."

The Buddha of Suburbia thus has the patina of times past. In addition to the nostalgia induced by the precise, detailed reinvention of the music and fashions of the seventies, Kureishi's novel also gives us that decade without the contradictions, reservations, or confusions experienced by living through it. Through artistic arrangement—and in retrospect—his novel crystallizes the decade's historical fragments.

One critic of the novel has identified "the central perception of the novel, which is that the Seventies were a decade in which almost everyone behaved as if they were teenagers."[19] Another critic has underscored today's suspicion of the seventies philosophy captured in Kureishi's story: "Soon Haroon is launched on a new career as a guru to the middle classes. 'Only do what you love,' he tells them, 'Follow your feelings.' A recipe for disaster if there ever was one."[20]

What is sometimes mistaken for the sixties, with its outlandish costumes and, more important, its uninhibited culture, is more properly attributed to the seventies, which exaggerated the preceding psychedelic decade rather as the Mannerist style exaggerated the Renaissance style. *The Buddha of Suburbia* reminds us "that many of the sins and shortcomings we instinctively blame on the Sixties actually belong to the Seventies. The Sixties swung to the tune of the young and the essentially powerless. It was in the decade that people with responsibilities, people with good steady jobs, people with families and mortgages, started to kick over the traces, to smoke marijuana, to wear bell-bottomed trousers, floppy-collared shirts, and kipper ties."[21] In Kureishi's created seventies, what was going on on the surface was in fact just what was going on. His generation accepts the sixties revolution as a given. Thus, as a critic of this initiation novel characterizes its portrayal of the decade, Kureishi's "Seventies are what happened when the Sixties hit the suburbs."[22]

The sixties social movements, characterized by bra-burning on campus, had evolved into the fires of urban rioting in the seventies. Following immediately upon the impact made by the flower children of the sixties came the next wave of youth, which included Kureishi, absorbing the earlier generation's dreams of the future.

But Kureishi is not a historian. His reconstruction of the decade is neither anthropologically nor historically based. Rather, today, readers find comfort in his seventies as he recreates both our identifiable and our distant past. And from the present Kureishi is able to recreate the seventies not as history, but as an appealing yesterday. Thus, in *The Buddha of Suburbia*, he creates a decade that both looks its part and looks apart.

Kureishi's story is understandable; it is laughable, too, in that the youthful Karim really doesn't have a clue. In the words of a London critic, "Karim has all the reasons for his likes and dislikes, but, alas, can't quite thread them together." [23] Kureishi makes Karim's youthful confusion identifiable in a decade he characterizes with surety—a decade in which political philosophies are toppled and racism pervades. A decade in which, in terms of religion and tradition, the deities of Asia give way to the gods of Empire and Rock, in which art's place in our pop culture world is questioned, and in which assimilation and identity collide. Kureishi gives his narrator safe harbor from his odyssey at the decade's—and the novel's—close. Yet as Karim Amir muses to find an answer, Hanif Kureishi writes that there is none. Societies continue. Societies change. And societies continue not to answer the questions, but merely to change the questions. Kureishi's seventies are not a decade in search of an identity, but, as he re-creates them twenty years later, a decade in search of itself.

AUTEUR *London Kills Me*

Kureishi had begun his first novel, *The Buddha of Suburbia*, in 1987, after *Sammy and Rosie Get Laid* premiered and with another screenplay, *London Kills Me*, written and held in abeyance. While all his projects begin with research, the years devoted to composing and drafting his first novel were, in the main, solitary ones, whereas the process of shaping his stage material and film projects involves collaboration with other people, including actors. Thriving on the change of pace involved in moving between the solitary act of writing stories and novels and the collaborative experience of screen work, Kureishi brings insights gained from one project to another:

When I began writing *The Buddha* I first started out being alone and with a subject, which was really race. The other thing I wanted when I wrote the book was total control, which I got. I didn't have any actors. I wanted that. That was important to me.

After writing the novel it just seemed natural to me to do my film that wasn't about race and to get out of the house. And so my choice was a practical thing. It was partly the change from the isolation of writing. The boredom of writing. Doing this thing alone, doing this huge thing alone drives me mad. And since I like being out, being around actors, that's what I wanted to do next.

In August 1990 in New York City, a month after handing in the manuscript of *The Buddha of Suburbia*, he started to plan the filming of his third screenplay—*London Kills Me*. This time, Kureishi was to con-

Fig. 11. Kureishi, as director of *London Kills Me,* supervises the shoot in London's Notting Hill. Controversy during the production of this film was treated as newsworthy in itself. (Still photo courtesy of Jacques Prayer.)

trol bringing his story before the camera, making his debut as film director. Returning home, he began his research for shooting that film in a London neighborhood that he knew personally. At this time, he still felt that he was able to mingle with the street kids whom he had pictured in his earlier works:

I spent a lot of time on the street with these junkie kids. Up the road, Notting Hill. Because it's such a mixed neighborhood. There's Pakistanis. There's a largely Caribbean community, an Irish community, a Spanish community, a Moroccan community. There's a lot of drugs: dealing smack, crack. Also there's a big college community. Stephen Frears lived there. Nick Roeg lived there. You know, big houses. My agent lives there. It is a vibrant area.

With the eye of a filmmaker, Kureishi adds, "And the streets are quite narrow."

With two screenplays already produced as motion pictures, Kureishi understood clearly that his primary task as a film director was to translate his written story into a visual one. Although he has always liked to vary his projects to take on new challenges, from the beginning it was evident that this project would present a greater challenge than any he had undertaken so far. Filmmaking is always a complicated process, but the production of London Kills Me was perhaps even more confusing than most.

The beginning of the project, however, had been clear-cut. After spending more than three years working on his novel, Kureishi wanted to work again with other people. Clear, too, was his motivation: after having been in complete charge of his prose story, he wanted more control over his film story than he had had in the previous film projects, by taking more responsibility in the cinematic storytelling process. As Kureishi himself explained,

Stephen (Frears) wasn't available; Stephen was making The Grifters. And the producer [Tim Bevan] said, "Maybe you should try doing this yourself." [Bevan] said, "I've worked with many first-time directors. I think we'll have a go. We'll get Ed [Lachman] in. He's a cameraman, experienced, you know, have a go."

Making the film was important to me. Stephen had directed my films; other people have directed my plays, and they made a lasting contribution. I wanted to see if I could do something all by myself, or whether I would be always working with other people.

The film is a story of contemporary London. So too was the filmmaking. Kureishi's reputation caused his London shoots to attract media attention. The press reported that the person upon whom Kureishi's main character was based was threatening legal action. No sooner had shooting begun than the production complications began to mount.

It was becoming increasingly obvious that the separation between what Kureishi writes about and who the author is was continuing to widen. Kureishi's white main character, Clint (Justin Chadwick), seeks a way out of Notting Hill's street world and into its gentrified neighborhood. The film follows the endearing grifter as he deals drugs, squats in a flat, uses and loses friends, services a limousine-liberal feminist, and cons his mother and her brute Elvis Presley–worshiping husband. Ultimately, through robbing his future employer, Clint acquires what he has pursued throughout the film—a pair of indispensable working shoes that then substitute for his old pair of ill-fitting, ruby-red cowboy boots—footwear loaded with cinematic consciousness. The last image of Clint, now ponytailed, is through the window of a trendy upscale bistro where he is working as a waiter. He has passed society's entry test and scaled the culinary heights of fresh pasta, el grande half-decafs, and designer mineral water, rising from street hustler to respectable citizen.

As director, Kureishi made changes on the set as he saw fit. As he himself explained, "I changed things. I changed the script. We changed things; you always do. . . . I tried to tell the story that I'd written." However, he knew from experience that a film script was not intended to be read, but rather was to be filmed as interpreted by actors, and that in translating this story into film, it would be necessary for him to switch from the mindset of creator to that of collaborator.

The experience revealed to Kureishi the problems encountered by a film director. He learned that he would address them differently in a second production. "I'd want more support, more money," he has since said, having realized that having more money enables a film director to confront his real enemy—time. "It's so hard making a film. What you need, really, is time . . . You don't need more money to pay the actors more; you need money for more time, another week, usually."

Today Kureishi considers directing another film possible, but unlikely. He has realized from his debut as a director that he is uncomfortable with the daily responsibilities of directing and also that he misses having a separate director with whom to thrash out his ideas: he feels that the collaboration between a writer and a director makes for a better screenplay as well as a better film.

To return to the making of *London Kills Me*, shooting of the film proceeded successfully. Press coverage continued, daily business was negotiated, and the film was made. Nonetheless, its production was haunted by tales of difficulties, drugs, and arguments, and it suffered mass rejection by the critics—in spite of which—and perhaps because of—Kureishi's cinematic/literary perspective has continued to evolve.

Although it wasn't the critical triumph that *My Beautiful Laundrette* was, and although it didn't receive the spectrum of reviews that *Sammy and Rosie Get Laid* received, *London Kills Me*, nonetheless, had some admirers. In particular, it found some critical success in the United States, where one critic wrote, "Directed and written by Hanif Kureishi . . . the story . . . has a bold, racy rhythm all its own."[1] But overall, it was poorly received and limited in distribution.

The popular critical reverence for Kureishi's status as an artist after his second film script gave way to the first critical rejection of his work in response to this next experiment. Kureishi had accepted the challenge of directing the film of his third screenplay, experimenting wearing two hats—that of writer and that of director. The critics nearly decapitated him twice.

Negative response dominated the reviews, although some of it was constructive, identifying the film's flaws. *Rolling Stone* magazine, however, dismissed the film in a review of little more than one paragraph in length. The critic concluded, "The directing debut of gifted screenwriter Hanif Kureishi is a crushing disappointment . . . Stephen Frears made the characters come alive; Kureishi does not . . . low in characterization, the film drowns in its own pretensions."[2] In a British review, Kureishi's debut as a director was, once again, more chastised than were his efforts as writer, but his writing too was found lacking. "Mainly it falls because it has precious little to say about characters who have precious little to say,"[3] complained the critic.

Comparisons with the previous Kureishi/Frears collaborations were unflattering. "Kureishi doesn't have Stephen Frears to hide behind any more . . . *London Kills Me* pushes none of the right buttons,"[4] wrote one reviewer. Some popular reviews of the film—and, more to the point, of Kureishi—extended beyond negative criticism to critical execution: "Hanif Kureishi has declared that . . . his directorial debut was made for the Saturday night Odeon crowd. Two men and a dog in an art house seem more likely . . . Kureishi displays little cinematic sense . . . This is a film to be endured, like a migraine."[5]

Whether positive or negative, however, critical reception is part of the filmmaking process. It is not unusual for films to engender critical disapproval. Moreover, film critics have a tendency to enjoy turning the knife.

Mentions of *London Kills Me* became almost rabid in their disapproval. One London critic declared in a 1993 article that Hanif Kureishi "came seriously to grief . . . by writing and directing *London Kills Me*, a film about a young drugs dealer in search of some shoes in order to get a proper job," and asserts that, as a filmmaker, Kureishi had "said he was influenced by de Sica's *Bicycle Thieves* [*sic*]. He was wrong."[6] This critical disapproval issued two years after the film's opening appears relentless—and gleeful—as does other negative criticism of the film. In 1994, for instance, the London press was still knocking the film, classifying *London Kills Me* as one of contemporary film's "real duds."[7]

It cannot be denied that the film exhibits the difficulties found by its critics. "I think, by his own admission, Hanif would say he's not a film director," producer Tim Bevan has said, continuing, in agreement with Kureishi himself, that "he doesn't really want to do that again. I think that he feels comfortable with the pen, and that's, as it were, his paintbrush, but he doesn't really feel comfortable with the camera. There's some great stuff in *London Kills Me*, but it actually fails to fly like his other two pictures did."[8]

The negative response identified some cinematic problems. Kureishi was, at the time this film was made, and continues to be, in the process of developing a new perspective concerning the dynamics of literary and cinematic storytelling. But this film was seen as missing the mark, leaving Kureishi's searcher, in the words of one reveiwer, "in Kureishi's moral limboland," merely wandering between film and literary conventions. According to the same reviewer, "a vacuum surrounds this innocent abroad, which Kureishi needs to fill with a story which suits the emotional conflicts and comic mishaps that naturally spring from his *Candide* tales. Then he will have fully integrated his two disciplines, the literary and the cinematic."[9] Kureishi's continuing work in both genres expands the critical analysis of him as well, permitting the comparative analysis of his storytelling in each genre in its own right, as well as when transferred—and translated—into another.

Kureishi's first screenplay had been celebrated for its earnest treatment of controversial issues. Kureishi's perspective was seen by critics as being essential to the success of *My Beautiful Laundrette*.

His next film was sometimes criticized as artificial because it did not come from Kureishi's personal experience. Yet, as with *My Beautiful Laundrette*, its earnestness was again recognized—although it was sometimes considered unbalanced and out of proportion; the *Economist* critic, for instance, wrote, "Politics weakens Mr. Kureishi's touch—as was apparent in his didactic and dismal second film, *Sammy and Rosie Get Laid*."[10]

Even Kureishi's earnestness, however, began to be questioned by reviewers of *London Kills Me,* some of whom labeled him as being increasingly didactic. A tendency to present political tracts is present in all of Kureishi's films, but it was seen by the critics as being more detrimental to his third film. His tendency toward politicizing had previously been masked by the collaborative effort with Frears; that is, Frears's direction had presented Kureishi's stories as cinema, not as political tracts on film.

Additionally, the criticism here of Kureishi's storytelling also reflected a disapproval of him as a celebrity of some notoriety. It was his notoriety that seemed often to be the target, with critics questioning how a successful author could understand the life of marginal street kids. It is not, however, the case, as such criticism suggests, that an author need be what he or she writes about; and the critic's concern should be the honesty of the story, not the celebrity of the author.

London Kills Me has also often been criticized for Kureishi's seeing his story not as a film director but as its writer. Kureishi is, after all, a writer, and it was his decisions as a first-time director that were here criticized. One London critic complained,

Kureishi is a good writer, though it could be argued that the louder he shouts, the less good he is. What he isn't yet is a good director, and *London Kills Me* bears all the signs of being pieced together to tell a wisp of a story in logical order rather than to make a film whose style mirrors its content with flair and dynamism.[11]

Another critic labeled the film's ambiguity as a negative element of the storytelling, and complained that "the complexity and ambiguity of the film's end is matched by the character of the triangular relationship of Clint, Muffdiver, and Sylvie." The same critic further illuminated the underlying irony in the film's characterization, point of view, and London milieu by noting the similarity of one of its key scenes to one in Nicolas Roeg's cult film, *Performance* (1970), claiming, "There is a bath scene that clearly refers to Roeg's bath scene in *Performance.*"[12]

Similarities between the two highly stylized films include the fact that both are about rock and both portray a marginal lifestyle; in addition, both films are set, and, indeed, *must* be set, in contemporary London. Both, too, are stories that blend the contradictions of an ironic world.

Fig. 12. Roeg's cult film *Performance* features a classic bath scene. Here Rolling Stone Mick Jagger enjoys his psychedelic bathing experience. (Copyright ©1970 by Warner Bros. Inc.)

But although Kureishi's bath scene is similar to a key one in this film that he has acknowledged as a favorite,[13] Kureishi's scene, identified by the critic as similar, is merely stylistically evocative of Roeg's, and not derivative.

Bathing is a characteristic element in all of Kureishi's films and most of his stories thus far. *My Beautiful Laundrette* concludes with Omar and Johnny washing each other up after Johnny gets wounded in a street brawl. Their bathing is an affectionate experience of intimacy and isolation, bonding the pair in the back room of their dream laundrette. In critic Leonard Quart's assessment, "What is the strongest about their relationship is seen here and in the film's concluding scene, where, after Johnny is beaten by his old gang, Omar tenderly soaps him and washes his cuts and bruises."[14] Evoking the same kind of intimacy and underlying eroticism of *My Beautiful Laundrette*, heterosexual lovers in Kureishi's second novel, *The Black Album*, also take to the tub, Deedee giving Shahid a bath after their extensive sexual encounter.

Bathing plays a part in *Sammy and Rosie Get Laid*, too, as Anna watches Sammy taking his bath but remains a distanced spectator. Despite his nakedness, Sammy bathes while remaining unexposed. Evoking the same paradox—nudity without vulnerability—Sammy and Rosie are later seen bathing together in a tub after Sammy, who admits he has already washed that day, announces that he and Rosie need to take a sacramental bath as a means of restoring intimacy to their relationship. In this second antiseptic bathing scene, Kureishi juxtaposes the couple's emotional indifference with their physical intimacy in the tub.

When Karim Amir takes a solitary bath in the TV adaptation of *The Buddha of Suburbia*, the audience is watching him. Karim anoints himself with romantic scents. He surrounds himself with candles. His bathing is a self-oriented ritual that evokes sitar music, cleansing him of Bromley and everything suburban. Karim prepares for a glamorous new life living with his father, Haroon's mistress, and Karim's dream lover—her son Charlie—at Eva Kay's house.

Although in directing *London Kills Me*, Kureishi made considerable changes from the screenplay, several scenes involving bathing remain, and the film's key scene is the bath scene that recalls Mick Jagger's tub scene in *Performance*. The scene illuminates how Kureishi, as writer and director, presents his characters' dreams. Moreover, by making reference to the scene in *Performance*, it also highlights the irony in Kureishi's filmmaking.

Performance's story line, defiantly film oriented, too, was, like Kureishi's film, an original screenplay—using, in the words of one film writer, "authentically subterranean material transmitted by David Litvinoff, a novelist manqué."[15] However, director Roeg had interpreted Litvinoff's written story.

London Kills Me's tub scene opens as a new day dawns, full of optimism. The mangy street people who squat in the flat look younger and more innocent as they sleep. Clint awakens Sylvie (Emer McCourt) who, like her pink ballet slippers shown earlier, is soft and graceful beneath the drug-addicted hooker she dresses as. They take a bath together, during which Sylvie, bare-breasted and free from her daily struggle for survival, nurtures Clint, who here seems like a little boy looking for acceptance. Muffdiver (Steven Mackintosh), a third member of the household, then discards his spotted silk dressing gown that gives him the air of a business executive and joins them, intruding in their tub.

The complex relationship of the three is characterized in this depiction of their interplay as a bathing trio. The scene contrasts the film's focus elsewhere on their frantic lives in garish costumes on the streets with the languid familiarity of their naked bathing. A process of characterizing by means of what characters say, what they do, and, most vividly, by the way in which they say and do operates in this tub scene.

Before Muffdiver joins them, Sylvie and Clint bathe and discuss their parents. Clint is unable to hide either his rash or his needs from Sylvie: not only is he in frantic pursuit of capitalistic success, he is desperate to realize his dream of loving acceptance—of finding a mother. Sylvie, shampooing his hair, is that earth mother—wise, supportive, unafraid to be giving. (Clint's search for the affection and warmth of a mother he cannot find is more obvious in the screenplay scene, in the conclusion of which he holds out a coat to Sylvie, warning "Mum" not to catch a cold. The film, though somewhat altered from Kureishi's published script, conveys this serenity through its shots.)

In the shot in which he crawls into their bath, Muffdiver's male nakedness is prominent. Subsequent shots cut the three characters' bodies into parts, hiding, shadowing, covering the trio in a fragmented composition, until Muff too slips under the communal water's calm. Actor Mackintosh remembers shooting the scene:

What can I say about it? I remember feeling critically nervous that day at being naked. And I remember the warm, sitting in the bath. But I remember we sat in the bath so long doing the scene that the water eventually went cold. And it all became rather dull. And I didn't really care about my being naked or what after a while. . . . Hanif talked a lot about [*Performance*] when we were doing the scene. Hanif drew a lot of comparisons and I think it was a big influence on him at that time. And I could see why when I subsequently saw *Performance* afterwards. But as I hadn't seen it in a long time, I couldn't really see then what he was getting at. . . . So, I wasn't drawing on Jagger or Roeg's film scene in the bath.[16]

When Muffdiver drops his silk dressing gown he is free to abandon with it the ambition and the control he assumes on a daily basis. The bathroom is dominated by a tromp l'oeil paradise on the wall, far removed from the gray of London, their squalid drug-pushing world, and the rest of the spray-painted squat. As the three bathe, inhibitions too have been discarded. Above the waist, all are naked, yet shots of the bare-breasted Sylvie are not primarily sexually suggestive, while the men's nakedness becomes romantic, playful, more childlike than explicit. Imitating their drug-money encounter of yesterday, Clint says of Muff, "I like him when he's like this . . . 'Where's my fucking money, you fucking bastards . . .' We're the same blood. I could touch you, I could. And you could kill me." To Sylvie, he says, "He could just wipe me out. Maybe he should. I make him feel soft. He hates anyone who does that to him. Even you. I wonder why he wants to be so hard."[17]

Underlying sexual tension between these three characters is evident. Conflict and the threat of violence is part of this tension. Sylvie is sleeping with Muff, and Clint is sexually attracted to her. Clint appears sexually attracted to Muff as well. The triangle is further complicated by the fact that Muff appears to maintain power over Sylvie and Clint, but it is unclear as to who really has the male power. Clint acknowledges his bond to Muff, who could kill him, and he—not Sylvie—has seen Muff's real nudity. When Clint blurts out that he knows the exposed vulnerability that Muff so desperately hides from everyone else, he issues a threat to Muff, and at the same time is sharing a secret with him.

In addition to these sexual convolutions, familial hypocrisy and contradiction are also elements of this scene. Kureishi's characters yearn for the security of love while at the same time they resent its choke hold on them. Muff fears the "boy" who is intimate with him; Sylvie enjoys the dependency of the "doll" that she mothers; Clint resents, flaunts, and yet seeks the ties to both Muff and Sylvie.

The tensions of the tub scene—together with its bathing characters—plays against the tranquil ritual bathing and the island paradise painted on the wall behind the tub. Muff, Sylvie, and Clint are all on their own, but their alternate lifestyle, their involvement with sex and drugs, does not assuage their childlike needs. Prior to this scene, the film has already shown us the infinite disappointments of their street routine and told us the delusions they make of their childhoods and memories. The bath becomes a respite in the abusive lives of the three. But in that moment, it is their reality.

The quicksilver moment passes not tragically but inevitably—because mutability is a human reality. Contradictions lie both in sexual and familial love. Kureishi's characters find delusion because all dreams are flawed. Thus, like passion, peace, or a drug trip, this bath must be a transitory experience. Therefore, the intense honesty of Clint's assessment of the bathers, too, must be splashed away in the frivolity of their bath play.

The continuance of this communal experience is simply too much for a hypocritical society. Dream remains essentially dream, usurped by reality. Thus this dramatic, almost lyric movie scene promises and ridicules simultaneously through its dialogue, actions, setting, and tone. Kureishi recognizes that the communion of the trio is contradictory. The paradise in and behind the tub is a created scene depicting a transitory moment. All of the elements are there for a powerful scene, even if in this story the scene reads better in scripted form than it operates on film.

According to Bevan, the film's producer, collaboration, an important part of filmmaking, was the missing element in *London Kills Me*: "I believe that all of the best films are collaboration. I've worked in many different ways. I've worked for some very fine talented directors, writers and all the rest of it. And I've worked on some very arty pictures. I don't ultimately believe in that auteur theory of filmmaking. I believe that the best films come out of collaboration."[18]

Kureishi recognized that if he was successfully to put his story on film, it was crucial that he have a director's perspective. The critical finding here that he failed to achieve this perspective in the film must not be attributed to inexperience or to an aesthetic rejection by him of the importance of that perspective in filmmaking. Kureishi himself agrees that the exchange between him as the writer and a director was missing. But more importantly as a cinema-aware writer, he has attributed this cinematic weakness to a flaw in the writing, and has gone on to identify the effects of that missing collaborative exchange on his storytelling.

Distinguishing between the roles of writer and director in the film better illuminates the immense amount of collaboration involved in making movies. Kureishi's response, therefore, not only expresses his attitudes about filmmaking, but further defines the aesthetics involved in the process:

I always thought that the writing in that film [*London Kills Me*] wasn't very strong either. And that the writing could have been more in focus. I think one of the things about working with a director is that it makes the writing tighter because you go through every scene, you know, you discuss it with the director and the director asks questions . . . If one was just doing it oneself, one wouldn't have the same kind of close observation. So I would say that in *London Kills Me* my directing was not the main problem, it was probably my writing.

As a writer, losing the director's input—since in this case the director was himself—hampered Kureishi's ability to write the screenplay. Producer Bevan has further clarified the difficulties of doing both. Kureishi needed to complete his process of screenwriting before he could take on the responsibilities of film directing. This division of writing and directing into separate tasks hampered the ongoing collaborative process that Kureishi had enjoyed during his work with Frears. As Bevan explained,

Because Hanif was the writer-director on *London Kills Me*, we had to go through strict drafts and we had to make the screenwriting side of it much more formal, if you like, because we had to get that right before we kicked off on the direction. So the process of arriving at the script that we actually ended up shooting was a long one. I think it proved to be slightly more painful for Hanif than the previous two films.[19]

Several reviews recognized the traditions of the film genre in which Kureishi worked. In retrospect, a relationship can be discerned in the tone of *London Kills Me* to the seventies nostalgia of *The Buddha of Suburbia*, on which he was also working at that time. The film evokes gangster films; youth films; the classic immigration story, *The Wizard of Oz*; rock movie musicals, like *Catch Me If You Can* (1989); and the Beatles films; one critic noted that "they stick to the Portobello Road area of Notting Hill, scene of the heady youth revolution of Colin MacInnes's *Absolute Beginners* (1986) and the exotic 1960's drug culture of Nicolas Roeg's *Performance*, to both of which it alludes."[20] The film's place in cinematic tradition is clearly suggested by these early reviews, but at that time there wasn't much investigation of the film as a genre film. The film is successful in these respects, and some of that success has become more recognized as the years have passed.

The heavy subject of the film seemed to demand that the story initially be considered as a "socially conscious" work, a term used to describe many of Kureishi's stories, from his first play. While this is a valid interpretation of the film, it is not the only one. It may not even be—in context—the most telling one. Even at the beginning a critical recognition of the film as a genre film did exist, but the film's place in that tradition should have been more fun: Kureishi is aware of the films of his youth, and there is a case to argue for connecting him with pop musicals. *London Kills Me*, therefore, could be seen as further illuminating a link between contemporary storytellers and film, between music and movie music. More, it exemplified dynamic contemporary attitudes among an expanding group of new filmmakers. As Kureishi explains,

It is much easier now to be involved in cinema than it was when I was a kid because in my day you couldn't see films. You know, you never saw *400 Blows*. Maybe it was on the telly once every three years, but you couldn't go to a video shop and rent it and watch it. Or if you went to the cinema, you had to go to [central] London, which was a long way away. And they didn't show *400 Blows* in my town; they showed Elvis films. So being influenced by the cinema depends on where you live. It's partly that, too, isn't it? Scorsese went to see the films he saw because of the part of town he lived in.

Kureishi's script, too, seems to have been misinterpreted in some of the criticism as a stylized narrative rather than a universal story. That is, at release, the story's underlying truth was simply dismissed. The depiction of the drug-addicted street people who populate Notting Hill was difficult for the London critics to swallow. At that time, Londoners' awareness of the street communities and urban, migrant society of their city was still a way off. This caused a real misunderstanding of Kureishi's story. "What I like about *London Kills Me* they still don't accept—that absolute world exists," says Bevan, explaining some of the film's critical rejection. "If you look outside my window every afternoon, it's the world that's existing right outside . . . And I think it was a remarkably accurate film, actually, and it's quite prophetic in many ways and I think it's much better than any of the homeless, quote, films made today . . . appalling movie[s] . . . [with movie] stars wandering around as the homeless."[21]

Although some critics did acknowledge this look into the unsavory street world they recognized as already existing in London, they saw Kureishi's story of the wounded worlds existing in London neighborhoods not as prophecy but as bitter social commentary. Derek Malcolm, writing in the *Guardian*, called the film "a pretty courageous effort, being about the kind of people who stand on street corners around London and make the rest of us walk a little faster past them."[22] And *London Kills Me*'s characters, however true, aren't the type of people who are appealing.

In America, where homelessness was already an unavoidable issue by the time of the film's release, Bevan, who was also the producer of the enormously popular *My Beautiful Laundrette* and the blockbuster *Four Weddings and a Funeral*, recognized another difficulty in finding an audience—namely, the fact that the film is inherently about London life. Such a theme would usually prompt curiosity in the United States. In this case, however, regardless of how accurate it was, the story's portrayal of street life was still too unappealing to attract an audience. According to Bevan,

It just didn't really work in America either; they didn't want to know about it. No one wanted to know about that world basically . . . not a bleak, cold place to be, you know. If you go back to *Laundrette,* there's an element of glamour about it, although it's about nastiness and all the rest of it. Daniel [Day-Lewis] is a very glamorous character, as was Gordon [Warnecke]. And although who knows where they were going to go, there was a distinct feeling of optimism, they were a part of Thatcher's Britain. They were the entrepreneurs and all of the rest of it . . . *London Kills Me* is about these kids who are a bunch of smack users who've got nowhere to go and who ain't even going there very fast. This isn't necessarily what people want to see when they look in the mirror, and I think that's partly to do with how that film was received.[23]

This negativity at first appears to be a fault in the filmmaking, not in the storytelling. But as Kureishi acknowledged, it was actually a writing problem: the characters in Kureishi's films are not among the most appealing in fiction. On film, the written characters demand softening through their casting. In *My Beautiful Laundrette*, Day-Lewis was glamorous enough to make the audience accept the National Front's Johnny as appealing. In *London Kills Me*, actor Steven Mackintosh, another casting coup as Muffdiver, like *My Beautiful Laundrette*'s glamorous neo-Nazi, makes his gritty character appealing.

Mackintosh's casting as Muffdiver occurred as a result of a misunderstanding—he had met with Kureishi thinking he was to audition for the part of Charlie in *The Buddha of Suburbia*, which he had wanted to play from the time he had first read Kureishi's novel. Instead, their meeting was about Mackintosh playing drug-dealer magician Muffdiver. The prospect of performing magic tricks gave Mackintosh pause. "That was probably the part of the script that scared me the most because I couldn't do any of that stuff," he has admitted. "And I had to. All I kept reading throughout the script was Muffdiver makes something appear and it drove me insane. I went to visit magicians everywhere. And I just sat at home every night trying to make handkerchiefs come out of my hand and balls pop out of my mouth and stuff." Aside from this, however, the actor was quite comfortable in bringing the rather despicable street character from page to film:

Muffdiver is a little bit hard to try to pin down. I think he's just into controlling people, really. He's just playing a power game with people. He's a rather cold person, a dealer, and wants to be seen as leader of the gang ... He's difficult. When you read Muffdiver on the page, you think, "Shit, there's not a lot about this person that's very nice." But I think there are moments, like with Mr. G, when he shows his vulnerability.... I'm not inherently nasty or wanting to be tough all the time; maybe subconsciously I bring that to the character without even knowing it. Maybe that helps in making the character I'm doing, who's supposed to be tough and rude and nasty, a little more three-dimensional.[24]

Kureishi's script created out of Muffdiver's drug-culture entrepreneurism screen material for the actor to work with, and Mackintosh himself added significant visual appeal to the film. His Mick Jagger–evoking bathtub scene is enhanced by his resemblance to another member of the Rolling Stones, Brian Jones, who, ironically, drowned.

Each of Kureishi's written story lines is in itself interesting, and, as he did in his other films, in *London Kills Me*, Kureishi again uses a large cast of characters whose stories, like those in *Sammy and Rosie Get Laid*, read in a disjointed way but overlap. Each role is well cast, from Clint and his odyssey and Hemingway and his mentoring to Muff and his grifter magic, Headley and his limousine-liberal antics, and Dr. Bubba and his sagacity.

With all this positive input, then, what is it that goes wrong in the film? The overriding problem with *London Kills Me* is that its story line does not allow for audience identification. In addition, the film story does go out of directorial focus—an accusation also leveled at Kureishi's screenplays for earlier films.

While the film script is literary and reads in an allegorical and ritualistic way, there are some halting moments in the film itself, which is a linear telling of the story. The distanced point of view which is so successful on the page does not completely transfer to the camera. A development of some of the movie images might have helped avert this problem. As it stands, however, the grisly images on film were seen to lack Frears's directorial balance and the cohesion of the earlier Kureishi films. Moreover, Kureishi's direction of the film was not seen as clarifying his use of cinematic images from the 1939 children's classic motion picture *The Wizard of Oz*.

It is the movie's ambiguity, not the story's, that confuses the audience, as Kureishi evokes Fleming's cinematic Oz odyssey without really addressing it. This film classic is brought to mind in Kureishi's film in everything from Clint's ruby red boots to his companions' travails as he seeks his place over the rainbow. But unlike the Great Depression's Dorothy, London's Clint never clicks his heels to go home again. Home and the maternal security Clint sought are too clearly an illusion. Muffdiver and Sylvie and the makeshift family Clint created on the streets disintegrate and implode. The irony is that Kureishi's street story is powerful in itself; it falters because in the final scene, when Clint, as a waiter in an expensive restaurant, finds himself in a whole different world on the other side of Hemingway's plate-glass window, the film's ambiguity gnaws at the conventions of the previous road film without being fully realized; that is, Kureishi's characteristic unresolved ending does not, on film, hold its own against its technicolor antecedent. Kureishi's Wiz-

Fig. 13. Hemingway (Brad Dourif, right) gives Clint (Justin Chadwick) the chance to give up drug dealing on the streets in exchange for becoming part of London's legal service industry. The promised new life lies beyond glass windows, separated from Clint's life on the street. (Still photo courtesy of Jacques Prayer.)

ard is not Oz's—he is the dual masters of Hemingway, pulling the strings to hoist Clint up among the productive and employed, and Margaret Thatcher, stringing Clint Eastwood up with the metaphoric ropes of consumeristic philosophy. Although as an author Kureishi refuses to limit himself from presenting that duality, as a filmmaker, he doesn't clearly show his ambiguous Wizard as a separate, new cinematic identity with dual cinematic impact.

The aimless, decadent, and cinema-absorbed characters of this film succeed in telling a story of contemporary street culture, often sparking intensely representative images of Kureishi's storytelling. But their ambiguity as cinematic images is seen to diminish the film's impact. Clint begins his pursuit of the sweet life dwarfed by a larger-than-life color poster of Anita Ekberg, star of Federico Fellini's 1960 black-and-white movie, *La Dolce Vita*. Advertising a movie-house revival of the film, the poster attracts Clint's momentary interest. The mise-en-scène commands the audience's attention: The static, painted celluloid goddess looms over the color and motion of Clint's reality. And as the sweet life and dreams collide, so their contradictions overlap and commingle. Here, Kureishi is successful in translating the dynamics of his literal storytelling to filmmaking. This shot is, simultaneously, an anthem to and a condemnation and parody of Eastwood's dreams. But these electronic pop culture contradictions are not fully developed into a film story; rather, they flare up, intrigue, and then are lost or minimized as clever mind games.

Additionally, cultural bias may have further hindered reception of this film. In Kureishi's earlier films, in which Asian characters sought assimilation into the contemporary London scene, the author's racial and cultural perspective had been new, and was critically controversial. An ominous undertow lurks in some negative reviews of *London Kills Me*—namely, an apparent disapproval of the fact that Kureishi has dared to tell the story of a *white* street boy's experiences. Asian critics had censored Kureishi in the first two films for selling out as their Asian spokesman. In *London Kills Me*, however, was the Anglo-Asian author now being criticized by white critics as well for attempting to tell stories that didn't fit into the Anglo-Asian subgenre?

Popular criticism, like anything else in our pop culture, can itself show evidence of trends—indeed, in their dealings with Kureishi, critics had been through several such trends already. And Kureishi himself can play the press at their own game as well as anyone. At times, indeed, he has benefited from the press coverage. Some of the negative criticism of this film is of him personally; that is, it is an attack upon his celebrity status—a status, paradoxically, that was generated in the first place by the same press that ended up criticizing it.

Kureishi himself provides a final comment on the negativity that greeted *London Kills Me:* "I couldn't just direct a first film and put it out; it had to become a big doo-da," he has acknowledged. "I regret making that film. I regret making it for the cinema, I mean. I should have shot it on sixteen-millimeter and put it on TV late at night. I should have done three or four films like that; I wish I had."

Filmmaking, like any art, must take risks in order to evolve. But in motion pictures such experimentation proves costly. Kureishi ended up paying a price for cinematic experimentation that went beyond that resulting from poor box-office receipts. As a writer, Kureishi likes to take risks, but as a filmmaker, he incurred monetary losses and public censure that were so high as to make further artistic experimentation on film too expensive a possibility. But as he had done from his theatrical experiences, so Kureishi learned from his experience as a film director. His knowledge of the process, production, and distribution of films would enhance his future cinematic writing projects, and his experiences as a filmmaker would provide him new subject matter for his storytelling.

ADAPTER *The Buddha of Suburbia* on Film

Although he at first declined to write

the screenplay adaptation of his novel, *The Buddha of Suburbia*, Kureishi changed his mind, and found himself in another productive film-making collaboration. He joined the BBC team producing his novel as a television serial to co-write the script with the serial's director, Roger Michell, whom he had known as a director at London's Royal Court Theatre. Kevin Loader, who had accompanied Kureishi to the Whitbread Award ceremony for the prizewinning novel in 1991, and who produced the series, remembers Kureishi's mood at the beginning of this project:

I think Hanif had a very bad experience on *London Kills Me*. . . . it is very hard to direct . . . And it is particularly hard to direct the first time . . . A lot of [the negative criticism] was unfair because I don't think some people realized what the piece was. I don't think they saw its antecedents properly. There's a lot in common with early sixties rock-and-roll movies. . . . It felt to me that sort of animal, with a dark undertone. On the surface its form goes back to a kind of sixties exuberance and innocence. The material is right and rather engaging. Interesting to compare what it was like in 1963 when *A Hard Day's Night* came out with something made in 1990.

If you have been mauled by the press, as Hanif was in *London Kills Me,* then you know how difficult they can be . . . [The mauling] was because his first screenplay had been nominated for an Oscar, . . . and I think he'd been getting away with it for too long. And I think that they just thought it was humorous that he was trying to direct a movie.

[Kureishi] is very aware of his responsibilities as a spokesman for his color and his generation . . . He works very hard for it and for the things he believes in. But there are occasions when he's had his fingers burned because he hasn't judged the press very well.

    . . . it is a very particular scene, the English media scene. It's very villagey, especially if you live in London. A lot of the time, it is the right-wing tabloid especially. If somebody starts something, then Hanif will take the ball and run with it . . . [The negative criticism] did go hand-in-glove with the public notion of having to bring down somebody who's very self-assured and is prepared to stick his neck out, prepared to take a radical position, not afraid to stand up and be counted. And I think some people probably struck out because of that.[1]

Roger Michell and Kureishi set up shop with a BBC secretary in Loader's office at the BBC's headquarters in London's Shepherd's Bush. It was an extremely compatible partnership, and it took them only six weeks to write the four one-hour-long screenplays. "It was more difficult for Hanif than it was for me," Michell has conceded, "because Hanif is understandably extremely close to the subject matter of the book. His father had died only months before we started working on that screenplay. When Hanif was writing, he was always, in a way, writing for his father's approval. For me it was quite easy."[2]

Michell remembers the pair of them confronting what they had determined would be their major stumbling blocks in terms of adaptation. The first of these obstacles was the fact that they wanted to translate the prose story into a story that would work on film. For the production team, this would involve incorporating precise historical details from the seventies—the adolescent era shared by Kureishi, Loader, and Michell—in order to duplicate the novel's depiction of the era without becoming an historical drama. The next problem that they foresaw, Michell remembers, was that of addressing the novel's strong first-person point of view without resorting to continuous voice-over. Finally, they would have to surmount the difficulty involved in replicating the ambiguity of the novel's ending.

Kureishi, Loader, and Michell also anticipated—accurately—a problem of censorship owing to the need to translate into film the novel's depiction of drug use, strong language, sex, and nudity. This outrage fueled much of the criticism by the tabloid press of the TV film, and questioning the taste (or lack of taste) of the program was an integral part of the critical response. The collaborators also correctly anticipated the waves of nostalgia that their seventies story would evoke. Guaranteeing yet another publicity bonanza, David Bowie was signed to score the music for the serial.

"Superstar David Bowie is such a fan of the novel, that he offered to write the title song when he heard that *The Buddha of Suburbia* was to be a TV series," proclaimed one national tabloid.[3] Almost every review of the program featured its connection to Bowie, and his music in itself was the subject of considerable additional press. Response to the latter was positive and identified its particular strength in *The Buddha of Suburbia*. "Karim's rites of passage story was appropriately serenaded by Bromley-born Bowie's *Ch-Ch-Ch-Ch-Changes*,"[4] wrote one critic, while another put into words the magic resulting from the choice of composer: "It's all wonderfully bizarre, and with David Bowie's apt score, highly nostalgic too."[5]

Thus, as in Kureishi's previous films, music again both captures the historical period of the seventies and prompts the nostalgia for that decade. Bowie, himself a figure of the seventies, was an ideal choice for the program. His music defined that period, and he was still a media superstar during the TV program's production. As the composer of its music, he defined the seventies depicted in that program, too. His reputation—as a musical rebel and as a figure of musical history—prompted a TV critic to posit the rhetorical question, "Who could be more appropriate than David Bowie to write a soundtrack that is a dazzling pastiche of Seventies rock 'n' roll?"[6]

The involvement of Bowie was "meta-musical," for he was also tied to fiction and autobiography, to Charlie—*The Buddha of Suburbia's* Bowie-loving, Bowie-like character—and to Kureishi himself, a fellow student at Bowie's Bromley high school. One review, for instance, characterized Charlie Hero as "Bromley's answer to Bowie, perfectly capturing that early David look—part shocked sprite, part dead fish."[7] Another noted Bowie's autobiographical connections to Kureishi's Bromley: "Another figure who straddled the artier and the less couth ends of pop in the early seventies, and whose scornful postures anticipated punk, was David Bowie—perhaps, after H. G. Wells, Bromley's most famous son."[8]

Bowie's enormous contribution was summed up in another review: "With incidental music by David Bowie, a cool period soundtrack and a major character modelled on an amalgam of Bowie and Billy Idol, *Buddha* manages to be both humorous and hip—no mean feat when you're dealing with the '70s."[9] David Bowie was thus able to translate into music Kureishi's history, humor, and hype.

Critics also confirmed the casting as having been another significant element in the success of the TV version of *The Buddha of Suburbia*. The producer, Kevin Loader, remembers:

Casting was remarkable, but . . . that was partly because Roger [Michell] was sitting in the office working with Hanif on the script. It meant [Michell] and I could start working on the casting much, much earlier. Normally we wouldn't have been able to because normally I wouldn't have been able to afford to bring him in. But he was on the payroll . . . [Kureishi] sat in on a lot of the casting as well, actually. He was very interested.[10]

Several members of the strong cast, led by Roshan Seth (Haroon), Naveen Andrews (Karim), and Steven Mackintosh (Charlie), had also worked with Kureishi on *London Kills Me*. Once again, as Charlie Hero, foil to Karim, Mackintosh played a difficult role. Evocative in terms of makeup, hair, and costume changes of stages in rock-music history from "glam" to punk, the brutal Charlie floats in and out of the plot. Mackintosh has admitted to having wanted to play this part ever since he first read the novel, before he had worked with Kureishi in *London Kills Me*:

I instantly just thought that [Charlie Hero was] a pip. I mean, it's the sort of part that is a peach. And I think it's a pretty hard part to get wrong—all the changes the character goes through and his desperate ambition to be a star at any cost. . . . it's a dream of a part, really.

And also there was a lot about the suburban upbringing of that character that I could relate to. . . . I'm a suburban. So, I understand that way of life and what growing up in a place like that means. Trying to get out and be something.

It's great the way the whole thing turns around. In the beginning, Charlie's always putting Karim down and saying, "You're not going to be anything. I'm going to be a star," and the focus is all on him. But then, by the time the story ends and Charlie is living in New York and he is a rock star, suddenly it's come full circle. And actually, Karim is very positive, things are happening for him. And Charlie is rather isolated; he's on the road and he's a rock star; he's achieved everything he wants. But he's quite lonely, really, and he's desperate for Karim's company and wants him to stay. When Karim leaves him, he's all alone . . . ultimately I think Charlie's a very lost soul, really. He's a very arrogant character underneath and the turnaround at the end shows that really he's very lonely. That ambition has left him very alone. I think that ambition can do that to people. It becomes such a strong thing in their lives. You follow that dream; that's all you follow—and maybe you get it, and maybe you don't—but ultimately, you're left with nothing. You didn't fulfill the rest of your life, then somehow you're empty of that ambition too . . .

I played Charlie Hero as close as he could be to the book, but it might not be exactly as Hanif envisions [Charlie]. I felt I had to make him my own. It was quite easy to do. I could draw comparisons with myself, that's the easiest way to approach it. If you look at a part and you see nothing within that role that's remotely like you or related to you, it's very hard to latch on to. I think I can use myself with most parts, but in the case of Charlie, it was instantaneous. I could hear his voice in my head as I read, as he leaped off the page. So it was great fun and glamorous . . .

I felt that the character was so very clearly written that although he wasn't in [the story] for large chunks of it, his presence when he was there was so strong and the scenes were so brilliantly done and funny and focused that it would carry. And I got a strong sense of his story carrying right through. You know, there were long periods when you didn't see him, but when Charlie came back, his hair was different or he had a swastika on his face or he had some other outrageous outfit. He would be rude to somebody or taking drugs or having strange sex. Also, even when he has long periods in *Buddha* when he's not there, they're constantly referring to him. Like his mother's referring to him, saying things like, "Where's Charlie? What's he doing?" You're always wondering about Charlie because Hanif keeps reminding you of his presence. In a lot of ways, I think Hanif would have spoiled it, to have Charlie in a greater part of the story, having more of this character who causes a sensation every time he turns up would become too much, or Charlie would become boring. . . . Roger [Michell] created a comfortable atmosphere, and everybody really wanted the whole thing to work. The feelings started off with Hanif's book, basically, the fact that the book has great impact on people when they read it. On anyone who's ever read it . . . Everybody had very strong feelings about *Buddha*.[11]

The fine TV cast assembled also included Susan Fleetwood (Eva), Jemma Redgrave (Eleanor), Nisha Nayar (Jamila), Brenda Blethyn (Mum), and Harish Patel (Changez). The actors in the large cast were generally well received and the casting praised. One critic found that "[all] the performances are impeccable," and described Brenda Blethyn as "divine" and Susan Fleetwood as "a one-woman Bohemian rhapsody."[12] Another critic raved about "a solid supporting cast including the incandescent Susan Fleetwood," and then singled out the three former cast members from *London Kills Me*—"the distinguished Roshan Seth" and "newcomers Naveen Andrews as Karim and Steven Mackintosh as Charlie Hero, both destined for greatness."[13]

Although Charlie Hero was identified by most critics of the TV program as a David Bowie–like figure, matching Charlie's character to an actual person had been an interest of critics since Kureishi's novel was first reviewed. Mackintosh found that such expectations put idiosyncratic demands on him, in terms of playing the role:

I'm not a great singer, but it was not really required . . . I just screamed my head off . . . I mean, it was all about energy; it was all about just giving off this kind of serious angry energy, which was great. I remember being in that club and feeling, "this is incredible." And when punk first happened, it must have completely blown people's minds because they had never seen this kind of aggression on stage before. I used that.

What was strange was I knew that obvious kinds of comparisons were going to be drawn between the character that I was playing and certain pop stars from that time. I didn't want to become too identifiable with one particular person. I very much had Billy Idol in mind because I knew Hanif knew Billy Idol from a while ago and I could see a lot from the book that I could tell was Billy Idol: the pouting, the turning up of his lip and all that. And I saw it very much, especially the punk era of it, as a Billy Idol thing. Well, there's the Sex Pistols too, of course. So I had a lot of people in my mind but Bowie was someone who wasn't really in my mind at the time. But then obviously when the program came out I thought

Fig. 14. Punk rocker Charlie Hero (Steven Mackintosh) galvanizes London in Kureishi's *The Buddha of Suburbia*. (Photo courtesy of the BBC Picture Archives, London.)

it was David Bowie and I was blind not to see it, really. There are a lot of similarities, especially in the earlier section, like when Charlie's dressed as a spaceman in silver and turns up at a party. I think, too, that I look like Bowie. This kind of angular, very bony face. So there was no model really for Charlie Hero, not even Billy Idol, no one person, actually. I wanted to pick elements, and I easily did—elements from different people—Johnny Rotten, Malcolm McLaren, Billy Idol, David Bowie, whoever—and make them into my mishmash.[14]

Critical acclaim was also earned by Harish Patel as Changez in his British television debut. Taking the risk of casting Patel in the part had paid off for the producer and director. Loader relates their casting trip to Bombay:

We went to Bombay to cast. Hanif didn't come with us, but Roger and I went with our costume director . . . because we knew we needed to find this character. And he is the one character in the book Hanif and we knew we had to get right. We went to Bombay. We were there for three days, and on the first two days we sat in our hotel room in the airport and it was cultural shock. It was a bizarre couple of days, actually.

But, anyway, two days went by and we hadn't really seen anyone when a friend called. And he said, "Well, how is it going? Have you found who you want?" And we said, "No, we haven't." He said, "Well, there's one other person," somebody who perhaps had never been outside of India in his life.

God knows how Harish knew how to do it. He doesn't know what the significance of Chislehurst is. But somehow he knew. I read the book shop scene with him at the audition and he just knew. We weren't sure of him, you know, because we met him the day we were leaving Bombay. But by the time we got back to London, we decided that we wanted him. And there was a lot of nail-biting: Have we made the right decision? Actually, at that stage we weren't at all sure, but we knew we didn't have any choice because we hadn't seen anyone else even remotely right. I thought we made the right decision, but who always knows?[15]

Patel's casting was lauded by one critic who also voiced the apprehension often felt by both supporters and detractors of novels when they are adapted into film:

As one of the few people in literary London who disliked Hanif Kureishi's novel, I approached the four-part TV adaptation with grave misgivings . . . Harish Patel as Changez, imported from the sub-continent for an arranged marriage, was irresistible. Watching him gorge bananas while being lectured on his duties in the grocer's shop, or drooling over previously unthought of sexual routines, it was impossible not to think of the late John Belushi doing a black-face routine.[16]

Satisfied with the music and the characters, the critics found that the adapters had further realized their intention of recreating the look of the era of Kureishi's novel with precise detail. Shot in super 16-mm, the production was historically accurate, with obvious care having been given to the costumes and hairstyles. "Roger Michell's direction was fast paced and attentive to all the necessary Seventies' detail," wrote one reviewer. "And the photography, by John McGlashan, was a hymn to the Betjemanesque splendours of South London's domestic architecture."[17] Critics were also aware, however, that the program was more than a historical recreation of an era, one of them concluding, "For all the fun it has with the period, *The Buddha of Suburbia* has a timeless relevancy that will put the wind up the flare-wearers of today."[18] The number of viewers of each episode was strong for a BBC production, and the series was a solid, critical success.

Although Michell had expressed concern about how to transfer onto film the ambiguity of the ending, critics have found the ending of the television version as ambiguous as the ending of Kureishi's novel. "This drama has split critics," declared one reviewer, "and depending on what side of the fence you're on, you'll either read a melancholy profundity into Karim's expression that forms the final shot, or you'll want to wipe the smug smirk off his face with an iron bar."[19] Describing the difficulty of transferring this ambiguity successfully, Michell has said, "Karim is a prose character, but on film he becomes a bit more human . . . [and] I was trying to reflect that final paragraph in the book when Karim is sitting there . . . to show the way he does feel melancholy, but he is happy."[20]

Several adaptations for the BBC production had previously been attempted, but Kureishi was compelled finally to co-write the adaptation himself. He became displeased with deletions and additions to his story and identified "point of view" as being the major adaptation concern. To Kureishi, continual reliance on first-person voice-over in dramatizing his novel was like watching illustrated talk. Adapting point of view is always difficult when moving from literal to visual storytelling, and Michell agreed that this was the most pressing difficulty for the adapters as they set to work collaborating: "We thought about that a lot. We thought: let's have voice-over narrative. Then we cut it out. Then we shot the whole film. And when we saw the rough cuts, we knew we had to do something, and spent the day sitting around working out ways to keep the novel's tone without voice-over everywhere . . . I think we succeeded."[21]

As he had done with Frears on earlier film projects, Kureishi again collaborated with the director, though in this case, writer and director were more involved in co-writing the script than Frears and Kureishi had been in the earlier project. The script is thus the result of a writer's and a director's vision of the story. In the prose version, the story is seen through Karim's eyes, but this had to change when the work was adapted for film, to accommodate the point of view of the camera, which records what Karim sees. Consequently, voice-over would often have been redundant. Instead, images were seen, then narrated, by the addition of voice-over narration under the film scenes. The story thus became visual and literal, and thereby twice-told.

However accurate the transference of the literary to the visual had been, the technique used in the film prompted much critical comparison with the novel. Some critics saw the film's dismissal of the literary device of first-person narration as a reasonable cinematic clarification. One reviewer, for instance, wrote: "What sometimes seemed slightly outlandish in the book, when filtered through narrator Karim's jaundiced schoolboy caricatures, has been triumphantly brought to life by director Roger Michell's exuberantly funny production of this affectionate satire."[22] Other critics, however, lamented that the novel's point of view had been lost in the screenplay, and viewers thus had to struggle to get into the mind of Karim.

Analyzing changes in the film adaptation from the prose source provides a comparative critical tool to illuminate specific elements of Kureishi's storytelling in both forms. It is inevitable that a film story will differ from a novel, however faithful the translation. Differences occur even when the novelist does the adaptation, as Kureishi did here. The author, who, before undertaking this adaptation, had been disinclined to adapt prose into film, explains:

In my novel I could really fill the characters out much more. I had unlimited time and space. With the TV *Buddha*, I knew I had to be concerned with plot.

The book had sold one hundred and fifty thousand copies in paperback. Five million people would be my TV audience. It was completely different. So it had to be pretty direct. I just wrote—I wrote it with the director—but I just wrote what was in the book. At first they had tried to be clever with it in various ways, but it didn't work. I just did it straight. It's the same as the book. It was very fucking difficult. I never wanted to do it. In principle I was all for somebody else adapting my book to film too, . . . but only if they did it right.

Kureishi was also disinterested in adapting anyone else's prose stories to film scripts. His adaptation of Brecht, although staged, remains unpublished, and he declined requests to adapt Salman Rushdie's novel *Midnight's Children* for the BBC and to translate a novel by V. S. Naipaul into a screenplay. He has explained his disinterest as follows:

I'm not a handmaiden to other people. It is not as if I haven't got any ideas. I have my own ideas; I want to do my own work. I've got things I want to write, so I said no. I am nervous about fucking up somebody else's book because I don't want my books fucked up.

When he did later involve himself with co-adapting Oscar Wilde's novel *The Picture of Dorian Gray* with Roger Michell, he jokingly explained that, in this case, he selected an author who couldn't fight back:

I haven't read *The Picture of Dorian Gray* in a long time, but I have always liked Wilde. And it hasn't been done . . . done right. There's a great part in it. I like the rest of the book. It's a great book. It is a nice job: a month, maybe a little rewriting, hanging out with Roger. And, of course, Oscar Wilde is fucking dead.

Humor aside, the fact that he agreed to take on the Wilde project was also a result of his satisfaction with the television adaptation of his own novel. Moreover, he had learned from the experience, which changed his mind about the dynamics of adapting. With a clear understanding of the difficulties involved in adapting authors, including himself, he could now see the link between fiction and film for himself as author, adapter, and collaborator. For him now, writing, movie writing, and writing for the movies are all interlinked:

I write a book. I redo it. Finish it. Make it good. It will take me two, three years. Either way it's a big job. Writing *The Buddha of Suburbia,* I knew it was a movie as well as a book. And I have always known the novel I'm writing now (*The Black Album*) will be a movie. I know that.

One critic, who was in agreement with this statement, insisted that Kureishi and Michell had, in fact, successfully translated Kureishi's literary point of view into a different medium by understanding that they were not trying to replicate the literary in the cinematic. He wrote: "As Karim, Naveen Andrews proves equal to the task of making adolescent blankness interesting—Kureishi's dry, detached characterization doesn't offer much in the way of grand gestures beyond the odd flourish of acid wit but, even so, Andrews lets you see that there is stuff going on behind Karim's pose of dispassionate observation."[23]

Karim acts the same in the television version as he does in the novel. The foolishness and exaggeration of his perspective remain the same. But in the process of this transferral to film, the story's main character also somehow became lackluster. According to a TV review,

Like many teenagers the character is vain, arrogant and self-centered. In the novel these shortcomings are redeemed by the humor, honesty, and unerring sense of irony with which Karim homes in on the more ludicrous elements of the '70s culture. The detachment that made Karim such an unusually objective narrator in the novel makes for a rather unengaging character on the screen. Television can't put us into his mind and whereas Karim is at the heart of the novel, in the TV version he's in danger of being swamped by the many outlandish people around him. We're not looking at them through his eyes, we're looking at him and them from the outside.[24]

In the novel, it is not only the case that Karim's first-person point of view is how the reader sees everything; without Karim, there is simply no story. The novel's universe exists entirely within Karim's mind. The previously quoted reviewer experienced Karim in the film version as a character in a story, not as he had experienced the story and Karim as told by Karim in the book. What had come across as ironic detachment in the prose point of view was seen, consequently, as uninteresting on screen.

The author of the novel is no more detached from Karim than he is from any other of his characters; Kureishi refuses to romanticize anyone. This detachment—and Kureishi's distance from his characters' story—proves a crucial element in his novel. He maintains that first-person, ironic point of view in his screen adaptation, too, and the varying critical responses to the story on film expose differing dynamics of the two storytelling forms.

Although the adaptation strategy sparked some new criticism of *The Buddha of Suburbia*, the TV version's depiction of the novel's sexual encounters, street language, and drug use prompted a furor. The tabloid controversy, censorship problems, and U.S. refusal to air the adaptation tainted its production. But these controversial elements and their critical reception reveal another characteristic of Kureishi's storytelling.

Sexual activity is frequent and graphic in the story. It is interesting to consider criticism regarding whether it has a genuine place in the story or whether it is simply sensationalistic. One television critic asserted that sexual incidents hampered the series, admitting, "I found myself blushing for the actors rather than enjoying the characters whom they were portraying."[25] Another critic suggested that "the sex, for one viewer at least, seemed like a gratuitous series of interruptions and really did get in the way of the acting."[26]

Kureishi, who considers "writing about sex and drugs a speciality," is aware that his story challenged the conventional standards of television fare, but argues that because his novel portrayed the seventies as a time of more permissive sex and drug use, the inclusion of these incidents in the adaptation was unavoidable. Loader remembers:

It was always known that it was going to be difficult, but I have to say, actually, the BBC were very supportive of us. We had one meeting as a team before we shot anything and agreed the number of four-letter words we could have. If you want to use "fuck" on the television, it has to be cleared at the highest level. Our first draft of the scripts, I think, had fifty-three "fucks" in it, and it was then, and it still is, very difficult to put these in home-grown products.

We knew that we were going to have to have some conversation with somebody about this before [we began shooting]; otherwise, we were going to have terrible problems in this production, which is really important. We didn't quite go through them line by line, although there was a lot of hilarity by going through some of them line by line. We could sort of sit there and discuss whether "Jesus fucking Christ" was going to be acceptable or not and Hanif would . . . say, "Well, that's one of my favorites, actually." We also discussed some of the sex scenes at that time.[27]

The creative team recognized from the start not only the risks they were taking, but the boundaries of television production. Consequently, changes that had to be made in depicting the novel's sex scenes as TV film scenes were acknowledged by the adapters. Thus, for example, although the group sex scene was transferred, the sado-masochistic sex scene involving Charlie in New York, witnessed by Karim in the novel, was played discreetly off screen in the adaptation. Instead of seeing it, the TV audience hears the scene while watching Karim's reaction to it. In Kureishi's own words, "There's no point in shooting a lot of weird stuff because they're not going to put it on anyway. I'd have spent two days on the phone with some guy from the BBC calling to say that it had to be cut."

On the other hand, the story was also praised by other critics for its historical milieu and its fictional cohesion: that is, Kureishi and the television collaborators were praised for succeeding in keeping the story intact in the face of such critical controversy. After the tabloid furor about the group sex scene in the third episode, for example, critic Max Davidson wrote that any thrill-seeking audience would be disappointed in the fourth episode, for "the integrity of the drama was so striking that it was almost as if its creator Hanif Kureishi was taking the mickey out of the people who want to jump on the bandwagon and label him a pornographer." Regarding the airing of the fourth and last episode, Davidson continued, "It is the context, always the context, that matters; and anyone who has watched this series will attest that it has taken a serious, well-rounded look at the strains of adolescence."[28]

Another critic supported the controversial segments by recognizing the work's satiric universe, arguing that "attitudes to many subjects—Asians, contemporary music, mysticism—have been represented and variously parodied, ridiculed or attacked, and it would be odd, given the time and attention that so many people devote to it, if sex were to be left out."[29] An awareness of context is necessary in assessing the reliance on sexual episodes in *The Buddha of Suburbia*, as actor Steven Mackintosh (Charlie) has argued in defending the context of the broadcast version:

I couldn't personally see anything whatsoever wrongful to anybody within the whole program. Okay, drugs are used and mentioned quite a lot through the whole *Buddha*. But they're in no way glamorized. I think that drug users are common in London, and so [they are too] in *The Buddha of Suburbia*—or *London Kills Me*. Saying that films glamorize drug use is rather a funny thing to say, you know. Ultimately, I think films just show the way things are. I mean, an audience should be granted as having a little more intelligence, really . . . If they want to watch something about people doing drugs, they're not necessarily going to go out and do them themselves. . . . And neither *London Kills Me* nor *The Buddha of Suburbia* is saying, "Wow, go out and try and do it." It's just that some of the characters are doing drugs. And they don't always have a great time. Charlie goes through a period of getting seriously messed up; he's hardly an advertisement for doing drugs. He's just somebody that has done them.

Actually, I think it's the sex, not the drugs, anyway, it's the sex element in Hanif that I think causes the controversy. You know, in *Buddha*, where the director takes Karim home to meet his wife and she wants to fuck him. They all of sudden get into this scene together—as in the book, I just thought it was a brilliantly funny situation. This naive young actor is being taken for a ride by this suave director who takes him home so his wife and he can get a hold of him. It's just such a funny idea. To actually see it on the screen in its full glory is slightly shocking, but ultimately very funny. Anyone I know who saw it didn't sit there going, "Oh, my God—shocking." They said, "Wow, that was so funny, that scene." It's about a whole situation. It's not about sex. That's what makes it funny. It has a context in the whole story. It's about Karim's journey. The idea that Karim gets carried away and taken to this director's house and suddenly finds himself having sex with about three or four different people. It's a very funny idea. This young boy suddenly being opened to sex in a major way. Because I think it's all done with a lot of humor . . . I think that comedy is very powerful . . . And it's to do with the whole story. It's not just a moment of sensationalism.[30]

Thus, regardless of the varying attitudes of critics toward censorship, the context of Kureishi's story was recognized as important by most.

Defending the artistic context of the story, for example, critic Christopher Dunkley asked, "While watching *The Buddha of Suburbia* did the oh-so-easily-shocked gentlemen of the tabloids really not notice that the big sex scene was supposed to be comical?"[31]

Ultimately, reviewers used *The Buddha of Suburbia* both to vilify and to promote censorship. Sex, nudity, and drugs remained controversial subjects for television, while new offenses were found in everything from its maintenance of yesterday's stereotyping to its negation of today's politically correct empowerment. Simultaneously, in one of the paradoxes of the multimedia world, outraged criticism became good publicity for the TV adaptation—whose production team was savvy enough to capitalize on it. Not only did the controversy not really hurt the series, it was used to attract a larger audience. Outcries of indignation increased its ratings.

Not only did the television adaptation add to Kureishi's celebrity, but more importantly, its criticism provided a different perspective from which to analyze his storytelling, further expanding understanding of his aesthetic. Kureishi's literary and film techniques—his storytelling methods—were better illuminated when scrutinized in this new comparative light.

six

AUTHOR AGAIN
The Black Album

The religious furor around Salman Rushdie's novel *Satanic Verses* began in India before the book was even published in Britain. The book was first burned by Muslims in England on 2 December 1988, following its UK publication on 26 September 1988 and its receipt of the Whitbread Prize for that year. A *fatwa* was pronounced the following February by the Ayatollah Khomeini, who offered a $1,000,000 bounty for the assassination of Rushdie by the Khorbad (June 5th).

While *The Buddha of Suburbia* was fueling its own controversies, Kureishi had been immersed in his next prose project from as early as 1988. He had scrutinized the incidents of book burning and rioting, as well as the reaction of the international community to the *fatwa*, and published his interests and concerns about the furor surrounding Rushdie's *Satanic Verses*, initially in nonfiction political analysis.[1]

As a man of strong opinions, he took a vocal stand against the censorship, violent threats, and terrorism, and used his celebrity to bring attention to the controversy. As an author, he set about finding a structure for a fictional story about London's turbulent eighties.

Although originally conceiving his fiction as a short story in its own right, by 1992 he envisioned it as part of a collection of short works. When he began writing a first version at the Venice Film Festival that September, he drafted instead a novel, with the working title *Mysteries of the City.* Feeling unsatisfied with that draft, he determined to rethink and restart the story. As he himself explains, his method of writing and revising his "eighties" story, which would become his second novel, *The Black Album*, enabled him to assess its evolution through its drafts:

I have been trying to write this novel for two fucking years, but I hadn't found it. I had written another draft [*Mysteries of the City*] before this draft, like half another novel, which was the wrong novel. I abandoned it. The abandoned draft had been about the same thing. But I realized it was from the wrong direction. I'm writing about the same thing now. Yet it is completely different. I had been writing about the media response to it, now I'm writing about the thing itself. I cut the media out, and now I'm starting to find the story.

In the earlier version a street hustler, Strapper, not unlike Kureishi's Clint Eastwood character in *London Kills Me*, preyed on Deedee's sense of responsibility. In the course of the later drafts, Strapper evolves from a main character into a drug-savvy, contemporary Artful Dodger whose major function, in the final manuscript, becomes a mechanical one: He brings Chili into Shahid's story and continues to move the story forward.

As the story gained momentum, the novel took shape. Kureishi described the work he was now doing on *The Black Album* as "making it better, longer, putting it in focus," and further winter revisions resulted in a new draft which was "fuller somehow, and better ordered. Better paced. Better developed." Claiming it now had "more characterization" and was "tighter," the author explains, "I had figured out, really, what I wanted to say. I made sure not to have too much in, and I put everything in the right order. Technical things like that."

While planning a television documentary in Karachi in early 1994, he put *The Black Album* aside, although he continued working on a short story that was published in *The New Yorker* that spring. The documentary was aborted, and he returned to revising his novel; at the same time, he considered compiling a short-story collection and began co-writing a screenplay. This frantic working pace continued into the fall of 1994. In March 1995 the novel was published, and following its release, Kureishi made personal appearances at book signings in London and lectured at the Royal National Theatre. The novel was released in the United States that fall, published by Scribner's. It met with mixed reviews, generally receiving more press in the UK than in the United States.

The sensationalism of his storytelling continues in this novel, which includes such incendiary incidents as a "rave" (street jargon for a gigantic all-night, drug-using dancing party at an abandoned or large com-

Fig. 15. Drug dealer Clint Eastwood (Justin Chadwick) is stripped by rival dealers at a "rave" in *London Kills Me*. (Photo courtesy of Working Title Films, Ltd.)

mercial site); there is also a divinely inscribed aubergine and a fundamentalist *fatwa*. Although again dealing with racism, Kureishi more plainly reveals his strong political liberalism in this second novel. Remarkably, *The Black Album* also provides Kureishi with an arena for his most mature love story to date. With all its sexual interludes and controversial politics, this novel is fundamentally about the temporary nature of love—provisionality—and assesses the mutability of love, religion, art, and, pivotally, belief.

Love is investigated as a sexual, romantic, and familial concept. In the book's central affair, the adolescent sexual fantasies of the main character, Shahid, come true when he beds an experienced older woman. His former teacher, Deedee knows and is willing to do things that would be unknown to most younger, more naive women. In an early episode set in a taxi on the way to a rave, Shahid plays upon Deedee's knowledge of street life as well. Her sophistication is extremely attractive to Shahid; first she teaches him about sex, and later in the novel, as Kureishi words her sexual experience, she entertains him as she "turns herself into pornography."

The monogamous relationship is what both characters need. Shahid finds in Deedee his dream lover—knowing, inventive, and erotic; and, likewise, Deedee finds in Shahid her dream lover—devoted, innocent, and prolific. Deedee's experience makes her attractive to Shahid; Shahid's youth makes him as attractive to her. The teacher knows what she wants, and in her young student, she has someone who does—and can be made to do—things an older man wouldn't.

From the start, their needs are not stereotypical, and their characterization finally challenges society's conventional gender roles. Deedee disregards Shahid's male need to be in control, and Shahid thoroughly scrutinizes and exploits his sexuality. Their affair illuminates the message that sex is power. In Kureishi's novel, power is dynamic. Shahid, reduced first to a powerless little boy and then to a sex object, becomes free to move from resignation to hedonism. Deedee first demands mastery and later chooses conspiracy.

Together, the pair live out a role-reversal fantasy. As storyteller, Kureishi manipulates sexual fantasies beyond the stereotypes of female vengeance and male nightmare. Through the fact that Shahid and Deedee are able to move beyond the gender biases of sexual perspectives and of accepting prurient voyeurism, he suggests that all sexual conventions are confining.

The characters' sexual roles are self-determined. Not tied to either sex's stereotypical role, they accept the eroticism involved in the wrestling for male and female power and lose the didactism of gender politics. Unburdened, Deedee and Shahid become much more dynamic lovers. Sexual fantasy and political role reversal coexist. Learning and experimenting, they allow themselves and each other to make mistakes and to hurt and be hurt. As Kureishi explains, courageous acceptance of love's provisionality underlies Shahid's and Deedee's affair:

[Power] shifts here and there, . . . as it does in all good relationships. What I liked about their relationship was the provisionality of it. Brownlow's Marxism or Riaz's Islam are quite severe strict religions, aren't they? Deedee's given all that up. Near the last lines of the book, she says . . . "As long as it's fun," which is provisional. She can only say who I'm going to be, what I'm going to feel, what I'm going to be—today—now. Then I'm having somebody else, or I'm going to be somebody else.

Shahid agrees they can be fluid in that way, as it were. And that sets a fluidity. It makes their relationship a good one.

The following comparison of a sexually explicit prose segment in the novel's three drafts reveals the author's process in creating the dynamic relationship. His refining of words to permit the nuances and contradictions in the couple's exchange of power to become understood without determining any hierarchy for these roles is achieved through his subtle but directed focus of language. While the incident related remains similar, the fluidity of the incident, its "provisionality," is illuminated in the revised wording.

Draft One

He wanted to be naked in front of her. He undressed with only a little shame. But her mind had drifted away, thinking of the past and how to redeem it. When she came back she saw him folding his clothes, and sat up.

"You're looking at me," he said nervously, "as if I were a piece of cake. What are you, what are you thinking?"

"That I deserve you."

"Yeah?"

"I'm going to like eating you. Come here."

She put her lips to his ear and enquired if there were anything she could do.

There was a lot, a backlog, he barely knew where to begin, the forbidden wasn't forbidden for nothing. "I'm fine, actually," he said, kissing her face in gratitude, trembling.

She knew to persist. She'd been wanting him to wear make up since she first saw him; she was certain he'd look beautiful.

His instinct was to decline. It wasn't, yet, his destiny to look like Barbara Cartland. But then he recalled their first night, when she told him that "yes" was a more interesting word than "no". Why couldn't he trust her; why shouldn't he give himself to her? In his dry mouth he tried yes, the first of many.

She fetched her bag and lay everything out on a white towel. Then she hummed and fussed, reddening his lips, darkening his eyelashes, applying blusher. It troubled him; he felt he were losing himself. What would she see?

Something shifted when he relaxed. There was no point in resisting. He didn't look at himself as she painted him, but he liked the feel of his new female face. He could be coy, flirtatious, teasing; a burden went, a certain responsibility had been removed. He even wondered what it might be like to go out as a woman, and be looked at differently. To examine him Deedee moved about; she got him to turn his head this way and that, and to put his arms here and there. Then, for her, he walked up and down on his toes, swinging his hips, his arms, throwing his head back. She hummed and nodded and smiled and sighed.

He bowed.

He took an orange from the bowl beside the bed and started to peel it. She crossed the room and put on a CD of Vogue. She went to the wardrobe.

Shahid is inhibited as he undresses before Deedee. He doesn't like to be naked in front of her, as much as he knows Deedee likes to see him naked. Remaining dressed, she becomes a more powerful spectator. She is lost in thought but quickly recognizes Shahid as he sees himself, her object to be devoured. Grateful that she promises the complete sexual pantheon to him to perform as a man, he is again reduced to a boy when Deedee demands not that they engage in sex, not that he be gratified in some role-reversal sexual fantasy, but rather that he perform for her as a woman.

Draft Two

He undressed only a little coyly. She had said she liked him naked while she was dressed. But when he glanced at her, he saw she had drifted away, thinking of how to redeem the past. He folded his clothes and stood there. She sat up and licked her lips. He shrank back. "You're looking at me as if I were a piece of cake. What is it you're thinking?"

"That I deserve you. That I'm going to like eating you."

He went to her on his knees; she put her lips to his ear and enquired if there were anything she could do. Hand in hand they went, once more, into the bedroom and lay on the mattress on the floor. There was a lot she could do; he had such a backlog he barely knew where to begin; the forbidden wasn't forbidden for nothing.

"I'm fine, actually," he said, kissing her face and trembling.

She knew to persist. She'd been wanting him to wear make up since she first saw him; she was certain he'd look beautiful.

"Now?"

"There's only now."

Surely it wasn't, as yet, his destiny to look like Barbara Cartland? But he re-called their first night; Deedee had said that "yes" was a more interesting word than "no." Why couldn't he trust her; why shouldn't he give himself to her? In his dry mouth he tried yes, the first of many.

She crossed the room and put on a CD of Madonna's "Vogue." Then she fetched her bag and lay everything out on a white towel. She hummed and fussed, reddening his lips, darkening his eyelashes, applying blusher, pushing a hard pencil under his eye. It troubled him; he felt he were losing himself. What would she see?

Something shifted when he saw that nothing would be saved by resisting. He couldn't see himself as she painted him, but he liked the feel of his new fe-male face. He could be demure, flirtatious, teasing; a burden went, a certain re-sponsibility had been removed. He didn't feel he had to take the lead. He even wondered what it might be like to go out as a woman, and be looked at differ-ently. He longed to play with this new sexual power.

To examine him Deedee moved about. Curtly she told him to turn his head this way and that, to place his arms here and there, to do more of this or the other. It was easier not to resist, even when she had him walking up and down on his toes, swinging his hips and arms, throwing his head back. She nodded and smiled and sighed as he went. Finally he bowed, took an orange from the bowl beside the bed and started to peel it.

The language revisions now suggest that Deedee drives him to do as she says—that is, to become more submissive, more "female"; Shahid realizes that as she has the power, it is inevitable that he be the passive object to her active aggression. He is thus described as "trembling . . . losing himself . . . [his] destiny"; he moves from asking, "What would she see?" to fearing that "nothing could be saved by resisting," then to admitting that it is "easier not to resist"; finally, the penis-suggestive "shrank" is used to describe how he has become. In conveying that Shahid must completely abandon his inhibitions, forfeit his male security, and, finally, deny his male identity, Kureishi makes this gender-role transfer-ence linguistically.

Simultaneously, revisions in Deedee's descriptors support her becoming increasingly male—that is, aggressive and powerful. First making Shahid an object for her examination, she becomes the active partner, thereby making him the passive one. Deedee becomes not only self-motivated, she also becomes self-satisfied. In the version of the exchange quoted above, her descriptors—some, such as "hard . . . pushing," suggesting male sexual attributes in themselves—gain momentum, from the strong "persist" and "certain" to the masterful "examine," to the smug "curtly" and "nodded," and, finally, to the self-satisfied "smiled."

Most dynamically, he turns Shahid's trying out of "yes"—"the first of many"—into an objectifying assessment by this character of the value of yes. The word now signifies the newly learned freedom he finds with Deedee. Wording Shahid's growing inclination to the transvestism is a powerful inclusion in this draft. Revisions emphasize an underlying inevitability in the dressing-up. Language used in the second draft makes this cross-dressing experimentation a more mutual experience than it is in the first draft. Yet the passage is still commentary-heavy—that is, the actions are explained. Stating the feelings and motivations of the characters in this way keeps the episode from taking off as story just yet.

Draft Three

He undressed only a little coyly. She had said she liked him naked while she was dressed. But when he glanced at her, he saw she had drifted away. He folded his clothes and stood there. Suddenly she sat up and licked her lips. He shrank back.

"You're looking at me as if I were a piece of cake. What are you thinking?"

"I deserve you. I'm going to like eating you. Here."

On his knees he went to her. She put her lips to his ear and enquired if there were anything she could do. Hand in hand they went, once again, into the bedroom and lay on the mattress on the floor. There was a lot she could do, he thought; there was such a backlog he barely knew where to begin; the forbidden wasn't forbidden for nothing. He said, "I'm fine, actually."

She knew to persist. She'd been wanting him to wear make-up since she first saw him; she was certain he'd look good.

"Now?" he said.

"There's only now."

Surely it wasn't, as yet, his destiny to look like Barbara Cartland? But he recalled, then, their first night, when "yes" was a better word than "no." Why be afraid? Live, if you can, here, tonight. Didn't he know how to trust her?

She crossed the room and put on Madonna's "Vogue." She fetched her bag and lay everything out on a white towel. He sat beside her. She hummed and fussed over him, reddening his lips, darkening his eyelashes, applying blusher, pushing a pencil under his eye. It troubled him; he felt he were losing himself. What was she seeing?

She knew what she wanted; he let her take over; it was a relief. For now she refused him a mirror, but he liked the feel of his new female face. He could be demure, flirtatious, teasing; a burden went, a certain responsibility had been removed. He didn't have to take the lead. He even wondered what it might be like to go out as a woman, and be looked at differently. She back-combed his hair.

To examine him she moved about, telling him to turn his head this way and that, to place his arms here and there, to do more of this or the other. It was easier not to resist, even when she had him walking up and down on his toes like a model; beyond embarrassment, in a walking dance, he swung his hips and arms, throwing his head back, pouting, kicking his legs out. As he went she nodded, smiled and sighed.

He bowed, took an orange from the bowl beside the bed and started to peel it.

While definite elements and phrases continue to occur, the author reorders them. As with moving the Madonna CD, Kureishi moves phrases around. The incidents remain the same but their new placement changes their impact. Continued polishing of the wording is again evident. Deedee knows, for instance, not that Shahid would look "beautiful" in makeup, but that he would look good. The new description of the transsexual experience suggests "appropriate," "right," not "aesthetically pleasing." Kureishi also deletes editorializing passages and scraps elements that read like stage directions wherever he can.

A most significant addition is that of the looking glass. Whereas in the first draft Shahid simply "couldn't see himself as she painted him," Kureishi now makes Shahid ask Deedee to help him see himself as she sees him. This request fundamentally alters the charge; putting into words Deedee's blunt refusal to provide Shahid with a mirror galvanizes the incident and expands the description into one of a dual power struggle.

Deedee's refusal to let Shahid see the woman she has made him into keeps him as her object and prevents him from using her as his female looking glass. The refusal strips Shahid more naked than he appears when, as a man, his female sexuality is exposed. And because Shahid is not allowed the comfort of seeing himself as a reflection, it is his female identity, not the mirror images of female and male identity, that is brought into focus. When Shahid is completely exposed, Deedee is dressed— "she liked him naked while she was dressed." Shahid now sees himself as naked as he was before her. And he enjoys it: from being made a willing feminine sexual partner, he has seen himself become a brazen female whore.

Final Manuscript

He undressed only a little coyly. She had said she liked him naked while she was dressed. But when he glanced at her, he saw she had drifted away. He folded his clothes and stood there. Suddenly she sat up and licked her lips. He shrank back.

"You're looking at me as if I were a piece of cake. What are you thinking?"

"I deserve you. I'm going to like eating you. Here. Here, I said."

On his knees he went to her. She put her lips to his ear and enquired if there were anything she could do.

There was a lot she could do, he thought. There was such a backlog, he barely knew where to begin; the forbidden wasn't forbidden for nothing. He said, "I'm fine, actually."

She knew to persist. She'd been wanting him to wear make-up since she first saw him; she was certain he'd look good.

"Now?" he said.

"There's only now."

Surely it wasn't, as yet, his destiny to look like Barbara Cartland? Then he recalled their first night, when "yes" was a better word than "no". Why be afraid? Live, if you can, here, tonight. Tonight was for ever. Didn't he know how to trust her? Why couldn't he trust her; why shouldn't he give himself to her? He had to. Oh, yes.

She crossed the room and put on Madonna's "Vogue." Madonna said, "What are you looking at?" He loved that track. Deedee fetched her bag and lay everything out on a white towel. He sat beside her. She hummed and fussed over him, reddening his lips, darkening his eyelashes, applying blusher, pushing a pencil under his eye. She back-combed his hair. It troubled him; he felt he were losing himself. What was she seeing?

She knew what she wanted; he let her take over; it was a relief. For now she refused him a mirror, but he liked the feel of his new female face. He could be demure, flirtatious, teasing, a star; a burden went, a certain responsibility had been removed. He didn't have to take the lead. He even wondered what it might be like to go out as a woman, and be looked at differently.

To examine him she moved about; telling him to turn his head this way and that, to place his arms here and there, to do more of this or the other. It was easier not to resist, even when she had him walking on his toes like a model. Beyond embarrassment, in a walking dance, he swung his hips and arms, throwing his head back, pouting, kicking his legs out, showing his arse and cock. As he went, she nodded, smiled and sighed.

He bowed, took an orange from the bowl beside the bed and started to peel it.

Gender portrayal proves characteristically dual. First, Kureishi employs conventional gender roles: he asserts that men are boys seeking willing whores—locker-room psychoanalysis—while women desire dominance over men—simple penis envy. Flaunting this role-playing, Kureishi highlights the absurdity of this sexual stereotyping and questions its security. But Kureishi doesn't simply reverse these conventional roles, he exposes their dynamic interplay.

And in the interplay Shahid finds that more than merely playing a role, he actually takes the role of the female. The passage forgoes dogmatizing about the male gaze. This is no treatise on victimization, and Deedee need not, therefore, usurp male dominance, as both lovers recognize her female power. And in the novel's most perceptive gender observation, for a moment Shahid feels not the embarrassment of playing the female role, but, rather, the power of being female. Shahid feels not as a woman seen by men feels; rather, he feels as a woman feels. He becomes not the traditionally passive female partner but an active one. Through his female compliance in the inverted reversal, Shahid confronts (or perhaps is made to confront) female identity. As Emily Brontë's revolutionary lovers in *Wuthering Heights* did in the nineteenth century, Shahid and Deedee take tentative steps in the literary portrayal of the convoluted powers of sex. The portrayal of these contemporary characters in Kureishi's explicit passage goes beyond both yesterday's demeaning stereotypes and today's tired revisionism.

Shahid vainly attempts to recover his male assurance; he bows in a typical, comic, theatrical male gesture. He knows that Deedee has taken control. She has revealed her mastery: she has exposed him completely. But inherent in that exposure is a certain liberation: because they have been made to see each other, they have freed themselves. In Shahid's cross-dressing, both he and Deedee have seen the male—his and hers—as well as the female—hers and his. In this erotic blur, the dynamics of sexual power have been clearly exposed.

Kureishi perfects his wording in the final version. Both the provisional nature of love and the reciprocity of lovemaking are exposed in his wording. The gender politics are now in the form of a story. Characteristically, Kureishi submerges his archetypal argument into his characters' idiosyncratic actions. He sets the episode in motion, creating a rhythm as specific as the Madonna musical track he identifies. He bombards his flamboyant prose with sensationalism. Shahid's dancing and performing becomes more overt, flashes of his nude "cock" and "arse" now propelling the scene into visual eroticism.

In a different but parallel reality, in the course of the novel, Shahid and Deedee's sensational love affair also becomes a bona fide romance. Thus, while experiencing sexual love, Shahid remains drawn to the power of romantic love. In a passage showing him to be the stereotypically protective male, he bravely journeys through the London rioting to get back to Deedee. Likewise, Deedee is shown to be the stereotypically domestic female when, amid the violence, she offers to make Shahid a home-cooked meal. Thus, as well as being unconventional, their relationship is also stereotypical. Kureishi spins a love story that is blatantly romantic: It takes place in turbulent times and, in Hollywood fashion, the couple's passion, if temporary, dominates the issues of political and social upheaval all around them. Kureishi ends his story not with political resolution but with the lovers' decision to see what happens. This complicated plot, therefore, satisfies the reader with an essential element of this contemporary romance—the solace of the Hollywood ending.

Like the tension between choices throughout the novel, the couple's sexy love story, if romantic and political, is, at root, provisional. Kureishi sets an adulterous triangle in motion. Deedee is married to an academic who ties her morally, sexually, and intellectually to her past. When the student Shahid and she cuckold Dr. Brownlow, they transgress incendiary racial boundaries and conventional morality. Terrorism and their involvement in a political crisis increase the impediments to their love's survival. The student-teacher coupling of Shahid and Deedee breaks the bounds of generation and flirts with professional impropriety. Thus, as the novel concludes, the couple is breaking with convention while grasping at conventional romantic love.

Shahid and his married-teacher lover experience more than just a torrid affair. They crystallize the gender struggles for power as well as the conflict between romantic love and power in contemporary sexual relationships. And there is more. As in the conclusion to Ernest Hemingway's *The Sun Also Rises*, these lovers glibly dismiss their fears of the future and flaunt the pain of their pasts as the story comes to an end. At the close of this novel about terrorism and censorship, the lovers are able to leave the reality of urban violence behind—if only temporarily. Sleeping late, they wake up to a continuation of their romantic dreams. They will remain lovers—for as long as the dream goes on.

As a setting for the novel's heterosexual romantic couple, London is portrayed romantically as well. In fact, the cosmopolitan setting is pivotal to the tone and voice of *The Black Album*. The novel feels irresistibly romantic. Using London as more than setting, Kureishi presents the urban milieu in a characteristic way. With a loving series of urban images not unlike the montages in the screenplay of *Sammy and Rosie Get Laid*, Kureishi spins a cinematic love story of and to the metropolis, contemporary London. The author acknowledges:

I am writing about London, what I like about London, and trying to write about London in a slightly romantic way, I suppose. There are good things to do in the city, like having breakfast in certain places, having breakfast with someone you've fucked for the first time. Fantastic. Wonderful. That feeling again. I think I'm more capable of writing for that irony now than I was before.

Accepting the irony in the lifestyle of residing in England's capital is essential to Kureishi's storytelling. Thus, the romance and optimism

he conveys in his storytelling is corollary to a fear and disgust of contemporary city life. The hybridity of his perspective enables him to write both respectfully and critically about an urban condition that he finds inherently complicated—namely, the multiculturalism of contemporary city communities. Shahid and Deedee exemplify today's mutable urban lifestyle.

Kureishi's personal experiences prompted an evolution in his storytelling. And *The Black Album* not only expands his portrayal of lovers, it continues to rework his portrayal of the interaction between son and father, even though Kureishi had suggested that Haroon and Karim Amir in *The Buddha of Suburbia* had worked through his exploration of this relationship: "I wrote many fathers," he acknowledged while drafting *The Black Album*. "There's a father in some of the plays, and I wrote him in *Laundrette*. I finally put a father in *The Buddha of Suburbia*. I have three or four goes at something, and then I leave it and move on. I was very pleased with the father in the *Buddha*, and I don't think I will write any more fathers for a long time to come. I'm finished with that now."

Biographically, Kureishi mourned his father and became a father himself while writing *The Black Album*. In this, his second

Fig. 16. Flower stands like this one near the Seven Dials are part of the London street scene.
Fig 17. A warning sign on a London tube train—evidence that terrorist threats are assimilated into the city's daily rush-hour routine.
Fig. 18. Street musicians are assimilated into the busy street scene near Covent Garden. (Photos by author.)

novel, he traced the power of a deceased father over his son. Apparent throughout the novel, the parental bond—as well as that of the lovers in the novel—is more mature than are those of his previous sons and fathers. Shahid has reached a further phase in his relationship with his father, compared with Karim in Kureishi's previous novel. As a man, Shahid finally confronts the resentment he felt as an adolescent at being measured against his father's expectations for him.

The story unfolds as Shahid compares his reality with his expectations. Papa exists only in Shahid's memory. Observations about him are questionable, unprovable, and, quite possibly, romanticized. Thus, similar to the effect of denying the story the immediacy of a first-person narrator, the characterization of Papa and son creates further distance from and suspicion about the incidents related in the story.

Shahid's relationship with Papa also reflects a common life experience—that of a deceased parent's continuing presence in an adult child's reality. Papa is part of Shahid's thinking. The relationship between father and son shows off a human ambiguity. Although deceased, Papa remains part of how the living characters live.

Papa can be characterized neither through his actions nor through his words, two fundamental methods of characterizing in prose; instead, he must be characterized through how his children remember what he did or said. Papa is thus a series of stories. Kureishi clearly controls his novel's focus by characterizing the father in this way, through selected characters' reminiscences of him.

The perspective that the grown children have of their deceased parents frames the characterization. Papa is seen only in a paternal role by Shahid, Shahid's elder brother, Chili, and Chili's wife, Zulma. Other characters in the novel knew Papa, but the memories of Tippo, Papa's brother, or of business associates and peers are not included in his characterization. Mum's point of view is conspicuously avoided, too. The technique gives the novel its cool, detached focus without authorial exposition of Papa: readers do not learn about a man, they read memories about a father. Papa exists—and is named—only as a father.

Zulma's and Chili's memories of Papa, like Shahid's, include Papa's reactions to them and interpretations of each other's memories of him. The dynamics of the clearly defined relationships create overlapping, sometimes contradictory observations that also have the effect of expanding our knowledge of the living characters. For example, while Zulma's memories of Papa center on gender differences and immigration, Chili's memories center on generational conflicts and economic status, and Shahid's memories center on philosophy and honor. This way of describing Papa thus also more fully characterizes Zulma, Chili, and Shahid.

Papa worked his way from clerk to entrepreneur in twenty-five years and died of a heart attack. According to Shahid, Papa, a successfully assimilated English businessman, was devoted to consumerism and distrusted the arts, advising his second son to "live in the real world." Disappointed with Shahid's bookishness, Papa preferred discussing sexual prowess with his elder son, Chili, to discussing Shelley with his "eunuch" younger son, Shahid.

According to Chili, on the other hand, it was his younger son's brains that Papa admired. Like Haroon and Karim in Kureishi's first novel, Chili and his father are portrayed as having initially competed, when the latter was alive, for "most macho" status. Later, Chili became merely a procurer of vicarious sexual adventures, bringing home stories of his sexual escapades; finally, he married Zulma to cater to Papa's needs. Having relegated Chili to running the family travel agency, Papa added to the pressures already placed on his first son by offloading on him the responsibility of care of his brainy little brother.

But we are then told that "Shahid adored and venerated his father; both he and Chili, in their different ways, wanted to be like him." The sons' competitive reaction to their father, fundamental to the conflict in the story, illuminates sibling relationships between brothers. It also reinforces the impact of parents, even after they have passed away, on their grown children. When Shahid watches Zulma pack up and move on, he still sees the forsaken Chili from their deceased father's point of view, not as a person or even as his brother, but as the place "where Papa's dream had been shipwrecked."

Papa's life is scrutinized as Shahid tries to determine whether he or his older brother would have been the greater disappointment to him. Papa lived a "decent life," but, we are led to ask, where did it get him? More importantly, where did it get his sons? "The poor fucker, worked his ass off, and for what? He wanted people to say how smart his sons were. But had they benefitted?" These are not merely rhetorical questions, they are applicable to every immigrant character, to every father's child. Shahid both acknowledges his father's frustrations and selfishly continues to wonder what his efforts gained him.

According to materialistic Zulma, who could always wrap Papa around her finger, now that Chili was a "scatter-head," the best way to benefit from their father's travails lay in Shahid's taking over his father's travel agency. Shahid doesn't doubt her assessment of how they can fulfill Papa's intentions, but ultimately he questions whether Papa was right in his expectations for his sons: "But this was different. Shahid had to admit that Papa was wrong and find his own direction, whatever that was." Shahid comes to understand the roles his father had determined for his sons as much as he recognizes Papa's failings and strengths. And his question is a signal of his education that is at the novel's center.

Shahid is the student who must question his teacher, the younger brother who must assert his identity, the son who must go his own way. In short, Shahid is made to assess love in its carnal, romantic, and familial aspects and to feel the power of each of these incarnations. More to the novel's point, Shahid comes to recognize the power of the belief in love, the human necessity of believing in love, and the inevitability of accepting the weaknesses of all human loves, thus permitting love of self.

The quandary that Shahid is in before he comes to this state of acceptance is especially dramatic in the predicament in which Kureishi's Asian college student finds himself, in the volatile London of the eighties, although Shahid's dilemma is identifiable to every parents' child. Shahid must accept the power of the past, learn to question what to believe about it, and somehow reckon with his assessment of it. This is unlike Riaz's dogmatic fundamentalism. Riaz glorifies the past and embraces everything about it. He denies even questioning it.

The violent conflict between fundamentalism and western progress in Kureishi's book is appropriately set in the academic forum — that is, the conflict is scrutinized by scholars, teachers, and students of both consumerism and the Muslim tradition. Kureishi's opinion of the censorship of the book and his refusal to accept terrorism are clearly given voice in the mindless violence of the riots, the comic search for a ceremonial broom handle, and the divinely inscribed aubergine. Shahid must determine whether he sides with the traditions of his forefathers or whether he should progress from the English cultural assimilation of his father. Kureishi does not question whether terrorism, dogmatism, or censorship are acceptable. In fact, one critic of the novel has asserted that Kureishi has revealed himself here "like the best propagandist . . . it's clear Kureishi comes down on the side of the angels."[2]

In fact, however, Kureishi uses Islam here as he has employed Thatcherism: It is neither vindication nor condemnation of either that he seeks; rather, he uses both as definite ideological beliefs to fuel his story. He has, indeed, admitted that he sees the similar power of these dissimilar philosophies, saying, "Islam is rather like Thatcherism. It's an intoxicating force to test yourself against."[3]

If not Shahid's only test, this is the one that provides the polar tension in the novel. The validity of the book burning itself is never a question—the question is, how powerful is each of the conflicting beliefs about sex, violence, god, and literature? Shahid is made to question how genuine, consistent, comforting, and defensible any belief is, whether it is the belief in love, in family, in religion, or in art.

Shahid is a reader and a lover of stories, and is translating a book of Riaz's poems. He has a bet with his brother Chili that he can't read a book and understand it. Deedee teaches a multicultural, non-canonical college course in which books are displaced as teaching tools by rock music and legends. At the novel's center is the burning of a book, a book judged to be unacceptable to the teachings of the Koran.

The novel's most controversial issue is in the burning of this book judged to be sacrilegious. The historical connections of the book burning, as well as its function as a plot incident, catapult it to the center of the novel. But although Kureishi does not condone the burning of this novel, he is not arguing in this novel in defense of a specific book. Rather, his is a story about the burning of a book, any book. "Above all," a critic has claimed, "*The Black Album* is a cheeky ode to the power and pleasure of literature."[4] The novel questions the nature of fiction and truth, reaffirming the rights of and need for storytelling in culture. The author recognizes the truth in creating fiction and investigates the need for the creation of the story.

Therefore, the book burners exhibit a number of motives, ranging from political to criminal, suggesting that even this act—like everything else in his fiction—will not be so easily labeled by the author. Integrity does not belong solely to either side, or to any one race, gender, or generation. Subjectivity is integral. Although as a man Kureishi has an opinion of censorship and does not shrink from making his opinion clear, as the author, it is his respect for the honesty of storytelling, and not his urge to promote specific beliefs, that structures his novel.

In *The Black Album* Riaz condemns what he deems to be the unacceptable treatment of religious dogma in a novel by its author. When Shahid transforms Riaz's writing into poetry rather than transcribing his political tract, he turns the fundamentalist political observations into poems so lush that he gets erections. Here, Shahid's translation of Riaz's writing reflects, in a second fictional turn, what Riaz has labeled unacceptable. Kureishi does not answer history; he questions the responsibility of any storyteller to convey realities and truths.

Exploring the dynamics of the place of art in society exposes the need for storytelling in the reality of our lives. Thus, the novel asks, "if art has no ties to fact, can it have, in fact, ties to truth?"

Kureishi's second novel leaves the question unanswered because asserting an answer, any answer, would manipulate the fiction. In short, if it were to give an answer to the question, the novel would itself become historical interpretation. To remain honest storytelling, in keeping with Kureishi's abhorrence of the novel's actions in history, historical fact-making is unacceptable. To remain an honest storyteller, Kureishi creates the entire fiction. He elects not to preach, but, instead, to tell his story:

The novel is concerned with stories, isn't it? Just as Riaz, as it were, invents Islam to suit him, . . . Shahid is doing the same when he rewrites Riaz's poems. When Shahid's with Deedee, she gets him to tell a story. When she masturbates, she tells him stories. When he masturbates, there are stories. There's always stories. It's a world of stories, the whole fucking book is made up of a world of stories, people telling stories . . . The point is that life is reinterpreted all the time as we live it, isn't it?

The novel openly questions religion in its depiction of conflict between eastern religious tradition and western progressive philosophy. It has a powerful current in the unstoppable avalanche of the book-burning frenzy. It depicts physical violence. It proclaims the pitfalls, contradictions, and hypocrisy of street society. In this book, Kureishi wrestles with issues of censorship, prejudice, and terrorism. The novel struggles to defend and define an aesthetic philosophy. It questions nationality. In the end, it demands a reinvention of identity. It is, therefore, a story not only of power but of mutability. It is a novel of movement, change, and action. *The Black Album* is, at its root, a story about provisionality.

Thus, the act of dressing up is done frequently by Shahid in the story. Dressed and undressed by Deedee, he becomes her fantasy—a little boy, and a woman. As telling is Shahid's dressing up in traditional costume, a white silk salwar, for his Muslim brother Chad, representing Shahid's quest to understand his identity that is at the center of the novel. Shahid is all—and none—of these identities, according to the author:

Dressing up has a new fluidity. . . . Chad dresses Shahid up—he makes Shahid wear a salwar. It's a really good scene. Chad says, "Hey, I want to dress you up. I'll bring you a present when you dress up." Really nice. And he gives Shahid this wonderful white, pure silk salwar. Chad dresses Shahid up, and he puts this cap on his head. And Shahid is standing there looking at him really embarrassed. And this scene contrasts, in a way, with the previous scene where Deedee dresses Shahid up. Shahid and Deedee dress up. Deedee becomes a guy who wears makeup; Shahid becomes a woman. If you're a Muslim, you can't play with your identity in that way.

Kureishi also uses changing costumes to carry an almost allegoric series of events in his novel. One of these is a red Paul Smith shirt bought by Shahid's brother, Chili, a clotheshorse from his designer suits down to his Calvin Klein underwear. The designer garment passes first to his shy, studious brother, Shahid, then, by default, to politico brother Riaz, and, finally, back again to Chili through his violence at the end of the story. As well as being an object to follow through the course of the story, the shirt also charts a ritualistic circle.

A sartorial banner, the red shirt passes to Shahid from Chili to assuage the latter's guilt by dressing his egghead younger brother up to his own standards as a passionate womanizer. When Shahid loses his brother's hand-me-down red shirt, he as blatantly dismisses his brother's consumerist values. Continuing its passage through the novel, the red banner next redeems suburbanite Shahid from his careless, naive loss of

Riaz's laundry. Shahid, who, to make up for the loss, gives Riaz the shirt, will later learn that he cannot as easily bring back traditional beliefs by wearing traditional garb. While Riaz wears the red shirt, he is unaware that he ironically appears to be the epitome of the western consumerism he loathes. Finally, Chili sees red, literally, when he sees his shirt on Riaz, flashing like the red rag before a bull. In a final altercation, he forces Riaz to return the red shirt to him.

Paul Smith's designer-clothing collection is housed in his shop on London's trendy Floral Street and is displayed in luxurious Knightsbridge department stores. His expensive designs are sold from Tokyo to New York, a rather modern turn on the traditional British sportswear look—slightly irreverent, funky, and expensive. An awareness of the significance of the red shirt demands not only fashion savvy, but a knowledge of fashion in and as pop culture.

This characteristic reference to English fashion is one of the elements cited by critics noting the English aspects of the novel as being representative of Kureishi's ties to English customs. One American review, if mixed, recognized the book's ties to both Kureishi and English tradition: "With Hanif Kureishi, expect an urban carnival . . . Like the rest of Kureishi's narratives, *The Black Album* is picaresque, tracing Shahid's collisions with the sparring classes, races, and religions around him."[5] The style, if not as comic as that of previous prose, is seen here as customarily outrageous. To another American critic, like Shahid's creativity at the typewriter, this story, if "blasphemous . . . [springs from] just the sort of rogue impulse from which novelists, and rock stars, take flight. And Kureishi, as fan and practitioner, would seem to make no distinction."[6]

Music, specifically the labyrinthine history of rock music, is again a recognized element of his storytelling here. A critic for the *Chicago Tribune* noted the relevance of music to the black story: "Kureishi has also served as co-editor of a massive anthology of comment and reportage on the subject of pop music (*The Faber Book of Pop*), so it is no surprise that *The Black Album* takes its title from Prince's recording, itself named in sassy response to the Beatles' *The White Album* . . . Prince is the idol of the novel's characters because he is 'half black and half white, half man and half woman, half size, feminine but macho.'" So, too, the *Tribune* critic finds the novel itself musical, written as it is with "the sounds and images of a strobe-lit rock concert."[7]

The novel is also noted as cinematic—that is, as being tied to the movies. Kureishi's use of movie images is scrutinized by the critics, as his career as a film writer, likewise, is credited. But Kureishi does more than merely employ film as a cultural common denominator. He does more, too, than create a fluid kinetic story. His novel not only recognizes the motion picture's rendering of dream, it builds upon it. While the "streets of gold" dream of the first half of this century had fueled the dreams of his Asian immigrant forefathers when they emigrated to England, Shahid's story investigates the price of pursuing that dream exacted from his own English-born generation descended from those immigrants. Consequently, although *The Black Album*'s Papa came to England hoping to live the dream he saw in the movies, his disillusioned English sons' dreaming can now only find life in the movies.

Their parents had come to England to make an affluent and stable life in a country not run by tyrants. Once this was done, their remaining ambition rested with their sons, particularly the eldest. Papa loved Chili, but would he have approved of him now? His most recent ambition was to make it in America, though it wasn't so much the voice of liberty that called Chili, as the violent intensity. Time and again he watched *Once Upon A Time In America, Scarface,* and *The Godfather* as career documentaries. He had even cursed their Papa—out of earshot—for coming to old England rather than standing in line on Ellis Island with the Jews, Poles, Irish and Armenians. England was small-time, unbending; real glory was impossible in a country where the policemen wore helmets shaped like sawn-off marrows. Chili thought he could be someone in America, but he wasn't going to go there poor. He'd get himself more established in London and then hit New York with a high "rep," or reputation.

The problem was, as their satirical uncle once stated, money had come too easily to Chili in the 80s. He didn't respect where it came from. "It's easy for people, especially if they're young," he said, "to forget that we've barely arrived over there in England. It takes several generations to become accustomed to a place. We think we're settled down, but we're like brides who've just crossed the threshold. We have to watch ourselves, otherwise we will wake up one day to find we have made a calamitous marriage."

Chili's plight as an assimilated dreamer is quite clear: He sold himself out to live on Easy Street. The alterations in the immigrant experience are understood through cinematic references, not historical ones. The author acknowledges his use of film history to image this historical transition in his fiction, commenting:

In the fifties and sixties, a lot of immigrants came to Britain from Pakistan and India. And many of them were really honest, and they worked hard, and they did well, and they wanted their sons to do well and so on. And they had the immigrant ethic. And it's kind of run out in Chili. By the time we get to Chili, the immigrant ethic, the work ethic, doing well, head down, studying—in England— has run out with him. The father did well, passed on the money to him. What did Chili do? He spent the money on drugs and women and clothes. And Chili doesn't have his father's earnest desire to do well in England, you know, because he's another generation like the Pacino character in *The Godfather*. He's not like the Brando character; he doesn't have—integrity. [Pacino] doesn't have any purpose . . . in *The Godfather*. Nor does Chili in life.

Other story lines propel the novel forward. Kureishi uses Strapper to weave the parts of the story together as he wanders the London streets, loosening the moments before the next destination. Shahid is in motion, riding the tube lines to move himself from one place and one story to other places and other stories. Deedee, too, is in motion, leaving her marriage behind. The couple's train trip at the novel's conclusion emphasizes that this is a story of passage. The train takes Deedee and Shahid not to anywhere, but away from London. They run away terrified by the fact that the past is usurping the future, but when they move back to London, they can only move forward by realizing their present.

The actions are conditional because life is provisional. The lovers weather their ordeal, and in the quiet, they promise to continue to do so—as long as it is fun. Rolling. Back and forth. Relentlessly. Unresolved. Like tradition and progress. Identity and assimilation. The ending is merely a pause in the characters' stories. And in a novel concerned with bleak issues of our paradoxical society, Kureishi's characters give their conditional love a human face.

By remaining unemotional in telling Shahid's story, Kureishi is able to keep the story honest. Human honesty makes the particulars of his story understandable, if not always specifically within a reader's experience.

Not limiting his creation of fiction exclusively to his own experience, however, Kureishi also draws the identifiable truths in *The Black Album* from archetypal models and universal human experience. His story of the eighties cannot be part of his own adolescent autobiography; instead, therefore, he frames his adult perceptions of that decade through a fictional adolescent main character.

Some reviewers criticize this second novel for once again employing a young hero. But this is merely Kureishi's stylistic choice. There are significant differences from Kureishi's first novel's hero, story, and presentation to distinguish the two novels. History is filtered in *The Black Album* by the main character's young observations, assuring that this second novel is more distanced. "The *Buddha* came to me in the voice of the boy as the boy's experience," Kureishi remembers. "*The Black Album* is a more objective novel, as it were. Obviously, it's about Shahid, his experience in his life, but it's not from his point of view in that way, not from inside his mind. It's a cooler book emotionally."

Shahid's process of analysis is supported by the structure and balance of the novel. The novel's comparison of his past with his present illuminates its investigation of tradition and change. The physicality of Shahid's adolescent affair with Deedee plays in tandem with the boy's intellectual probings with Riaz. Just as it portrays both raves and lectures, so it also presents contradictory philosophies, as Shahid weighs possibilities, determines his own values.

Throughout his fiction, Kureishi's individualistic characters reveal their human sameness. The appeal of the characters is in their honest creation. Thus readers understand characters like—and unlike—their experiences: the province of artistic instruction. *The Black Album*'s Hat genuinely loves Shahid as his friend. Each is individual in the way that all lovers are: hopeful, dreaming, and conniving; and each is also from a family that is, as most families are, complicated and unpredictable, sometimes forgiving beyond reason and other times arguing to the point of erupting into insoluble conflicts. Kureishi expresses the recognizable in the honesty of his lovers; he writes the identifiable in the families that he portrays, resembling as they do the myriad families of our contemporary world.

Shahid vacillates between belief and worship, between fiction and reality, between intellectual pleasures and simple pleasures of the body, between cultural assimilation and cultural identity. He confronts the quandary in which today's immigrants find themselves. Kureishi finds the truth in the human predicament, which he treats not as a mandate to preach answers, but as his rationale for storytelling.

An incident of literary censorship is integral to the novel. As a man, Kureishi has certainly made his attitude toward the Rushdie *fatwa* clear— he has definite opinions on book burning and its effect on literature. But as an author, it is not his autobiographical beliefs that drive the story; rather, he is writing about Shahid's fictional search for an answer amid a maze of contemporary contradictions, and he is writing, too, about fundamentalist Riaz's fictional search, and about buppie Chili's fictional search. It is his genuine fondness for each of these characters, if not for their beliefs, that characterizes his storytelling.

Kureishi's second book received mixed reviews. His literary reputation—that is, the canon of his work that preceded this novel—was sometimes misused as a critical measuring stick for assessing this story. Undeniably Kureishi's reputation affected the response to this book. Reviews—particularly American ones—quite often used more words comparing this book (unfavorably) to *The Buddha of Suburbia*, a far more critically acclaimed and popular novel, than they used analyzing it in its own right. Even the novel's supporters often made this unfavorable comparison. This is often the fate of second novels. Unarguably, *The Black Album* does have context in Kureishi's work and has some strong ties to his previous storytelling. But these ties should not be permitted to shape critical response to it.

My Beautiful Laundrette and *Sammy and Rosie Get Laid* are concerned with Anglo-Asian urban issues, while *London Kills Me* portrays the drug milieu of a young London hustler, but at the conclusion of each, all their youthful main characters are, like Shahid, left in a new place facing different questions. *The Buddha of Suburbia*, likewise, opens with Karim living in the suburbs on the edge of the explosive 1970s and leaves him on the brink of the conservative 1980s. Kureishi's second novel is more distanced and less comic than his screenplays and first novel, but a hybrid perspective remains central to the stories, while youthful characters are once again involved in flamboyant incidents. The seri-

Fig. 19. Anna (Wendy Gazelle) photographs the burning of the London neighborhood that illuminates the conflicts between Rafi (Shashi Kapoor, center) and his son, Sammy (Ayub Khan Din, left), in *Sammy and Rosie Get Laid*. (Photo courtesy of Working Title Films, Ltd.)

ousness of the fundamentalist movement and the conservatism of the times make *The Black Album* a story of a different London. And whatever the decade, the location in which Kureishi chooses to study maturation remains the same: London.

Although less comic and more historic than *The Buddha of Suburbia*, the second novel is also brought to a conclusion while remaining necessarily unresolved. But unlike the earlier novel's conclusion, which leaves Karim perching on the eve of Thatcherism, the fact that *The Black Album* leaves the eighties for the nineties gives this political novel a less melancholy conclusion. Shahid wants to believe in something; he is searching for something to believe in. Pledging his love to Deedee on a train carrying them away from the seething streets of London, Shahid chooses at that time to believe in love. That choice compels him to embrace the present.

His acceptance of the present prevents Shahid from also accepting the religious philosophy to which he has been exposed during the furor over the banned book. Indeed, Shahid never accepts dogma, creed, or solution, leading him to reject the values of 1980s London as well. Shahid is a more definite character than Karim; he makes a choice not to commit. When the lovers agree to stay together, it is understood by both of them that it is a provisional choice. They are traveling, on a holiday, on the move. Thus, like the historical dynamics of the international community's dealings with the *fatwa*, Kureishi's fictional world remains vigorous. He only gives his main character temporary respite from the questions still stalking him on the London streets. *The Black Album* questions whether answers exist, just as it insists that the questions themselves do—and must—change.

AUTHOR IN PROCESS
Love in a Blue Time

While promoting *The Black Album*, Kureishi continued to compose, adapt, and collaborate, enjoying the stimulation of moving from project to project. He revised a draft of his adaptation of Oscar Wilde's *The Picture of Dorian Gray* for film treatment, oversaw the publication of *The Faber Book of Pop*,[1] which he co-edited, and composed short stories.

Kureishi has been interested in writing short stories throughout his career. Sometimes the short fiction has been part of the process of creating a longer work or a source to be adapted into another medium. Early in his career he had drafted *My Beautiful Laundrette* as a three-page short story before determining to tell the story in a screenplay. *The Buddha of Suburbia* had first appeared as a short story, too, and Kureishi had originally conceived *The Black Album* as two novellas.

At other times, he has been attracted to the immediacy of storytelling in the short-story genre, two examples being "With Your Tongue down My Throat" and "Esther." Explaining his attraction to writing short stories, Kureishi says, "They are so fast, so immediate, they are able to catch up with your life." He feels free to experiment with "new ideas and new moods" in his short stories.

In Kureishi's first published short story, "With Your Tongue down My Throat," half-sisters Nadia and Nina exemplify not only the paradox of Anglo-Asian politics, but the tensions between the dreams and the reality of Asian immigrants. It experiments with a female voice in its point of view within a point of view and allows Kureishi a mirror look at racism.

Nina imagines her sister far away in Pakistan as "a girl . . . sitting under a palm tree, reading a Brontë novel and drinking yogurt. I see a girl being cuddled by my father. He tells stories of tigers and elephants and rickshaw wallahs." Her fantasy, rooted somewhere between Kipling and Tagore, is an eastern version of *The Cosby Show*. Nina's fantasy of her sister is a childhood dream of a faraway land with a loving dream daddy.

Upon actually meeting Nadia in London, Nina sees not only that she bears no resemblance to her fantasy image, but also that her dream has been colored by bias.

You're smaller than me. Less pretty, if I can say that. Bigger nose. Darker, of course, with a glorious slab of hair like a piece of chocolate attached to your back. I imagined, I don't know why (pure prejudice, I suppose) that you'd be wearing the national dress, the baggy pants, the long top and light scarf flung all over. But you have on F. U. jeans and a faded blue sweatshirt—you look as if you live in Enfield. We'll fix that.

When the sisters meet, Nina realizes not only that Nadia is not the Indian miniature drawing she had fantasized her to be, but that she looks too suburban and removed to fit into Nina's young, working-class, often unemployed London crowd.

When Nadia dresses Nina in her national costume, she wraps Nina in the identity of which she dreams. Nina describes "the Pakistani dress I'm wearing now (with open-toed sandals—homemade). It's gorgeous: yellow and green, threaded with gold, thin summer material." Nina now sees herself as part of her dream, the princess of her tradition. Since the dream of Elsewhere has eluded her as a hybrid Londoner, she dreams she can find it by accepting her Asian heritage. She can't wait to wear the costume, and puts it on for her trip to collect her unemployment money.

When dressed as she had fantasized her Pakistani dream sister to dress, Nina becomes the object of racial abuse in London. In a fast-paced episode, Kureishi first satirizes white liberals, then goes on to decry racist white bigots. Nina, looking like "a lost woman with village ways and chickens in the garden" in her national outfit, is given leaflets and assistance numbers from crusading communists when entering the community center. Nina makes out that she understands the patronizing stance adopted by the liberals, telling them, "I'm oppressed, you see, beaten-up, pig ignorant with an arranged marriage and certain suttee ahead." Then, while returning from the community center, she stops to buy white wine for dinner and meets with abuse from a passing group of toughs on a bus who see her Pakistani costume. They balance the two-sided prejudice against her by shouting racist slurs: "Curry breath, curry breath, curry breath." No longer a Londoner anymore, but instead an Asian, as she walks the streets of her hometown she is ridiculed by everyone from political theorists to street gangs because of her national costume.

Later, the sisters travel the streets dressed as Londoners. Nadia now recognizes their exile as Asians in the west. She becomes increasingly aware that the separation she feels from the English who have achieved her dream in London is greater now, as she walks with Nina in white London, than it was when she merely dreamed of it far away in her affluent Pakistan. The London that is Nina's home is "filth" to Nadia; their father has filled Nadia's head with his dreams of a gorgeous and civilized London past, not of the reality of the modern city she sees. The only way for them to regain a glimpse of the dream is to immigrate again. To do so, Nina and Nadia must journey to another urban class in London. Nina says:

We'll have to get the bus and go east, to Holland Park and round Ladbroke Grove. This is now the honeyed London for the rich who have preservatives in their conservatories. Here there are *La* restaurants, wine bars, bookshops, estate agents, more prolific than doctors, and attractive people in black, few of them aging. Here there are health food shops where you buy tofu, nuts, live culture yogurt and organic toothpaste. Here the sweet little black kids practise on steel drums under the motorway for the Carnival and old blacks sit out in the open on orange boxes shouting. Here the dope dealers in Versace suits travel in from the suburbs on commuter trains, carrying briefcases, trying to sell slummers bits of old car tyre to smoke.

And there are more stars than beggars. For example? Van Morrison in a big overcoat is hurrying towards somewhere in a nervous mood.

Kureishi's short story exposes both sides of twentieth-century immigration. In Pakistan, Nadia sees the west as the rich, pop-culture world of the movies, a world in which expensive urban neighborhoods are tinged with a pinch of tasteful decadence: designer drugs, celebrities, and well-dressed danger. This is not, however, the London Nadia finds when she moves there. From her life in London, on the other hand, her sister Nina imagined Pakistan as an exotic, uncorrupted landscape, and thought of Nadia's life there as being softened with the security of living in a westernized family touched by the mass media. This, likewise, is not the Pakistan she actually finds when she goes there. The actualities of both homelands are as different from their fantasy versions as they are from each other. And, ironically, they are, in many ways, the same. Both characters find that they cannot find a home at home. Nor can they find a better Elsewhere merely by emigrating to another country.

Kureishi's expanded immigrant dream matches society's expanding perspective. The comic writing masks the brutal realism, and the author's stylistic use of parenthetical intrusions linguistically supports his hybrid point of view. The hyphenated cultural identity of his insider/outsider narrator is distinctive. Although by no means the first storyteller to have done so, Kureishi's adopting various points of view underscores the universality of storytelling, beyond limiting any point of view merely by the generation, class, sexual preference, nationality, and gender of the author.

The reader ultimately finds out that it is really Howard who is telling the story as he assumes Nina would tell it. Kureishi uses this device not only to show more clearly how Howard sees, but, more interestingly, to expose how Howard sees Nina. Racist, sexist, and immigrant-related prejudices, as well as racial, gender, and generational attitudes, are exposed by employing this trick perspective. Howard, for instance, advises Nina to take lots of pens to Pakistan, telling her, "It's a third world country. They lack the basic necessities."

After Howard is revealed as the narrator, the story concludes on a somber note as he admits that he regrets the loss of any real chance of putting himself into Nina's life. Thus, he too lives in dream rather than reality—in his fiction. As he describes it, "The bus moves on and I watch until it disappears and then I go inside the flat and take off my clothes and have a bath. Later, I write down the things she said but the place still smells of her."

Kureishi also experiments with the technical operation of storytelling in this early short story. For example, when the narrator receives a letter from another character, he/she addresses the reader directly in apposition. The relating of plot incidents as author, then through a narrator, and then through a narrator's narrator creates a heightened focus in the story. If somewhat cumbersome, the point-of-view-within-a-point-of-view device emphasizes the artfulness of the story—that is, that it is not a seamless slice of life, but, rather, a stylized work of art.

This literary framing operates like the motion-picture camera lens that frames cinematic storytelling. By framing his story in this technical way, Kureishi makes the reader aware that every story changes with the point of view because every narrator tells a different story.

According to the author, introducing this split narrator made him aware of his insecurities in creating a female narrator:

You know the girl in "With Your Tongue down My Throat." . . . A young Asian girl, a student, came to see me the other day. She said, to my surprise, "Oh I really like your story; I really identified with that girl. I was annoyed when you did that to me at the end, when you put her story through the mouth of the guy." She asked, "Why did you do that?" And I said, "Because I was scared that if I didn't, people would think I meant all women are like that." And I realized that the politics of the seventies had haunted me for ages.

Kureishi is suggesting here that, in part, his sensitivity to seventies politics affected this choice in his earlier fiction. Changing the point of view is noteworthy in that context. However, his concession has a place not only in his autobiography, but also in the evolution of his storytelling. The male author, having attempted to tell a story from a female point of view, then went on to experiment with expanding his storytelling to include other gender, national, and racial perspectives. This early story of racial discrimination and hybridity illuminates Kureishi's rejection of any subgenre labeling that limits the universality of human experience.

Kureishi chose to expand his short story "The Buddha of Suburbia" that was published in a 1987 periodical. "Esther," another short story written while Kureishi was waiting for the publication of *The Buddha of Suburbia* as a novel two years later, remained as a short story. This story is interesting in terms of what it reveals of the author's evolving style.

"Esther" exhibits Kureishi's characteristic techniques, but it is the story's differences from Kureishi's other work that cause it to stand out.

Ray is a professor who walks out on his students while directing them in an Ionesco play because he is "bored by them." Described as "in his early forties and immature," and shy to show his body because of a crippling disease, Ray is unsuccessful with women "even though he'd advertised in *Time Out*," and prefers to be serviced by prostitutes and "to sit smoking in the airless, modern college room, looking out on the London traffic, his poor feet on a chair, *Blonde on Blonde* playing as he lectured on American literature of the 1960s." He writes an essay on Wilkie Collins, includes Joe Orton in his lectures, and is patronizing in his "polite indifference." Then he meets Esther.

Lolita she is not: Esther is "in her middle fifties, but now that women in their sixties were wearing track suits and taking up windsurfing, she seemed older. She wore the sort of shoes women pruned roses in." Ray chooses at first to dismiss her, but she is tenacious, always asking "the right and yet the wrong questions, the most tormenting." When Ray attempts to tell her his most personal secret, his failure in dealing with women, she interrupts him with the confidence that her husband is having an affair.

Ray gives her the draft of his book on Dickens to read, goes to the National Theatre with her, and attends a dinner party at her home with her husband and some upper-class Londoners. At the dinner table, he is forced to defend the 1960s when they are attacked by her husband, a Thatcher conservative politician. But in retrospect, Ray doesn't mind the evening too much; after all, "how long was it since he'd examined his beliefs?"

Later Esther confides to Ray that she visited her husband's mistress to confront her, but found her quite a "decent woman, kind and sensitive." Esther is so upset by the confrontation that she gets sick to her stomach. After ministering to her sickness, Ray is forced to drive her home. He is furious: "for God's sake, he didn't want his mind full of these people's lives, their genitals, their self-inflicted problems! England was teeming with people suffering because of this government, people in bad housing, the unemployed, children in rotten schools. He started to despise Esther, and resented the weakness of his involvement with her."

Weeks later, when she meets Ray again and announces that she has terrible news, Ray thinks, "terrible to you, who have nothing more important than the intricacies of human relationships to think about." What Esther has to tell him, however, is that the mistress has committed suicide. Ray writes letters to the papers to expose the affair. He causes a government scandal, and Esther's husband is ruined.

The story concludes six months later, when "Ray woke up to find he'd lost interest in the whole thing." Esther and he remain friendly—she brings him a cake and they go to the theater together—but he never tells her what he did. The story ends as he visits a whore; as he sits while the stoned woman lays naked next to him, Ray notices that "the bed stank of cigarettes, and she smelled of petunia."

The story is consistent with Kureishi's storytelling themes, techniques, and interests exhibited in his other work. His politically aware and honest social criticism of the self-serving pragmatists of the 1980s stings, but it is balanced by Kureishi's comic swipes at the burned-out activists of the 1960s. The story features other Kureishi dualities, too: He sets literature, for example, alongside a parody of the exploitation of that art; Ray's stasis at the conclusion supports Kureishi's portrayal of his social contradictions; and Ray's indifferent awareness of socially conscious issues does not displace his lack of humanity.

The story also exhibits Kureishi's characteristic structure. Opening with energy, Kureishi gets right into his story with Esther's remark, "You are obviously a sensitive man." The dialogue immediately creates an ironic tension between Ray and Esther. The story remains unresolved by a conclusion; the ambiguous inactivity in the ending, with the prostitute smelling of petunias as Ray lies with her in a bed smelling of cigarettes, is also typical of Kureishi—the story simply stops rather than ends.

"Esther" assumes a knowledge of London literary circles, authors, and politics. References to authors, even when arcane, carry weight as descriptors. For instance, while he gets his laundry done by his mother, forty-year-old Ray talks about Trollope with his dad; and he describes a former student by declaring that he still reads Hunter Thompson. Fashion, too, is again used to portray character, the costuming of Ray and Esther characterizing them within the first few paragraphs of the story. Music, albeit not the major soundtrack it becomes in other Kureishi stories, is used as a reference point in the story: Bob Dylan and the firebrand days of 1960s social revolution are now reduced to background music in Ray's college classroom as he smokes and stares out the window.

Writing short stories gives Kureishi the opportunity to take chances. Unlike with films or novels, Kureishi is able to write short stories with "total control" and without investing a financial fortune or years of his time. Kureishi recognizes the benefits:

If I started writing a film script today, when would it be on the screen? It would take me six months to write it. Maybe six months for them to raise the money. Then we fuck around for six months before we start shooting. Then we shoot. Then we edit it. Then we put it out. It wouldn't be out for two years, at least two years. Maybe three years. And with a novel, two, three years, the same thing. As you know, *The Black Album* was at least three years. But short stories are like writing fucking postcards.

Kureishi uses the genre as a forum for experimentation. And his experimentation widens the fictional universe about which he writes. The recognition that race is an important issue and that race is a significant theme in the author's storytelling does not limit him to that theme or to Asian characters. Race is not an issue in "Esther," a story about white characters. An assumption that he must write about race or should write about Anglo-Asians supports a labeling of storytelling that Kureishi refuses to acknowledge.

I don't think being black or female so pervades a writer's mind that all experience is different from that of whites or men. Besides, the job of the writer is to invade his characters' minds, and they can't all be the same. They can't all be exactly like him . . . But the idea of writing is for one person to speak to a deep part of another and overcome the determined isolation of categories. Generally, writers who put themselves into categories aren't very talented and are published because they're gay or feminist, or black. Their writings are subgenre works that don't say anything to people outside the group. They're not literature.[2]

"Esther" is not a comic story. As Kureishi has said, he "writes stories from different places in [his] life." Kureishi did not see this story as comic. The same would later be true of *The Black Album*, but in that case, disappointment at this change in tone colored its reception. Unlike *The Black Album*, "Esther" was allowed by critics to stand on its own, rather than be compared with Kureishi's comic writing.

While the settings in Kureishi's other stories are gritty, this story comes from a different place: it is a story of academia and a more genteel class. Street society, a milieu Kureishi used again in *The Black Album*, is not the world of this story. By the time he wrote "Esther," Kureishi was a celebrated writer and a personality, and the London he wrote about now had to include that reality. Kureishi himself is not apologetic about this upscale addition, claiming, "I've changed, of course, as we all change. The people I know and the places I go are more up-market now, but I don't regret this—it would be pretentious to sit in Brixton just to get material."[3]

"Esther" also gave Kureishi a chance to feature older characters. Although he has written elsewhere about other older characters, the main characters in his other stories are young men. Their flamboyance dominates these stories. In Kureishi's characteristic recycling of characters, Ray appears to have been an early working of *The Black Album*'s Bronlow, a well-worn, worn-out academic who searches for life's answers in classic 1960s rock. If Kureishi's universe has previously been that of musicians, magicians, and street hustlers, this short story gives him a forum to create characters from the other London worlds he knows just around any London street corner.

More than a story of passing through initiation, "Esther" is a story of refusing to relinquish antiseptic disinterest. Its middle-aged characters, already initiated into society, face disillusionment. Unlike his other fiction, this is not a story of adolescent entry into society. As he does in "Esther," Kureishi gives older characters prominence in his later short fiction. Yet because "Esther" comes from this "different place," Kureishi chose not to include it among his stories collected in *Love in a Blue Time* in 1997.

During 1995 and 1996, Kureishi wrote short stories with an eye to publishing his first short-story collection in 1997. This collection promised to illustrate characteristic elements underlying his stories, to continue the evolution of his themes and stylistics, and to expand the breadth of his storytelling.

The title story for this collection had been in Kureishi's mind since

1991, when a fictional idea had attracted him at the Venice Film Festival of that year. Although from 1991 to 1995 he worked primarily on the story that became *The Black Album*, drafting "In a Blue Time," the short story that he had conceived at the film festival about a film director facing life after Thatcherism, remained a simultaneous project during these years.

Kureishi likes reading and writing short stories, and he likes the fact that their publication process is so quick. Working on a number of short stories simultaneously with his novel gives him the chance to "run as many as five on his computer screen" and create, compose, and revise his short fictions as he chooses.

Some, such as "With Your Tongue down My Throat," are concerned with his most recognizable themes: race, immigration, and familial conflicts. Some—again, such as "With Your Tongue down My Throat"— are written in a comic voice, while others investigate new techniques. Still others, such as "In a Blue Time," investigate new subjects, characters, and settings and are not comic writing.

Kureishi drafted "The Revengers' Tragedy" and "My Son the Fanatic" in late 1993 and worked on them and other projects in 1994. He published the first of the two completed short stories, "My Son the Fanatic," in *The New Yorker* in spring 1995.

"My Son the Fanatic" centers around the problems experienced by Parvez, an Anglo-Asian immigrant, and his son. The setting is the world of late night, a world of cabbies, dealers, and whores in north England. Parvez, a Punjabi and a taxi driver for the past twenty years, is frustrated by his son Ali, in whom "his dreams of doing well in England would have come true."

Parvez notes that his son has discarded his fashionable clothes, computer discs, and videotapes, dropped his white girlfriend and other English friends, and become distant and irritable. At first afraid that his card-playing cronies will blame him for Ali's peculiarities, Parvez finally solicits their advice, and agrees with their admonition to "to watch Ali scrupulously and to be severe with him." This severity, the short story's climax, leads Parvez to commit violence against his son.

Parvez has considered himself an Englishman, enjoying western life as well as hoping for western prosperity for his son. Ali, however, accuses Parvez of abandoning the traditions and religion of his heritage: "Ali then reminded Parvez that he had ordered his wife to cook pork sausages, saying to her, 'You're not in the village now. This is England. We have to fit in.'"

Parvez and his son continue to argue as Parvez attempts to make his son understand him. But Ali remains adamant, telling his father, "My people have taken enough. If the persecution doesn't stop, there will be jihad. I, and millions of others, will gladly give our lives for the cause." Weeks later, during a cab ride, Parvez's friend, the prostitute Bettina, is insulted by Ali in her failed attempt to defend the boy's father. Parvez takes the boy home and later, infuriated, he bursts into Ali's room as he prays.

Parvez kicked him over. Then he dragged the boy up by the front of his shirt and hit him. The boy fell back. Parvez hit him again. The boy's face was bloody. Parvez was panting; he knew the boy was unreachable, but he struck him nonetheless. The boy neither covered himself nor retaliated; there was no fear in his eyes. He only said, through his split lip, "So who's the fanatic now?"

Clipped simple sentences and sparse exposition give the story a lean, hard-hitting edge. The short-story genre suits Kureishi's storytelling here, since there are no subplots that might distract from the impact of its central power struggle between Parvez and Ali that implodes to its inevitable violent conclusion.

There is a philosophical division between Muslim fundamentalism and the Asian immigrant dream. The economic and social system in England affronts some immigrant beliefs while it is itself at the heart of what others believe in. Earlier in the story, the author reveals this underlying tension in the postcolonial Asian community: "'But I love England,' Parvez said, watching his boy in the rearview mirror. 'They let you do almost anything here.' 'That is the problem,' Ali replied." Ironically, this exchange occurs in the rearview mirror, with Parvez watching Ali while driving his taxi. The image suggests the conflict: Parvez has accepted the western work ethic and is driving a cab to provide Ali with western comforts; Ali, however, will not go along for the ride of western consumerism. He has seen his father sell himself out and he refuses to do so. The dream must tear apart as it cannot go both forward and backward—forward to include western morality, consumerism, and liberalism to satisfy Parvez, and backward to retain eastern asceticism and conservative values to pacify Ali in the back seat.

The violence is ugly, simple, and unadorned. The rhetorical question at the end, asked by Ali of his likable father—"So who's the fanatic now?"—assaults any sense of narrative resolve. The question is more than a clever paradox, it is a contradictory axiom of contemporary English society that is central to Kureishi's storytelling. Here, the hybrid author picks at the scab of Asian assimilation into an Anglo society; the wound festers. His technique simply to stop a story rather than to resolve it is appropriate and powerful in this story, whose truth is not impeded by Kureishi's biographical experience or liberal philosophy. This is a contemporary question, to which there is no simple answer: "he knew the boy was unreachable, but he struck him nonetheless." Violence is not a solution here; it is an inevitability. According to Kureishi himself,

If there is to be a serious attempt to understand present-day Britain, with its mix of races and colours, its hysteria and despair, then writing about it has to be complex. It can't apologize or idealize. It can't sentimentalize and it can't attempt to represent any one group as having a monopoly on virtue.[4]

Kureishi is not tolerant of the violence, but he understands Ali's threats and Parvez's frustration. He knows racial violence and urban terrorism in the UK, and his point of view sheds further light on the growing violent threat of this second-generation immigrant who demands a return to the traditions of Islam. Kureishi tells this story not from the son's point of view, as is the case in his other portrayals of father-son relationships, but through the eyes of the sausage-eating Parvez.

The father here fights to keep his dream that of his son also, rather than see Ali follow his own dream of a past that his father has chosen to forfeit. Asian Parvez believes in the English tradition, and that is where his dream lies. Ali, however, insists that, in following his dream, what Parvez has left behind was—and is—the answer.

This short story boldly assaults yesterday's definition of English society—Parvez does not fit the stereotype that all English today are white—and shatters, too, stereotypes of Asian immigrants, expanding the definition of the Anglo-Asian community. Clearly a different man from his father, Ali is a seething revolutionary. Kureishi flaunts the animosity between father and son and reveals the tensions within the Asian community in England. In depicting this struggle between father and son, Kureishi brings the conflict between modernism, fundamentalism, and consumerism boldly to the center and proclaims that immigrant assimilation in the west and immigrant traditions from the east constitute an important English issue. Both of his Asian characters in this story are, after all, English, and changing English society cannot therefore afford to marginalize this religious conflict, because Asian-Anglos are thus already an integral part of its newly defined English nationalism.

Kureishi felt that "there was more to the story to tell," and after "My Son the Fanatic" was published in *The New Yorker*, he began working on an expanded version, as he had done earlier, after the short story "The Buddha of Suburbia" was published in *Harper's* magazine. He began this expanded version while continuing to work on other short stories, this time turning to a film adaptation rather than a novel. The film, shot in 1996, was screened at the 1997 Cannes Film Festival, with a UK release scheduled for later that year. It stars noted Indian actor Om Puri, Rachel Griffiths, and Harish Patel, who had worked with Kureishi in *The Buddha of Suburbia* playing Changez.

Kureishi, aware of the necessity of expanding his short story to create a film script, added incidents, scenes, and characters. By including the white Fingerhut family and the broken engagement of Parvez's son (named Farid in the film) to the Fingerhuts' daughter Madelaine, he illuminated Farid's assimilation into white England. Making Fingerhut a police inspector emphasized the police presence in the racial and religious turbulence of the northern city in which the story is set. Kureishi also wrote new scenes depicting Farid's involvement with the fundamentalist movement, thus focusing his involvement with Islam. Farid, with the support of his mother, Minoo—another character created for the film version and featured prominently in the script—challenges Parvez by insisting that a visiting mullah (a Muslim holy man) be housed in their home. Kureishi further explored the tension between Anglo-Asian philosophies and lifestyles by adding Parvez's lifelong friend Fizzy; the relationship between the two is reminiscent of Anwar and Haroon's relationship in *The Buddha of Suburbia* and of that between Nasser and Papa in *My Beautiful Laundrette*.

Kureishi's realization that "My Son the Fanatic" includes a love story had prompted the short story's inclusion in *Love in a Blue Time*, a prose collection he saw as "stories about love." It was this love story that Kureishi wanted most to expand on film—a story of extramarital love in the coupling of white prostitute Bettina and Asian taxi driver Parvez. Although their mutual attraction is suggested in the short story, their adultery becomes central to the film story. Other adaptation decisions resulting from Kureishi's experience are his introduction of a German tourist who pays Parvez to pimp and pander for him and his depiction of the abusive, violent manner in which Parvez treats his wife, Minoo.

The inclusion of encounters with local prostitutes, city violence, and racist bigotry gives the film a more gritty tone than that of the published story. Moreover, the added scenes crystallize an underlying unrest in the story, not only in the main characters' conflict, but in contemporary English society.

Like Kureishi's earlier essay "Bradford," this film is set in England's industrial north. Although shooting of the film took place elsewhere in northern England because the political situation in Bradford was deemed too volatile, it was still plagued by protests and threats from groups of Islamic fundamentalists who were offended by the prostitution, adultery, and alcohol consumption depicted in the film. Kureishi met with these groups during the filming and worked closely with the film's director, Udayan Prasad. Although a Hindu, Prasad was a happy choice for Kureishi, who has said that he "felt from the beginning that the story should have an Asian director." Kureishi admired Prasad's directing and felt that the veracity of the film was enhanced by their collaboration as screenwriter and director. Although in another different but successful collaboration, Kureishi and Roger Michell had fashioned the screenplay of *The Buddha of Suburbia* together, Kureishi's experience with Prasad more closely resembled his early filmmaking collaboration with Stephen Frears, in which Kureishi had written the story and Frears had directed it.

The central change from the published version in *Love in a Blue Time* is that in the adaptation, Kureishi made Parvez a more unlikable character. Thus, although in the short story the reader might easily have had sympathy for Parvez, who is made the object of his own son's threats and scorn because of the boy's religious conversion, Kureishi's script and the film adaptation denied this advantage to the father. As his son accuses him of being, so Parvez actually is corrupted and his decline into western decadence is visualized. In the film version, Kureishi showed his understanding both of storytelling and of storytelling for the camera. A clear example of this is the scene of marital rape that he wrote in the knowledge that it "wouldn't get on the screen, but . . . sure [it] would be in the published version of the film." Both the scripted scene and its deletion from the film exhibit Kureishi's understanding of the business and production of motion pictures, as well as of the dynamics of cinematic and prose storytelling. Kureishi employed the differing screenplay and film versions as a means of telling his story more completely.

The short story climaxes in an ambiguous line of dialogue. This technique, significant to the short-story tradition, is effective in the prose piece, but Kureishi realized that to translate this ambiguity as powerfully onto film, he couldn't rely just on a climactic conversational confrontation between father and son. As a film writer, adapter, and director, Kureishi knew that he had to include action and visualize his story to make the struggle between his characters as telling on screen. He thus added scenes depicting wedding-plan confusions, drunkenness, adultery, the police presence, violence, and the mullah's visit to transfer the back-and-forth wresting of power among his short-story characters into elements that would succeed on film. The film adaptation reveals that just as disillusionment and religion in England are integral issues in Kureishi's story, so also are racism, class, poverty, and unemployment.

In 1996, Kureishi completed and published another story of Anglo-Asian racial prejudices, "We're Not Jews." This third-person story is Kureishi's most tender rendering of childhood disillusionment. It is another compelling look at racist London, but from a different perspective—that of an innocent young child.

The story's action unfolds primarily on a bus ride as a white mother and her Anglo-Asian son are taunted by racist neighbors, a father and son, both named Bill. Mother remembers the father from their childhood days, when they shared an air-raid shelter. Because she is white, Mother is at home in her neighborhood, where her marriage to Azhar's Asian father has made her a despised intruder. Bill and Bill accuse her of being the worst kind: a traitor, someone who was one of them until she became "worse. Goin' with the Paki." Mother knows there is no solution, because were her husband ever to go back home as he threatens, they would have to move to a strange land which she and her son—and her husband, too—have never really seen. Finally confronting the hecklers, "[Mother, who] refused to allow the word 'immigrant' to be used about Father, since it applied to illiterate tiny men with downcast eyes and mismatched clothes . . . managed to say, 'We're not Jews.'" Here, Mother reverts to invoking a hierarchy of prejudices, distinguishing her Asian husband, who writes novels, from the Jews she has been brought up to believe are intruding immigrants; her son Azhar, meanwhile, mistakenly thinks Jews are the blacks in South Africa whom he knows his father is prejudiced against. The meanness of all racist epithets is revealed in the sequence. The altercation causes Mother to become sick when they leave the bus.

Kureishi knew that the story "would have to wind up with the father" because thoughts of Father are significant throughout the story of Azhar and his mother. Father dreams of being an author, and his rejected manuscripts—Mother makes Azhar hide them so that Father will have hope—clutter the garden, hidden like an alcoholic's bottles.

Mother and son arrive back home and, in the story's final paragraph, where Azhar is greeted by his father, Kureishi moves to the boy's relationship with his Asian dad. Beer bottles surround Dad's typewriter in the garden, where he and his extended Asian family are listening to cricket on the radio.

[They speak and laugh in] Urdu or Punjabi, using some English words but gesticulating and slapping one and other [*sic*] in a way English people never did. Then one of them would suddenly leap up, clapping his hands and shouting, "yes—out—out!" Azhar was accustomed to being with his family while grasping only fragments of what they said. He endeavored to decipher the gist of it, laughing, as he always did, when the men laughed, and silently moving his lips without knowing what the words meant, whirling, all the while, in incomprehension.

Azhar has learned to live in an adult world run by adult rules that he does not understand, and whose traditions, values, and prejudices he knows but does not comprehend. He keeps his mother's secret, imitates his father, and takes his place in the world he has been given.

The adults in the story have already exposed the feelings that make them who they are. In their world, sheltered in his family's love, Azhar need not face the cruelties of the outside world. He is home. Yet in this story, Azhar's happiness is an unthinking one. The story leaves him whirling in the childhood memories that will color his philosophy as a grown man. The scars of prejudice will commingle with the security of family. His loss of innocence is a mark of his Anglo-Asian heritage.

Early in his career Kureishi recognized that in his longer works, humor was needed to soften the ugliness of the prejudice he presented there. "In fact," he said, "satire and irony are probably the only ways we can approach the complex problems of our time. At the moment, everything is so horrific that if you wrote straight social realism people wouldn't be able to bear to watch it."[5] Yet racism and prejudice in this story operate without the balm of Kureishi's comic tone. He is able to deal with the brutality of racism in a short story without feeling the need to soften it with humor. He uses the structure of the short story, with its single climax, as an unadulterated expression of prejudice and an unrestricted look at bigotry. The clearness that the short-story form provides is particularly evident in the final paragraph of "We're Not Jews," in which the contradictions in prejudice are choreographed.

From 1993 until 1996, Kureishi continued to experiment with the short-story form. He drafted more stories for the collection *Love in a Blue Time*. Kureishi's experimentation is most obvious in two stories in this collection: "Lately," Kureishi's homage to Chekhov; and "The Tale of the Turd," Kureishi's storytelling foray into the fantastic.

An admirer of Chekhov, Kureishi enjoyed the process of retelling Chekhov's story. Although contemporary morality and language in Kureishi's story obviously differ from those elements in Chekhov's nineteenth-century story, noteworthy, if more subtle, thematic and stylistic storytelling similarities between the two writers are revealed by this project. Both, for example, are concerned with class. Chekhov's Caucasus seaside resort setting is peopled by characters who operate within a predetermined social order and from a code generated by this social hierarchy. Social conventions are pivotal issues in "The Duel." So, too, in the retelling, Kureishi's characters also operate within a class system. Thus "Lately" reaffirms how Kureishi's storytelling uses class-conscious contemporary English society to give his characters' actions context. For both authors, social setting provides an opportunity for the discussion of the politics, philosophy, and art of the times. The social manipulations of sex are also found in the work of both authors, albeit in a less graphic form in Chekhov. Both are interested in the dynamics of sexual relationships in society: sexual boredom haunts Chekhov's Layevsky in his tired affair, and ennui is often the fate of Kureishi's characters, too.

In the same way that Chekhov, as a playwright, relied on dialogue as a prose technique, Kureishi, a scenarist of the next century, uses dialogue to move his prose forward. The length of Chekhov's story also suits Kureishi, who, throughout his career, has been drawn to the tradition of novellas; like "Lately," both "With Your Tongue down My Throat" and "In a Blue Time" are long stories, and although *The Black Album* became a novel, it was originally conceived by Kureishi as two novellas.

Kureishi's other most obvious experimentation in *Love in a Blue Time* is with the fantastic. "The Tale of the Turd" was originally considered "too dirty to publish" as Kureishi prepared this collection, but it appeared in a London small magazine in late 1996. In this flamboyant story, reminiscent of William Burroughs, Kureishi details a fiancé's fantastic experiences in the bathroom of his girlfriend's parents' home, where he is a dinner guest. In a second streamlined draft, Kureishi concentrated on events in the bathroom. This first-person story sympathetically reveals the fiancé's disadvantages—he is out of work and older than the girlfriend he hopes to marry. His embarrassment is understandable when he abruptly needs to use the bathroom during a dinner given by his girlfriend's family in order to meet him; the host, an undistinguished academic of the same age as his prospective son-in-law, the host's teacher-wife, and their giggling daughters—including the visitor's fiancée—loom just outside the bathroom door, from where he fears they can hear him. He tries to assure himself that even the queen shares the same human toilet habits, but this thought doesn't give him much comfort in the situation in which he soon finds himself. He becomes distraught as he fights a battle with his turd, grown and biting at him with sharp teeth, and compelling him to take a Kafka-like journey into human excrement.

A December 1993 draft entitled "The Revengers' Tragedy" illustrates Kureishi's short-story writing process as well as his experimentation. Changing the title to "D'accord Baby" during the story's first revision, Kureishi expanded and refined it in its revisions into winter 1995.

Just as the title became more coyly political, so the shorter, earlier drafts evolved into a less definite and less obvious story. Characteristic of the author's rewriting, the plot incidents remained similar while the tone changed significantly.

In this story Bill determines to sleep with his wife's lover's daughter to get even with his wife for her adultery. Ironically, as the rewrites became more impressionistic, Kureishi characterized his main character more clearly. The name of the woman Bill beds becomes both more exotic and more romantic. Bill's adultery following his wife's marital infidelity is changed from an expository prose fact to a philosophical probability in the character's treatise on marital fidelity. The French pop tune Bill and Celestine originally dance to becomes a romantic and dated waltz. Recurrent imagery of taxicabs is introduced to mirror Bill's actions and lack of movement in the London traffic. The story clearly becomes one that is told through Bill's perceptions rather than exposition by the author. The plain incidents of the story are submerged in the hopes, fears, and regrets in Bill's mind.

A pivotal scene, the leave-taking between Celestine and Bill, becomes more focused through the revisions. The addition in the January draft of her calling him "old man" as he leaves conveys simultaneous pity, affection, and candor. Middle age, not sexual revenge, therefore, becomes the story's theme. Thus, as Kureishi ties the story more clearly to Bill's paradoxical musings about his midlife adventures, he also works into it the definite tone of a third-person narration concerning the adultery element.

The opening is abrupt and the premise definite: Bill plans to avenge himself against his wife and her lover by sleeping with the lover's daughter. But Bill is never quite as sure of anything that happens in the story after he has proclaimed his intention. He questions their decision to have a child and the commitment it will demand. Bored with his wife anyway, he doubts his marriage and is disillusioned by the institution of marriage itself. Yet, as a cuckolded husband, he remains determined to exact his revenge.

He is equally undecided about his career: The success he has achieved is bland, he knows the game too well, he has too many distant friends, and he has bartered art for commercial success. But he is comfortable and used to that lifestyle, and is sure that the romantic poverty that accompanied the idealism of his youth would be unappealing and unsatisfying to him now.

He measures out his life, inventing challenges and tests—he did it with his daily gym workouts in the eighties, he has done it with drinking, he has done it with progeny, and he does it now with reading, approaching Proust with the same logical methodology he uses to plot his marital revenge. He measures his revenge with the same precision with which he lays out his condoms, determining that one vengeful act will suffice, as will one condom. He is passionate about getting his revenge, not motivated by sexual passion. This comes at a time when Bill is wrestling with the insecurities of midlife and is reckoning with his mortality. He is painfully aware that "if he were to do anything worthwhile at this age, he had to be serious in a new way." Yet his seriousness, deftly undermined by Kureishi, turns out to be just as unsatisfying to Bill in his middle age. In his realistic scrutiny of life's passage, Bill also realizes the silliness of his middle-age quandary—he quickly corrects his Hemingway romanticism that he feels the earth moving during his cosmic lovemaking with Celestine with the comic assessment that the beds are merely separating under their rutting.

Bill throws himself with gusto into his one-night stand with Celestine, even to the point of agreeing to punch her when she insists she deserves it. The implication is that this is the blow, deflected now onto his lover, that he rationalizes that he should have given to his unfaithful wife before deciding instead to go to the pub. The blow is not his act of violence—the lovemaking is; nor is the blow epiphanic—Bill learns nothing from it. His main hope, in fact, is that Celestine's father will have the opportunity to inspect his handiwork; such an outcome, indeed, is part of his revenge.

The aging Bill is exposed as painfully adolescent in this story that is pervaded by a feeling of male locker-room antics. He likes the fact that his friends admire Celestine's legs, and announces their anticipated sex to his cronies as a clever French pun. He is boastful and, just as he had longed for his friends to see him riding in a luxurious limo in the States, after he has had sex with Celestine he wants his contemporaries to envy him for having mounted her and wishes they could see him lying naked in her bed.

After their night together, Bill finds comfort in the rain when he leaves Celestine's flat. The revenge accomplished and behind him, Bill walks through the London streets, cleansed by the rain that takes the place of the shower he had wanted after their lovemaking but was not inclined to take in her flat. Bill is content to stroll by himself along the city streets. Traffic becomes a pleasant blur and his walk becomes imagistic in this story that is peppered with taxicab imagery.

Earlier that evening, for example, Bill and Celestine had hailed a cab, but instead dismissed it and planned their tryst. Bill had also considered escaping into a cab when buying their dinner wine. Thus, at the story's conclusion, now walking at his own pace, Bill finally lets the traffic go by, embracing the journey.

This bittersweet feeling in the fading, urban glow is reminiscent of the conclusion to Fitzgerald's dirge to Paris, "Babylon Revisited." It is an introspective and resigned musing, in which Kureishi depicts London in a different time and creates a different mood than he does in his earlier stories.

"In a Blue Time" is the other story Kureishi was contemplating while he worked on *The Black Album*. In this long short story, recreational drugs and champagne mix with talk of a villa near Perugia and of diaper-changing tables. It is peopled by such characters as "girls with Home Counties accents, most of who [*sic*] appeared to be wearing cocktail dresses," who manage London film production offices, and a sixteen-year-old boy, "naked apart from a Lacoste crocodile tattooed onto his chest," who, in a London flat, checks the pulse of the lover he is mounting. The story centers around the different lifestyles of Roy and Jimmy, best friends when they were at college together, but now in different London worlds. Now Jimmy lives day-to-day by "scrounging," whereas Roy lives with his wife, Clare, who is expecting their first child, while he awaits his big film break. During the story, Kureishi, involving the friends in drinking bouts, drug buying, reminiscing, and mutual self-introspection, raises the questions of which of them has succeeded and which of them is happy.

Waiting for film producer Mundy to raise the money to put his feature-film deal on track, Roy remembers the film world of the eighties in which he made his money directing commercials: Immersed in the world of cinema, "'a bit more Bergman,' he'd say, 'Or do you fancy some Fellini here?'" Elsewhere, we learn that "Roy asked seven people if they

could recall the name of Harry Lime's English friend in *The Third Man*."
Roy is dependent on the movie-business world and enjoys spending
money breakfasting at Soho's Patisserie Valerie, shopping around Covent
Garden, and taking taxis. But when he is with the hand-to-mouth Jimmy,
he is ashamed that his designer velvet jacket "sang of style and money,
and made him look as if he had a job."

Jimmy, in contrast, barely remembers yesterday. He lives for beer,
Jack, and drugs, always looking for somebody to sleep with and a place
to sleep, although he has slept out on the street on occasion. He knows
how to mesmerize Mundy by sharing fragments of his unfinished film
treatment with him; he knows, too, how to undermine Roy's film
project—by telling Mundy that Roy has a substance-abuse problem. Even
though Roy is uncomfortable talking to Jimmy in front of his wife because "[s]omehow he had caused her to resent any life he might have
outside her," Jimmy ends up moving into Roy's house, and knows how
to flatter the pregnant Clare by suggesting that she looks "a bit like Jean
Shrimpton."

Kureishi had previously written other stories posing the question of
whether upwardly mobile merely means selling out: Clint in *London
Kills Me* and Karim in *The Buddha of Suburbia* face the same question.
In "In a Blue Time," he juxtaposes Jimmy's continuation of his youthful
seventies freedom with Roy's acquisition of familial, financial, and professional responsibilities in the nineties. The conflicts are again between
marginal and conventional lifestyles and artistic and commercial success, but these older and wealthier characters live in a different time
from the seventies and eighties of earlier Kureishi stories and face different class conflicts from those of Clint and Karim. The nineties setting
illuminates the differences in these conflicts.

Like "D'accord Baby" and "In a Blue Time," "Blue, Blue Pictures
of You" is set in the nineties among London's artistic community. Stylistically, it recalls Kureishi's storytelling from before the *Love in a Blue
Time* collection, in that the style is urbane and light in tone, while the
narrative revolves around the sexually explicit—here, the sexually revealing photographic project with which a photographer becomes involved. Ambiguity begins with the title and continues to the conclusion,
with the fast-paced story being propelled forward from the opening, with
its provocative first line.

The story is romantic and features a narrator who begins by admitting that he came to this story as someone "who used to like to talk about sex." He confides that he did, "at one time, consider collecting 'a book of desire,'" and that had he finished his book (or, as he acknowledges, even started it), the story he is going to relate would most certainly have been included. Kureishi's use of the past-tense "used" and "at one time" makes the reader aware that something happened to change the 1990s narrator of the story before his telling of the photographer's story.

The narrator tells the reader that the story he relates in the following pages was told to him by Eshan, who "photographed 'artists' but also considered himself, in private, 'some sort' of an artist." Eshan is a married man with children who fantasizes about the lives of Brian, whom he met in a neighborhood pub and from whom he has heard intimate sexual details, and Brian's girlfriend, Laura. Eshan's "passion" is to photograph those whose work has "meaning"—to capture the "moment of truth in the features of people seeking the truth." It is the photographic sexual involvement Eshan has with Laura and Brian, whom he photographs having sex, that comprises the story told by him to the narrator, and by the narrator to the reader. Like the photographic session of Brian and Laura's lovemaking, Kureishi weaves voyeurism and the reality, romance, and delusions of sex into the fabric of the story Eshan tells.

The story is peopled by nineties Londoners who seek out colorful city pubs frequented by the unemployed, the hapless, and junkies, and who end up becoming "characters" of the pub themselves. Kureishi unfolds his story of the photographs like a piece of urban folklore. He suggests an oral tradition of cosmopolitan legends passed from pubgoer to pubgoer. As in the much earlier short story "With Your Tongue down My Throat," Kureishi again builds on the nuances of different points of view. As told in the first person, this story is more believable and approachable, while the framing of the incidents as a narrative told by someone to someone else, as the episode related passes in its telling from person to person, gives the narrative a sense of urban mythmaking.

The story portrays lifestyle fantasy ("perhaps Eshan envied Brian his enchantment, and Brian Eshan's stability"); sexual fantasy (Eshan wonders about Laura and Brian while "lying in bed with his wife, as they watch TV, read nineteenth century novels and drink camomile tea");

and epiphany ("[Laura] was tired of it: she was even tired of being in love: it had become another narcotic"). But at the end, after they burn the photos of Brian and Laura, and Eshan leaves Laura playing the drums, Eshan is changed, but it is an ambiguous change: he hears Laura's drum playing—or Laura's moment of truth—"all the way to the end of the road." Kureishi's ambiguous ending of the story told by the photographer to the narrator mirrors the narrator's changed attitude when he introduced Esham's story at the beginning by revealing without explanation that he too has changed and forfeited his faith in romance. Thus this story of passage echoes a loss of romanticism both in the photographer's story and in the narrator's opening frame.

Two other stories written during this time, "The Flies" and "Nightlight," make up the collection. "The Flies" is a more fully realized journey into the fantastic than "The Tale of the Turd." In it, Baxter, a husband and father, finds his flat infested with flies. When his wife finally notices—because, like Baxter's, her wardrobe has been destroyed—she blames her husband that she has "nothing of her own left" and he feels guilty. The pest exterminator, who informs them that he is a "Microbe Consultant," orders full service, leaving three imported packs and a bathtub device, and deigning to return only when and if "we are available." Baxter surveys the infestation in the rest of the neighborhood, beginning "at the top of the street, wearing an acrylic cardigan purchased from the charity shop, inedible combat trousers, and a coat." He finds that the whole neighborhood is infested with flies. When one couple denies their infestation, Baxter "opens a door and notices an object standing in the bath. It is a glowing blue pole, like the one in his flat, and it seems to be pulsating." At another house, he joins a party and, as he begins his seduction of a neighbor, she admits, "'Most of them got flies round here. Except the newly-weds and adulterers.'"

The fly infestation persists and, as his last stand against the flies, Baxter finally turns to Gerard Quinn, a philosophical talker. "Despite all the ardent talk, the flat remains infested. [Baxter's wife] claims Gerard is making Baxter self-absorbed, and that he no longer cares about her and the baby." And, at the story's end, on a walk, Baxter looks to the sky and fixes on a cloud. "The cloud, as he walks towards it, seems to explode. It separates and breaks up into thousands of tiny fragments. It is a cloud of flies which lifts and breaks, sweeping upwards into the indifferent sky." The story's ending echoes the quotation from Calvino's *The Argentine Ant* which introduces it: Baxter sees no future, but instead, merely a "dragging on . . . into new troubles." Kureishi has admitted to liking "the symbolism in the story," which is more developed than in "The Tale of the Turd." It is set in nineties London, but Kureishi underscores the universality of his symbol throughout the story. "There are people now who think they can talk the contagion away," he explains. "Like people who think they can pray for rain, they won't accept [that the fly infestation] is a biological fact of nature." Accepting the story's symbol of decay and disillusionment, Kureishi rationalizes the infestation: "'People all over the world endure different kinds of bacteria." Then he poses a rhetorical question: "'[T]he century is old . . . what do you expect?'" Kureishi's story symbolizes human identity being devoured by conventions. Baxter expresses that loss in his recognition of the course that his marriage has taken. In bed with a lover, he thinks of his wife:

[I]t is dawning on him, as love dawns on people, that at times he does hate her; hates the way she cuts up an apple; hates her hands. He hates her tone of voice and the words he knows she'll use; he hates her clothes, her eyelids, and everyone she knows; her perfume makes him nauseous. He hates the things he's loved about her; hates the way he put himself in thrall to her; hates the kindnesses she shows him, as if she is asking for something. . . . Without thinking, he gave her his life. He valued it less then, and now he wants it back. But he knows that retrieving a life takes a different courage, and is crueller.

Baxter finds his life being swallowed up in a lifetime of his wife's idiosyncrasies. He resents it, but he does not have the courage to do anything about it. Thus, as symbolized by his walk under a legion of flies at the story's end, Baxter will continue merely being alive, while the flies eat away at his life.

"Nightlight," also written in 1996, is a story about weekly nameless sex in a basement. On the surface a typical "Kureishi sex story specialty," the narrative is again different from Kureishi's stories dating from before *The Black Album*, as it is set in the nineties, is concerned with more mature characters, and is darker in tone. The third-person point of view antiseptically presents the descent into darkness of a nameless man in his mid-fifties. A divorced father, he has lost interest in family, profession, friends, and society. All that remains of him is his obsession for his Wednesday sex. When the woman stands him up, he falls apart: "One Wednesday the cab doesn't draw up. He stands at the window in his dressing gown and slippers for three hours, feeling, in the first hour, like Casanova, in the second, like a child awaiting its mother, and during the third like an old man." When the woman does show up, not only does he lose himself in their anonymous sex, he finds solace in it. The network of images in the story is bleak. Desolation haunts the descriptions of London life and references to aging are frequent. Kureishi's main character, whose "existence [is] drudgery," is out of sync with his own life. Other than the multiple sexual climaxes he reaches in the basement, "[i]t is as if the gears of his life have become disengaged from the mechanisms that drove him forward." He is borrowing to survive and "at work his debts increase." He is "losing his hold and [questions] does it matter?" He lives in a "small flat, [drives an] old car and [has] a shabby feeling. . . . He has never anticipated this extent of random desolation." He has gone from woman to woman, destroying most of them. "Five years ago he left the wife he doesn't know why he married, for another woman, who leaves him but doesn't explain why. There have been others since. . . . He begins to think he can make women insane." Disgusted with these women, he wonders "why one ends up resenting people for not providing what one hasn't been able to ask for." He wonders whether, "after so many years of living, the expensive education, the languages he imagined would be useful, the books and newspapers studied, . . . he [is] capable of love only with a silent stranger in a darkened room." He hates to go out, but "in the house his mind devours itself; he is a cannibal of his own consciousness. He is starving for want of love." And he sees London as a city of hordes of people even more carnivorous than he is, feeding on their victims' blood: to him, Londoners "are on the move from wife to wife, husband to husband, lover to lover. A city of love vampires, turning from person to person, hunting the one who will make the difference."

Kureishi has here written another graphic investigation of sex, but the sexual partners in this story are far from the young and handsome Charlie and Karim in *The Buddha of Suburbia*. Although Kureishi had portrayed mature lovers earlier, in Rafi and Alice in *Sammy and Rosie Get Laid*, "Nightlight" turns a brutal light on middle-aged sexual intercourse, without any softening touch of romance, emotion, or nostalgia.

The jaded main character's need for passion is expressed in a fierce human paradox: "There are few creatures more despised than middle-aged men with strong desires, and desire renews itself each day, returning like a recurring illness, crying out, more life, more!" This is Kureishi's most rigorous, unromanticized depiction of male, middle-aged sexual desire to date. Yet "Nightlight," with its harsh recognition of the inevitability of death, ends as unresolved as Kureishi's earlier stories of initiation. Embedded in his cruel wording of the desperate struggle to stay alive is the indomitable human need to survive. The conclusion, linguistically mirroring the character's sexual encounters earlier in the story, is resigned to this contradiction: "But what does that matter? As long as there is desire there is a pulse; you are alive; to want is to reach beyond yourself, into the world, finger by finger."

Stories in this short-story collection more often portray older characters and more mature themes than do Kureishi's earlier works, and the collection suggests a new breadth in Kureishi's storytelling. His need to experiment with new techniques and themes is well served by the genre. A frank investigation of contemporary sex, race, and prejudice is still at the center of the stories, in which Kureishi continues to balance ridicule and regard for human conduct while respecting human nature. But he has expanded the fictional world about which he writes, and in addition to the comic voice of his earlier stories, in the stories comprising *Love in a Blue Time*, he experiments with storytelling in different voices.

"We're not Jews" is quite serious—in Kureishi's words, "more sincere, if you value sincerity"—and the overriding mood of "In a Blue Time" is melancholic, while other short stories that Kureishi wrote at this time include lighter, more comic works, fantastic tales, stylistic exercises, and a children's story, thus continuing to offer him new vistas. The characters range from successful middle-aged, white Londoners questioning marriage to young Asians facing adulthood and Fundamentalism in racist England.

Kureishi turned to the short-story genre because it suited the immediacy of new issues while giving him a forum in which to experiment with new themes and techniques, as he crafted new stories in new genres. But *Love in a Blue Time* demonstrates that the universality of storytelling remains cardinal to him.

WE ARE FAMILY
Lovers and Love in Kureishi

The differences that distinguish Kureishi's writing from the rest of English literature are more obvious than the similarities. So, too, the racial and social issues that he writes about more noticeably break away from than adhere to conventional subject matter. His plot incidents include buddy masturbation, terrorism, and murder by sex aid. His characters include Asian entrepreneurs, lesbian politicos, limousine liberals, and drug-using academics.

Nonetheless, portraying love—whether sexual love or love of family—is fundamental to Kureishi's art, and he universalizes this portrayal with his infectious sense of humor. Regardless of the wide range of new elements that define his contemporary relationships, their humanity provides a common bond. No matter what the cultural taboos, politics, sexual preferences, or restructured family roles are that his writing details, identifiable human truths are at the core of his storytelling.

The depiction of sex from a no-holds-barred perspective has resulted in a good deal of Kureishi's notoriety. He deems writing about sex a specialty. This interest may in part explain his movement away from writing for the stage: movie screenplays and prose, particularly novels, are more likely forums for including sexual description. In his first film script, his most celebrated couple, Johnny and Omar, are depicted as having an explicit and erotic relationship. The story's interracial, homosexual bonding breaks from convention: there can be no marrying and living happily ever after for these lovers.

Johnny and Omar are not only controversial bed partners, they actively assert their sexuality. In a scene within the laundrette, they couple passionately in the back office. In a scene outside the laundrette, Johnny accepts Omar's money while tonguing his ear to taunt a National Front street gang. The boys try to build a relationship incorporating Johnny's neo-Nazi tendencies and the cruelties of his past and Omar's resentment and self-serving opportunism. Their involvement exists against all odds in terms of gender, race, and class. Kureishi gives them a genuine affection for each other, but it is the unconventional sex between them that provides the sparks.

The political and racial conflicts Omar and Johnny confront are illuminated in their sexual encounters. As Kureishi explains, "If a black and white couple are screwing, it involves color, class, and relations between the sexes. Human relations are meeting points for a whole complex of social arrangements, and that's why I like to write about them."[1] And their flamboyant sexual encounters, whether comic, affectionate, or sensational, illustrate their identifiable, human motivation.

Avoiding a conventional literary resolution, Kureishi ends the screenplay with the boys bathing. He knows that an easy resolution is an untruth for his gay characters of mixed races. The obstacles facing them are formidable and there can be no pat riding into the sunset in his fiction. Thus the ambiguous ending is appropriate to his storytelling. But because the characters are written as people rather than as conforming to previous racial or sexual stereotypes, they also convey the human potential for hope in their contemporary struggles.

My Beautiful Laundrette is really a story of hope, a true romance. Whatever the particular idiosyncracies, sexual preference, race, or class of the partners, they are attractive, likable, and believable enough to gain audience involvement. Nationalism, ambition, and racism create the philosophical conflict in the narrative, but hope motivates Omar and Johnny. As such, theirs is a cinematic love story and, because the last scene remains ambiguous, Kureishi pulls off a hopeful ending.

Ironically, Kureishi did not gain audience identification with his next screen couple, Sammy and Rosie, his most conventional couple to date. In *Sammy and Rosie Get Laid*, extramarital sex was again graphic and frequent, but it was the antiseptic marriage of the title characters at the core of the story that was questioned critically. This marriage, and not the couple's flamboyant sexual escapades, was seen as an impediment to audience identification with the story.

Because the married pair remains more unapproachable than many of Kureishi's more controversial lovers, marriage becomes a social issue in this movie, while sex, within and without marriage, appears as a desperate political statement. Human pulse and passion is lacking in the story. The writing is not clear enough to elicit understanding, nor are the main characters likable enough to attract sympathy; indeed, their characterization was even construed by some critics to exemplify Kureishi's prejudice against marriage and the conventional, white middle class.

The criticism has some foundation, for until 1995 Kureishi's work included a rather small and unflattering range of married white characters. Regardless of their class, marital status, and race, Sammy and Rosie are uninvolving characters, and their marriage is aimless and confining. But they were created early on in terms of Kureishi's evolving new perspective, before he had a strong grasp on it. However, they were written beyond stereotypes, and are actually among Kureishi's most provocative creations, and it is thus also possible that, as with the nomadic street society of *London Kills Me*, their characterization was simply ahead of audience acceptance.

Had he created them ten years later, Kureishi could perhaps have characterized Sammy and Rosie more clearly; today's film audience could definitely better understand Sammy and Rosie than did the audiences of 1987. Forerunners of a new kind of movie character, they desire commitment but flaunt free love and revolving sex. Ironically, this downwardly mobile, loveless couple of ten years ago becomes quite identifiable today among cosmopolitan, jaded pseudo-liberals, reflecting the high esteem in which romantic love continues to be held—in fact, the adulterous Sammy and Rosie make committed love—married love—an ideal. In the movies as in the nineties, loveless sexuality prevails, while marital security remains the unfulfilled dream.

Sex in this film illustrates the yearning among modern lovers to find meaningful sexual fulfillment, not merely temporary—if continual— sexual gratification. By the end of the movie, Sammy yearns to feel something genuine, but he actually doesn't feel anything.

This romantic yearning amid the brutality and random sex of street society is even more overt in *London Kills Me*, whose characters include whores and hustlers. The plot activities include sex and back rubs, the screenplay discusses oral sex and sex for pay, but love is painfully absent.

And this nihilistic landscape may explain some of that film's critical rejection as well.

Writing novels permits Kureishi expanded descriptive possibilities in terms of depicting his characters' sexual exploits. The Herculean sex life of *The Buddha of Suburbia*'s Karim Amir takes off as soon as he unzips Charlie's flies in his Beckenham attic. As one critic noted, Karim's youthful masturbatory illusions fuel the novel: "Karim Amir is squeezing a favorite penis (not his own) to Pink Floyd's 'Ummagumma.' He's 17 . . . Karim is no Janis Ian inventing lovers on the phone."[2]

Criticism of *The Buddha of Suburbia*, particularly of the TV adaptation, hinted that Karim is in love with Charlie, thus creating a homosexual tie between Kureishi's first novel and his first screenplay. While there is indeed a tie between the two, to say that it is the homosexual love affair is a simplification. Here again, Kureishi is not writing about the politics of gender per se, but rather is inviting identification with unconventional characters by writing about the humanity in their actions. Karim is aware that Charlie loves him egotistically, as a looking glass, as it were. Karim's boyhood adoration of Charlie is also reflective of ego. Obsessed with the male sexual member, the boys are in love not with each other's maleness but with their own. They are experiencing a hormone-related avalanche of sexual awareness: puberty.

Karim's affair with Eleanor is again an uninhibited, interracial sexual encounter. Their heterosexual intercourse provides his means of assimilation into the white London scene. But it is also a continuation of his adolescent sexual exploration. Karim is in love with power; Eleanor is a prize of his ambition. But Karim's desires correspond to his human political agenda; the young man seeks himself through mounting her. In short, although *The Buddha of Suburbia* is a cosmopolitan sex extravaganza that details the juiciest stories, the novel's barrage of hetero-, homo-, and autoerotic sex never overwhelms the story.

Like Kureishi's screenplays and first novel, his second novel, *The Black Album*, is peppered with unconventional sex. But because he is able in this work to establish the humanity of his characters, their motives become understandable. Thus Shahid's process of maturation is identifiable and the excess of it is appealing as well because of Kureishi's comic style. Furthermore, the focus on the romantic heterosexual love

Fig. 20. Haroon (Roshan Seth, left) and Karim (Naveen Andrews) make a separate peace between generations at the conclusion to *The Buddha of Suburbia*. The dynamics between father and son remain pertinent in Kureishi's storytelling. (Photo courtesy of the BBC, London.)

story, in which Shahid and Deedee find a love powerful enough to take on the establishment, leads to a pairing that is not only Kureishi's most romantic, but that is one of his most appealing to date.

Other universal and unique aspects of loving are also illuminated in Kureishi's comic characterization of parents, children, and siblings. His stories portray a wide range of familial relationships, although some are more frequent and appear to be more interesting to him because of his personal experiences. One of his ongoing themes, in his own assessment, is "the bond between fathers and sons."

Just as his main characters are often seen to reflect autobiographical characteristics, so other characters also often show specific characteristics of the author's Asian father, who emigrated to England from Bombay when the rest of his family moved to Pakistan. Kureishi himself acknowledges his father's influence on his writing:

[My father] was a domineering, but also a dominant man . . . He imposed himself on you. He was also an interesting man to write about. . . . My dad was a civil servant for all of his life, but he used to write. He used to write very early in the morning. He'd write from five-thirty . . . When I was a kid, all I could hear in the house when I woke up was his fucking typewriter downstairs pounding. Bang—bang—bang—like thunder.

The familial pair of father and son is portrayed as a dynamic relationship throughout his writing. His treatment of this fundamental male bond evolves through the course of his work, so that while his novels are told from the viewpoint of the son, "My Son the Fanatic," the short story Kureishi adapted for the camera in 1995, is told from a father's perspective.

In creating his fictional characters, Kureishi draws from his own life experiences, whether autobiographical or imaginary. Every character, however, whether taken from actual or imagined events, is somehow real. While some characters are more easily tied than others to the author's life, all are tied to his creativity, a link that he himself recognizes: "There's no more of me in *My Beautiful Laundrette* than in 'My Son the Fanatic'; no more in *The Buddha* than in *The Black Album*. I'm in all of them in every way . . . Yes, I suppose [Karim Amir] is more of a stand-in for me, but they're all stand-ins for me in a way, in different, very complex ways."

His fictional sons are often second-generation dreamers who have been born into the disillusionment that their fathers found. Often they are the grown children of aging fathers living in a hostile land. Sometimes the sons are Asians, sometimes they are white men coming of age in an England so changed that their fathers refuse to recognize it. Quite often the sons are of mixed races. But always Kureishi's "sons" determine to live different lives from those that their fathers lived and to dream different dreams from those that their fathers dreamed.

Kureishi's stories render the universal experience of a son's growth from his father's boy into a man in his own right, a necessary step in maturation. His first screenplay, *My Beautiful Laundrette*, detailed the relationship of Papa and Omar. This father and son were distanced by Omar's determination to succeed financially at any price and by Papa's escape into reclusive alcoholism. Omar's separation was—and was depicted as—unresolved.

Papa is not supportive of Omar's ambitions. He is suspicious and disapproving of Omar's lifestyle. Without leaving his bed, but armed with a bedside photograph of Omar's deceased mother and a bottle of gin, Papa fights to dominate his son's life with his dreams. In their first appearances together, Papa plans Omar's future by telephone while Omar performs simple daily tasks for his father.

Omar is the passive and silent object of other people's ambitions throughout the film's early scenes; his life is planned for him. In a later scene, a bleak plunge into their domestic routine in which Omar sits on Papa's bed cutting his father's toenails, Omar interrupts his father's planning for him to make his own telephone plans with Johnny. After Omar begins his sexual relationship with Johnny, he is again seen with his father in their flat, but in this scene, it is Omar who talks. Papa, after a trip to urinate on the balcony of their flat, is now lost in his dreams and needs Omar's help.

Although in early scenes Papa always only appears with Omar, he is paired with Johnny in the final, pivotal scene that expands the universality of their conflict. Mirroring an earlier scene in which Nasser had tried to graft his entrepreneurial dreams onto Johnny, white Johnny now becomes the object of Papa's paternal maneuvers. Earlier, it is remembered, Nasser had tried to graft his entrepreneurial dreams onto Johnny. The generational and cultural conflicts are shown to overlap even more when white Johnny is seen as a son by both Papa and Nasser.

A paradox of our multicultural society is inherent in *My Beautiful Laundrette*—namely, the fact that separatist racial dreams in our white society merge without blending: Johnny needs Omar, while Nasser and Papa need to use Johnny. The universality of the humanity of this relationship between generations regardless of the couple's race, nation, or class is thereby underscored. The device makes the continued power struggle in this unresolved relationship brutally clear. There is no resolution between son and father, either in the story or in the film.

In the only scene between Johnny and Papa, Papa at last appears as promised—but nearly twelve hours late—at the grand opening of the laundrette. In the paternalistic encounter, Papa turns that failure into success by dismissing the superficiality of western A.M. and P.M. time divisions. His discussion with Johnny continues in this knowing and ironic tone. First Papa reminds Johnny of the failures of Johnny's ambitions, undermining the boy by playing on the guilt of his past. Having thus gained dominance over Johnny, Papa asserts his paternal ambitions for Omar. In cajoling Johnny into assisting him in seeing his son achieve his goals, Papa makes Johnny a surrogate in fulfilling his own fatherly plans for Omar.

A father's desire to realize his hopes for his son is an understandable motive. The encounter between Papa and Johnny reveals another, equally identifiable motive—that of parental manipulation. Papa garnishes his manipulation of white punk Johnny with racial guilt and prejudice. He relentlessly pursues what he sees as right for his son, even to the point of being willing to use the bond between Johnny and his son—a homosexual relationship of which he insinuates both his knowledge and his disapproval—to direct Johnny's influence on Omar. In a burst of apparent openness toward Johnny, Papa actually reveals the lengths to which a father will go to accomplish his unyielding agenda for his son.

In a later scene, the only one between Papa and Nasser, and both characters' final appearance in the film, Papa comes face to face with his brother to talk about their experiences as fathers. Nasser, who is a father only to girls, has been driven to return from his western ideas to tradition and seek his contemplative brother's advice. The brothers, dev-

Fig. 21. Papa (Roshan Seth) and Johnny (Daniel Day-Lewis) have a nocturnal meeting in *My Beautiful Laundrette*. Papa uses every parental device he can muster to make Johnny accept his plans for his son. (Photo courtesy of Working Title Films, Ltd.)

astated that their children have forfeited family traditions, discuss their failed plans.

Outside the window of Papa's flat, quick shots of passing trains obliterate Nasser's daughter, Tania, who stands on the railway platform, and who, like their hopes (and figuratively like Papa's white wife, who committed suicide on these bleak urban tracks), has disappeared by the time the train has passed. The brothers embrace in mutual failure. Papa returns to drinking gin in bed, where we first saw him.

The brothers' conversation is really about this struggle for power. Having failed with Tania, Omar, and Johnny, they realize the inevitability of their failures as sons through this disappointment they have both suffered as fathers. Both had dreams—albeit different dreams—of lives for their children, and both must now accept—as did their father (as must all fathers?)—that they will lose their children to their children's own dreams.

Hanif Kureishi 184

When Omar last appears in the film, he has, unlike Papa, moved from where he was at the story's start. The film's ending is a tentative one, but Omar has definitely taken the step of severing a son's dreams from a father's. No longer pictured with Papa, Omar is shown at the story's conclusion happily ministering to his white lover: Inside the windows of the laundrette, the couple bathe in the office of their dream enterprise.

Written with identifiable father/child elements, the story relies on the truth of all of its characters, by means of which the audience can identify with the story's conflict. Its particulars portray racism, homosexuality, and Asian immigration in London. But the story's theme evokes Wordsworth's "the child is father of the man" cycle, imaging the painful passage from child to adult.

The Buddha of Suburbia also leaves the story of its main protagonist, Karim, open-ended, but in this case father and son, Haroon and Karim, share the final scene as they had shared the opening one. Although again offering no resolution, this novel therefore suggests a more satisfying bonding of father and son than had Kureishi's earlier screenplay.

It opens as Karim, still a boy, first sees his father as a man. It closes as Karim, now a man, reckons with the realization that his father is, like him, only another man. Haroon's pantless handstand in the opening scene foreshadows his topsy-turvy marital infidelity, and Karim is assaulted by Haroon's failings, ranging from a bad sense of direction to a bad sense of marriage. Finally, however, Karim is able to qualify his opening observation—that Haroon's only foresight was in growing chest hair—as a son's melancholy questioning. Upon his return to London from New York, Karim realizes that Haroon's ascetic philosophy might be sincere.

The father and son are introduced as they participate in a typical adolescent power struggle, in which Haroon orders Karim to help him practice his yoga. Kureishi quickly propels Karim and Haroon from father and son into the role of "pals" as the two conspire to hide from Haroon's wife, Margaret, what they have just found out about each other—namely, Haroon's sexual infidelity (he is involved with Eva) and Karim's sexual unconventionality (he is attracted to Charlie). This is at best an uneasy truce between a father and a maturing son.

Through the course of the novel, as Karim thrashes about to find his way, so does his father. Although at the novel's close both men find themselves in new places, the fact that they have both undergone changes does not mean that they have arrived at a mutual destination. Father and son have not yet come to understand each other. Nonetheless, they have come to a realization: that each of them has/is something to understand. Karim and Haroon accept the existence of each other's philosophies, while neither comprehending nor respecting them. This is a more satisfactory phase in this complicated relationship than that of other fathers and sons in Kureishi's earlier work, but theirs is still a relationship viewed from a single vantage point. Kureishi continues to write about this relationship from this perspective in *The Black Album*. He wrote from the perspective of a father in "My Son the Fanatic." He knows that he still has "more to say about sons and fathers" after adapting "My Son the Fanatic" to film.

Kureishi continues to explore familial dynamics in his portrayal of other blood relationships as well. Although the father-son relationship is more overt throughout his stories, his more subtle mother-child pairings are also noteworthy.

Omar's mother is deceased in *My Beautiful Laundrette,* but her suicide on the train tracks haunts the story; her photograph on Papa's bed stand sustains her presence throughout it. Sammy's mother does not appear in *Sammy and Rosie Get Laid,* but even in her absence she continues to separate Sammy from his father. Half-white and British, Sammy is a stranger to his Asian father, more at home in the western world.

Even when present, as Clint's mother is in Kureishi's directorial film debut, *London Kills Me,* mothers are still distant from the story. This distance leaves Clint searching for a mother's love in another. Living in London's Notting Hill, he fantasizes Sylvie, his girlfriend and flatmate, as a maternal figure while seeking his birth mother in a journey to the countryside. In his quest, he romanticizes the maternal relationship, seeking the innocence of childhood. Desperate to escape his drug-dealing life on the streets, his need to find this contentment is ever present in Clint's story.

Clint's need for a mother's love is illuminated in the bathing scene. Bathing is a ritual of contentment, a symbolic return to the warmth of the womb. In the warm water, Clint again finds innocence. His adult nakedness is protected by the water as Sylvie washes him. He knows childlike simplicity and safety in her ministering. Tended by Sylvie, Clint is as unashamed of his nakedness as he is of his rash.

Although Clint is threatened when he angers Sylvie's lover, the father-figure Muffdiver, Sylvie restores calm in the bathing fantasy enacted by the three in the tub. When Muff throws off his entrepreneurial garb and joins them naked under the warm water, the three bathe in serenity. Clint finds the security of family love in this daydream bath that up until now, as a derelict on London's streets, he has been denied.

A second cleansing episode in the country mirrors this earlier dreamlike bathing scene in Notting Hill. On a pilgrimage to his mother's bucolic home, Clint again attempts to cleanse himself of the gritty street life he lives in London. However, the water from Clint's shower upstairs leaks through the ceiling and floods the derelict cottage, causing the furious Stone, Clint's stepfather, to burst into the bathroom.

Stone's expulsion of the insecure boy from the comfort of the shower into stark reality humiliates Clint, as Stone scrutinizes his adult body in the shower. With no warm bathwater to hide him, Clint must stand there, his skin rash exposed, nude, emaciated, and vulnerable before Stone. Stone will not allow Clint the comfort of dreaming that he has any place in the life of Stone's wife, and because Clint has angered his stepfather, he is deported back to the streets of London.

Leaving the house, Clint has an image of himself as a child at the kitchen table with his mother. The mother cuddles her little son in a ray of warm sunlight. This daydream reverberates in the same way that his illusionary escape into the bathwater did earlier. But ultimately Clint must return to the gritty city streets and the adult life that threatens him.

Symbol and reality overlap as Clint's reality incorporates dreams. In the Notting Hill bath-scene fantasy, for example, Sylvie is a mother-figure protecting Clint, whereas in reality, she is mainstreaming heroin in another second-floor room. As another example, while at Clint's mother's house in the country, Muffdiver is first shown in one scene disguised in Stone's Elvis jumpsuit in the hall. But Elvis-impersonator Stone reclaims the suit to become the intruding father figure.

In other examples of dreams invading Clint's reality, father-figure Muffdiver does not displace Clint in his daydream bathing, but his stepfather, Stone, does obliterate him in reality, and whereas Clint's dream mother tends to him in his bath, in reality his mother confronts him for stealing Stone's shoes, refusing to take the abuse that protecting Clint from his stepfather will bring her. Unwilling to act as his mother, she dismisses the boy, acting instead as Stone's wife. Stone, now dressed as Elvis in the jumpsuit—not in dream, but in the illusion that is his reality—leashes his vicious watchdog, making sure his unwanted stepson Clint clears out for good. Unlike in the earlier bathtub scene, there is to be no calm water, no serenity for this family trio.

The mother-son relationship in *London Kills Me* becomes powerful not as a symbol but as reality, as the story reveals that Clint yearns for acceptance, while his mother simply does not care enough to defend him against Stone. When thus unencumbered by representationalism, sensationalism, and literary symbolism, the honesty of Kureishi's portrayal of familial relationships again underscores the impact of his storytelling. Far from distorting the universal human truths conveyed in Kureishi's characterizations, the flamboyant idiosyncracies add color to them.

In *The Buddha of Suburbia*'s Margaret Amir and Eva Kay, Kureishi depicts both a mother and the woman who would take her place. Abandoning his mother, Karim moves in with his father and his mistress, Eva. While Haroon waits for Eva, Karim begins his domestic routine with her by taking a luxurious bath, after which she reads to him. Taking childish pleasure in selfishly keeping her from his father's bed, Karim becomes her little boy, a substitute for her son, Charlie, who has in turn abandoned his own mother. A later confrontation scene between Karim and his mother Margaret proves equally provocative. In this scene, Karim, by now bored with his new life with Haroon and Eva, has finally gone to visit his mother, now living with his uncle Ted and aunt Jean. Following his parents' split, Karim has reordered his own life to his own satisfaction, and is determined that his mother's function in that life is to make him happy by being happy. That is, Karim is determined that Margaret should act in the way that he thinks his mother should act. He brings her what he remembers to be her favorite candies, and finally coerces her to make him happy by enjoying her favorite pastime, sketching him.

Karim will neither bear the responsibility for her problems nor accept the burden of her unhappiness. However, he becomes desperate when she will not recover, and resents the fact that Margaret has become an unhappy woman who is imposing on his adult life rather than simply remaining his mum, supportive of him yet selfless, as he remembers, needs, and demands her to be.

Karim's relationship with mother figure (Eva) and real mother (Margaret) remains dynamic throughout the novel, with Eva marrying Karim's father and Karim having to learn to allow Margaret to let go of their family history—for Margaret, her affair with a younger white lover has made her grown Anglo-Asian son part of a completed phase in her life, not the continuing center of her existence. When she replaces her husband Haroon in her life, Margaret severs her tie to her son's Indian blood. Margaret comes into her own, both in her personal life and in her career, and when she establishes her new identity, it is no longer merely that of being Karim Amir's mother, it is as a person in her own right.

Karim is anxious to free himself from his father as part of his process of growing up: The son escapes his father's domination and asserts his independence. His separation from his mother, on the other hand, is not something he wants, and is therefore a more traumatic experience. Karim feels cut off from his mother. To him, as his mother she should always be there, in the background, nurturing.

In *The Buddha of Suburbia*, as in Kureishi's other fiction, fathers represent the public aspect of maturation. They often become the object of embarrassment or scorn until their sons have separated from their dreams and expectations for them. Sons grow up by separating themselves from their mothers as well, and in doing so, forfeit forever the innocence of childhood. The loss of the security of childhood is the price Kureishi's boys must pay to become men.

There are considerable cultural implications of the role of mothers in Kureishi's work, in which they exercise their power in a quiet way. Kureishi also suggests that autobiographical experience may formulate his aesthetic philosophy regarding mothers: "My mother was important in my life too. But she is important to me privately. I don't feel that I particularly want to write about her, for others to read about her."

Kureishi's short story "With Your Tongue down My Throat" expands his parental characterizations to include the relationship between fathers and daughters. As well as portraying daughter Nina, who deals with a distant Pakistani father in the east and a white mother in London, the story also portrays Daddy's little girl, Nina's sister Nadia, who hitherto has lived with her doting dad in Pakistan. Kureishi's inclusion in this story of differing gender perspectives in his portrayal of fictional families is an interesting experiment, even if the device of ventriloquist narration hampers its overall effect.

Although the father-son relationship remains more significant than any other relationship in Kureishi's work, he has portrayed other parental relationships. "With Your Tongue down My Throat," for example, also differentiates between traditional Asian expectations for Nina and her permissive, postfeminist lifestyle in England. It does so in the form of interplay between her stepmother and the women in her father's Pakistani household; the relationship between Nadia and Nina, and among Nina, Nadia, and her mother, who all share a flat in London with the mother's boyfriend, further contrasts traditional eastern family roles for women with the more volatile western roles.

In this short story, Kureishi extends his look at parents and children to embrace two different societies, neither of which the reader may be familiar with, although a universality transcends these social settings, allowing all readers to identify. Readers may not have experienced being of mixed race in London or in Karachi, living on the dole in England with a visiting half-sister, or, as in *The Black Album*, living in posh Knightsbridge with a drug-addict husband: these are the colorful characters' life experiences, particular to his plots. But readers do know the desperate adolescent urge to fit in. They have experienced the contemporary nuclear family's expansion through modern marital conventions, today's transient lifestyles with the increase in geographic mobility, and the contrary value systems confounding the process of growing up. The resultant difficulties of asserting an identity and setting up one's own life are recognizable in all his characters' experiences.

Kureishi also portrays relationships between siblings, usually of the same sex. Nasser and Papa in *My Beautiful Laundrette*, for example, are immigrant brothers who came to England hearing very different drummers. Allie in *The Buddha of Suburbia* is a conservative of the Thatcher era, while his brother Karim is a free spirit. In "With Your Tongue down My Throat," Nadia and Nina change places with each other to test their blood ties as women and sisters who have lived in different worlds. In *The Black Album*, Chili is a designer-label bon vivant, while his brother Shahid is an intellectual struggling with religion, sex, and art.

Uncles are also featured in Kureishi's writing, from his first screenplay's Uncle Nasser through Uncle Tippo in *The Black Album*. When grown, this uncle character often holds different immigration philosophies from that of his brother, the father of the main character. Although sharing common experiences growing up, these brothers choose different directions in life and provide Kureishi's younger characters with examples of the different, often contradictory, choices open to them. Nasser and Papa in *My Beautiful Laundrette* are as different as Papa and Tippo in *The Black Album*, even though the two works are separated by a decade.

In-laws further humanize family roles. An interesting depiction of a relative in the expanded family is Uncle Ted in *The Buddha of Suburbia*. Distinguished as a working-class British character and a perpetual family outsider, in-law Ted is a henpecked husband who admires his philosophically inclined brother-in-law Haroon for living outside his working-class ethics. Unlike his wife, with her racist patronizing of Haroon, Ted appreciates, even envies, his Asian brother-in-law's cultural differences. White Ted provides his family with a workaday, western pragmatism that is in contrast to Haroon's eastern philosophy. Zulma, the influential daughter-in-law in *The Black Album*, like many other Kureishi characters, sabotages fictional Asian stereotypes. Living in western London, she uses her Asian heritage to please and manipulate men.

London Kills Me expands Kureishi's portrayal of the reality and the romance of family life. In the relentless abusive behavior of its streetwise young characters, freedom conflicts with conformity, loneliness with independence, and purpose with desperation. Kureishi's story of a band of homeless addicts, pimps, whores, dealers, and hustlers facing life on the London streets apparently strays far from family portrait, but familial love bonds his homeless characters together. So, too, do guilt, necessity, insecurity, and competition, which, more than anything else except blood, characterize a family.

The interdependency of Muffdiver and his street gang reveals the idiosyncratic company of grifters to be as much a family as any other in Kureishi's fiction. As fatherly love characterizes Haroon and Karim in *The Buddha of Suburbia*, so the dynamics of family are applied to Muffdiver and Clint in *London Kills Me*. Similarly, just as brotherly love propels Nasser and Papa in *My Beautiful Laundrette*, so family dynamics in Kureishi's "In a Blue Time" make it easier to identify with filmmaker Roy and vagabond Jimmy. In his most recent film adaptation, *My Son the Fanatic*, Kureishi counterpoints the struggle for dominance of the decadent Parvez and his fundamentalist son with the brotherly relationship of the Punjabi taxi driver and his lifetime friend Fizzy. All of these family relationships make the unconventional antics of Kureishi's characters more understandable.

Kureishi's characters strive to change their histories. They end up regretting having changed their traditions; and they find that they cannot change their identities. Like families everywhere, members of Kureishi's families exhibit contradictory ideas, feelings, and experiences, thwarting, supporting, and loving each other. So, too, family relationships are depicted as complicating life. The old wisdom that people need to learn how to relate to one another is a consistent, if frustrating, lesson in Kureishi's storytelling. He continues to expand his portrayals to include what is identifiable in the dynamics of contemporary relationships. Race, sexual preference, politics, and class are varied among his characters and roles are expanded and challenged: in *The Buddha of Suburbia*, lifetime friends Anwar and Haroon become brothers, as do Parvez and Fizzy in the film *My Son the Fanatic*; while Muffdiver's street band in *London Kills Me* acts as a family.

It is Kureishi's respect for who his characters are, if not for what they do, that makes them identifiable. Gay mixed-race entrepreneurs take a chance on their dream laundrette in one story; a husband and wife accept Elvis as part of their marriage in another. Kureishi's fictional universe includes drugs taped to scrotums, store bombing, and sleeping out on the street—subjects foreign to most of his audience. His hybrid families are beyond stereotype: in one of them, two sisters are brought together when all they have shared is a biological father; in another, a son is voyeur to his father's adultery with a one-breasted woman; and in still another, a daughter-in-law argues about terrorism with a despot to the accompaniment of frenzied female violinists in a restaurant. But this world becomes understandable because the characters—on every side of the issues—are drawn with honesty.

The author neither demeans nor glorifies how his characters act; he simply tells their stories. And these stories detail widely diverging plots, from the comic theatrical adventures of *The Buddha of Suburbia* to the

Fig. 22. To the accompaniment of violinists, Rosie (Frances Barber) argues with Rafi (Shashi Kapoor) in a restaurant in *Sammy and Rosie Get Laid*. As the exchange of insults becomes more frenzied, so does the music, providing both soundtrack and commentary in the scene. (Photo courtesy of the British Film Institute.)

political turmoil of book burning in *The Black Album*. But his characters always remain identifiable. In short, what characters do is believable because Kureishi wants readers to recognize in the individuality of his plots the understandable humanity of his characters. Kureishi explains:

First of all, I want to make an enjoyable experience, so when you read a book, you will gain pleasure; it will entertain. But, secondly, I would like to write about issues which are important morally, that one needs to think about, like race or religion. In *The Black Album,* I suppose, I want to share what it might be that makes people become fundamentalists. I portray book burning as being foolish, but that fact is also banal; I want to show, too, why it may be that people get involved in it. But I try to leave [a situation] open. A book or a film can be read by me, I hope, in many ways. *The Buddha* was slightly different, but the *Laundrette* is open. *The Black Album* is also open, and it provokes many questions, I hope.

As a man, I have my own views, but as a writer, I would never make a case for anybody—or for anything . . . I have done that in the past, I think. Now, I try and make the argument or the debate as dramatic as possible . . . I try to write a book in which one can see from many views. I see Zulma's view, Chili's view, Shahid's view, Deedee's view, and Riaz's view of the world. And all these worlds are mixing in with each other, aren't they? As a writer, I would like to say I don't believe in anything. As a man, I may have my own opinions and preferences. But as a writer, I have to create many different kinds of characters, and I try to exist in all of those characters.

Wide-ranging though his characterizations and plots may be, Kureishi does not condone all of his characters' activities—some of his characters, after all, murder, cheat, and terrorize. Nor does he respect all of his characters' philosophies—his characters include racists, sexists, and hypocrites—or all of his characters' institutions—he satirizes churches, governments, the arts and entertainment industry, and academia.

Nor does he provide answers to the contemporary problems that are the issues he deals with: terrorism, racism, poverty, drugs, and disillusionment abound in his stories, and their contradictions are simply incorporated into the plot. Likewise, he refuses to romanticize: his marriages are often stifling, his children are sometimes ingrates, and his social reformers are usually phonies. He tramples on the conventions of acceptable language—racial epithets, religious slurs, four-letter words, and vivid descriptions of sexual and bodily functions pepper his fiction—and political correctness is ridiculed. His is the world of a generation in movement and his cinematic perspective and distinctive hybrid individuality color his fictional stories. But it is the identifiable humanity of this world that establishes the storytelling art of Hanif Kureishi.

Thus when Kureishi compiled his first short-story collection in 1997, he chose to include stories about different aspects of love. When Kureishi adapted his story "My Son the Fanatic" to film, he expanded the story because he recognized that there was "more to be told. . . . I want to tell a story about lovers, a man who falls in love with a woman who is not his wife." Love and lovers remain integral to Kureishi's storytelling, from his theatrical love triangle in *The King and Me* (1980) to his most recent publication, *Love in a Blue Time*, seventeen years later.

OVER THE RAINBOW
Immigrant Dreams

Kureishi identifies immigration as a central theme of his writing. The dream of someplace better burns in his characters and the quest to find the dream dominates his stories. While the search for this Elsewhere motivates many of the characters, others—Kureishi's immigrant characters—grapple with the disillusionment, alienation, and loss of identity that acquiring their dreams has cost them.

Kureishi's portrayal of a variety of immigrant characters has continued from his first play, *The Mother Country*, in which Imran questions his life in Asian London, through his recently published story, "We're Not Jews," in which a mother and her son are the object of prejudice. Sammy, Clint, Parvez, and other characters in all of his stories between these two works dream of finding a better life. Each is an individual, and all break the immigrant stereotype.

Emigrating from Pakistan to London with his brother, *My Beautiful Laundrette*'s Uncle Nasser is superficially an assimilated personification of the classic rags-to-riches dream. He has worked his way up the ladder in Western society through ambition. And he has learned how to work the system. "In this damn country which we hate and love, you can get anything you want," Nasser advises his London-born racially mixed nephew, Omar, when taking him under his wing. "It's all spread out and available. That's why I believe in England. You just have to know how to squeeze the tits of the system."

Although Nasser and his brother immigrated to London together, the two of them have widely differing views on how to achieve success there. Papa insists that the way to prosper in this strange country is through education, while Nasser knows that money is the key to Western advancement. Unlike Nasser, Omar resents the racial abuse he has encountered. More Western than his white lover Johnny, he develops unbridled ambition. "I'll want everything done now," Omar demands. "That's the only attitude if you want to do anything big." More fully revealing the resentment he feels and the lengths to which he'll go to grasp his dream, Omar later harangues Johnny with, "I want big money. I'm not gonna be beat down by this country. When we were at school, you and your lot kicked me all around the place. And what are you doing now? Washing my floor. That's how I like it. Now go to work. Go to work I said. Or you're fired."

Relinquishing his history, Nasser abandons eastern traditions. He takes on British values with the same gusto with which he acquires a British mistress. Nasser's home life, especially his relationship with his brother, suggests that he also feels loss—but the entrepreneurial dream is foremost in Nasser's mind. "But we're professional businessmen," he concludes, "not professional Pakistanis. There's no race question in the new enterprise culture."

These characters are more complicated than Kureishi's previous immigrant figures. Once Nasser becomes a successful British businessman, he dons the mantle of wise mentor and generous benefactor. In a racial role reversal, he smugly condescends, having already proudly fulfilled his immigrant quest. Now a patronizing Englishman, he muses about rescuing white, National Front Johnny from the streets. "I wish I could do something more to help the other deadbeat children like him," he says. "They hang around the roads like pigeons, making a mess, doing nothing."

Johnny clearly puts into words the fantasy that Nasser is living out when, at a gala party at Nasser's suburban home, he affronts his lover/employer Omar with a question: "What does he think he is, your uncle? Some kinda big Gatsby geezer?" A "big Gatsby geezer" is an excellent appellation for the Asian uncle who achieved riches despite the price paid in terms of loss of integrity and denial of his heritage. A character beyond tradition, a Platonic invention of himself, he resembles Gatsby, the twentieth-century dream figure, a citizen of the money-making class, identified with gentrified wealth. An icon of the rags-to-riches dream,

Fig. 23. Nasser (Saeed Jaffrey, right) introduces Omar (Gordon Warnecke) to his mistress (Shirley Anne Field) and to the good life in the west in *My Beautiful Laundrette*. (Photo courtesy of Working Title Films, Ltd.)

Fitzgerald's Jay Gatsby, despite his financial success, was, like Nasser, never able to gain what he wanted: that which he had left behind.

Salim's wife, Cherry, is another dislocated immigrant character in *My Beautiful Laundrette*, having achieved her place in British society through her husband's corrupt drug-dealing profits. Although residing in London, Cherry never considers London home; she is a Pakistani, and still lives in Pakistan in her dreams, even while she is in her own comfortable London flat, hosting a dinner party. On meeting Omar, for example, she criticizes his unfamiliarity with Pakistan and his family, the culture they have both forfeited in order to live in England: "You stupid, what a stupid, [Pakistan]'s my home," she tells him. "Could anyone in their right mind call this silly little island off Europe their home? Oh, God, I'm so sick of hearing about these in-betweens. People should make up their minds where they are." It is not where they are that Cherry wants clarified, but who they are. As she holds court at Nasser's affluent party among the Asian women, she maintains her Asian life in London; she is merely performing her routine in a foreign residence, while continuing, in her dreams, to live in her homeland.

However, Cherry is inevitably faced with the reality that she is living not at home but in this unwelcoming land. Sitting in her car under a London roadway, she tries not to see the white street toughs out the windows on a late-night rampage, but the gang members press their faces and bare buttocks against the car windows when they recognize that "Pakis" are inside. Their banging and hooting become more insistent. No longer as confident in her answer to their racism, the frightened immigrant in a strange land knows "in-between" Omar is now her only hope. Cherry screams for his help.

Papa and Nasser, as well as Omar, Johnny, and Cherry, all find flaws in the dreams of Elsewhere, and this is a theme that continues to pervade Kureishi's stories in a progression—and regression—of new immigrant attitudes. Kureishi expands his investigation of such attitudes later in *The Buddha of Suburbia*, in which he portrays the dreams of another pair of immigrants, Anwar and Haroon, as well as those of their children. Like Nasser and Papa in *My Beautiful Laundrette*, Anwar and his childhood friend Haroon also immigrated together from Bombay to London and went on to live very different lives in the pursuit of their dreams. Like the gap between Papa and Nasser's divergent dreams and Omar's ambitions and Cherry's resentment, Anwar and Haroon are separated by a generation from the younger wave of Asians in London.

In *The Buddha of Suburbia*, Kureishi also created Changez, imported by Anwar from their subcontinental homeland for an arranged marriage to his daughter Jamila and to take over Anwar's grocery shop in south London. Changez comes to London not, as his father-in-law did, to pursue wealth—fortune is not his dream. The novel distinguishes between the quest of Anwar, the hard-working, docile Asian who came to England to work, and that of his son-in-law, the slacker Changez, who emigrates to experience every sex position he has read about, from those in the Kama Sutra to those described by his "patron saint Harold Robbins."

Anwar and Changez may share a common cultural tradition, but their attitudes are antipodal. Beaned by a can of vegetables thrown by his culturally frustrated father-in-law, Changez blatantly refuses to pay any attention to learning how to run Anwar's shop. Outside the shop Changez avenges himself against Anwar's demands and kills him, hitting him over the head with a dildo.

While Anwar will not tolerate his daughter Jamila's sexual or political activities, Changez watches while his wife dallies in sexual encounters with her "cousin" Karim, bears a child fathered by another political dissenter, and conducts a lesbian affair. Jamila studies and protests through civil disobedience; her husband Changez accepts her activities and visits a Japanese whore. British-born Jamila, on the other hand, is as different from her mother, the Princess Jeeta, who lives in London, as Changez is from Anwar. She is different, too, from her counterparts in Asia, one of whom Changez would have married if he had remained in Pakistan.

The reading lists of Changez and Jamila display the differences between Asian and Anglo-Asian cultural perceptions. Although Changez pursues "the classics," they are not, unfortunately, "Virgil or Dante" as defined, if negatively, by Karim Amir, but "P. G. Wodehouse and Conan Doyle . . . Randolf Scott . . . Gary Cooper . . . John Wayne"—in contrast to the list of Jamila, which includes "Angela Davis, Baldwin, Malcolm X, Greer . . . and Plath . . . and other vegetarians." Jamila is in search of a political solution; Changez is in search of pop culture.

Consequently, here the contemporary world culture, from the intellectual to the inane, has spread far beyond national boundaries and redefined today's immigrant quest. Kureishi reveals not only the distinctions between Changez and Anwar, but other inconsistencies between them and Jamila. Tolerance is not immigrant Changez's tradition, just as feminism is London-born Jamila's philosophy. And their Asian attitudes evolve in their new country. The new immigrants are sometimes in line with the cultural crosscurrents of the twentieth century, at other times embraced by them, and at still other times haunted by them.

This convoluted revisionism in the depiction of the immigrant dream runs full circle in Kureishi's later stories. In a 1995 short story, "My Son the Fanatic," he portrayed the fundamentalist Asians who abhor every contemporary, grafted western dream. The son, Ali, rejects his father and clings to his Islamic roots. He is a hostile westerner, but more than that, he is a hostile Englander, a contemporary immigrant dreamer, as he resents the fact that he is living in contemporary times, whether it is in England or in contemporary Pakistan. Terrorism is his lifestyle: The immigrant dream has changed from nightmare to manifesto, in a violent explosion.

This evolution of the immigrant dream to today's revisionism is also an essential element in Kureishi's second novel, *The Black Album*. Riaz, Chad, and Tahira, like Ali, determine to amputate the dream of western consumerism that has sullied their religion. Nuances in the dreams of the novel's other characters illustrate the subtle changes that lead to the realization that the philosophical immigrant dream has again turned from a geographical expression into a chronological one.

Born in England, the Asian Chili is the antithesis of the bumbling Changez. He is a savvy, urbane womanizer. Zulma, his wife, is also his antithesis—even if she is the successor to Asian women in seventies Britain like Jamila (a generation away from communes and marches, Zulma is more comfortable dashing about in her sports car). As it has for Riaz, therefore, for Zulma and her well-dressed husband, Chili, the immigrant dream has still another twist.

Chili, whose parents were suburban travel agents specializing in group tours for an Asian clientele, grew up affluent in England and is a fop, a drug user, and a hedonist. Chili has substituted Georgio Armani for Angela Davis:

At home Chili had a wall of suits, linen for summer, wool for winter, arranged according to colour, hanging in his wardrobe like a spectrum. There were cashmere coats; there was a drawer full of sunglasses, inscribed with the designer's name; a cupboard full of electronic toys, calculators, video players, a portable CD, personal organisers, all in the unyielding colour of that time, matt black. His shorts were Calvin Klein.

He had caressed these things and stood for half his life before the mirror. Shahid [his brother] had always been prohibited to touch them, though on special occasions Chili would invite him to gaze at them and at parties he'd open his jacket to people, displaying the label and laughing. Another room had been converted into a gym where he was "redesigning his body." In the drive Tippo cleaned his cars.

In the novel's first draft, Zulma resides in contemporary London. She is another young, attractive in-law to the main character in the role of a supporting character. Unlike *My Beautiful Laundrette*'s Cherry,

Zulma is a modern, independent woman. And although she is a liberated western woman, unlike *The Buddha of Suburbia*'s Jamila, she enjoys her wealth, not the pursuit of social justice, in London.

Kureishi details Zulma's evolution as an immigrant dreamer. She is not only caught between cultures, she is, like Jeeta and Jamila in *The Buddha of Suburbia*, also caught in contradictory gender dreams—at times, she is more a woman of her generation than she is a woman of her race. Zulma also amalgamates the eastern ideals in *The Black Album* that belie a simple distinction between those of the present and those of the past. In later Kureishi stories, the immigrant dream becomes further complicated by adding emigrational throwbacks to ancient religious conflicts. In "We're Not Jews," Azhar's father and mother could avoid their racist London neighborhood by going back home. But the white mother was born on this street and the Asian father has never even seen India. Parvez in "My Son the Fanatic" is every decadent, western failing his Fundamentalist son loathes because Parvez has become a Briton while his son, born in England, is desperate to return to his ancient religions and traditions in a homeland he has never seen. The dream is thus becoming more complicated as contradictions expand both the immigrant's previous and present search for an identity.

In contrast to her husband, who appears, in his drug addiction, to be a victim of the west, Zulma appears as the victor, reminiscent of the female protagonist who wins out at the close of an American made-for-TV movie: she likes to dress in "canary Chanel" with "jangling gold jewelry"; a reader of "*Vogue, Elle, Harpers and Queen*," she is prone to prefer "instructive literature with photographs" to the "merely imaginative"; and her flat is well decorated, highlighted with art "lifted from Pakistan's unprotected monuments."

Zulma determines to start a western journal with some of her "girlfriends," covering the issues that, in her view, concern women today—fashion, weddings, and babies—as well as topics other than the things that she thinks "girls" like to think about, such as abortion and politics. Thus she is *My Beautiful Laundrette*'s Cherry as she would have evolved a decade later, and in terms of the generation and gender that she represents, she greatly expands Kureishi's portrayal of the dynamic immigrant dream. As he developed Zulma's character in the novel's later drafts, Kureishi recognized the significance in her evolution:

Characters like Cherry and Zulma are part of a Western education elite that exists in many third-world countries, many of whom have been educated in America. They live in Pakistan, Saudi Arabia, or African countries, and they speak English. Yet, in other ways, they're part of their own cultures, too. They are a common elite class. I suppose Zulma represents that. In some ways, she is alienated from her own country. Obviously, she's not a peasant; she's not part of the people, but, of course, she's part of the country, too. And she could never be part of this country. She lives in both countries, kind of international elite, I suppose, the prime example of whom is probably Benazir Bhutto. She's the finest example of that kind of Zulma-Cherry character, isn't she?

These modern western Asian women illuminate a new immigrant dream. And the modern dream also includes the paradoxical retroactive yearnings. In Zulma's case, this revisionism is sarcastic. "Next time I'm going to be demanding an arranged marriage," Zulma tells Shahib after her husband Chili, now a drug addict, has turned dream into hallucinatory nightmare. "This free thing has gone too far."

In his involvment with drugs, Chili resembles Salim, Cherry's husband, but unlike Salim, Chili is no longer merely selling to the westerners—he is a drug-abusing westerner himself. Kureishi made the distinction in "The Rainbow Sign," his essay relating his first trip to Pakistan: "I was even told that [heroin's] export made ideological sense. Heroin was anti-Western; addiction in Western children was a deserved symptom of the moral vertigo of godless societies." In "My Son the Fanatic," cab driver Parvez has become a pimp for a German tourist whom his religious son can no longer tolerate. Kureishi's comic style and objectivity toward his characters enable us to see how the dual threats of fanatical terrorism and brainless consumerism are now in tandem in the immigrant dream.

By including the paradoxes in his depiction of the changing immigrant dreamers, Kureishi presents their volatile perspectives. Gender, racial, and generational differences are further expanded by the religious differences between characters. Having been denied entry into their Elsewhere and having rejected assimilation into the new as well, immigrants create new classes in western and eastern societies, revealing another class of contemporary immigrant dreamers. These immigrants have to deal with questions from many sides about free speech, customs, religion, and consumerism. They have ties to their homeland in the past, to their homeland in the present, to western society both in the past and in the present, and to the dynamic Asian communities in western society. The characters show both the evolution of today's Asian dreaming and the author's perception of the nuances and contradictions of the immigration process:

As you know, life in Pakistan, in India, changes. But immigrants who came here keep the same attitudes that they had when they were young in Pakistan, in India. It all seems rather backward. Issues of arranged marriages, for instance, in Pakistan and India today may be more liberal there now than they would be for Asians here. . . . Yes, yes. And now all of a sudden . . . we're all very aware of the conflicts between religions. This religious conflict doesn't necessarily have anything to do with my British identity—or with British identity at all—it has become another thing, a new thing.

One couldn't have predicted in the sixties that in the nineties young people who were born and brought up here would be asserting their Muslim identity in quite such a right-wing way. Who would have thought such an odd thing could happen? . . . the young are less likely to take any shit. And they're tougher. They organize. They go on the street, being British and being Asians at the same time.

It is not the validity of the immigrant's search that is here in question. It is not the irresistible romance of the promise offered in emigration that is here in question. Rather, it is the mutability and melancholy of the dreamer underlying Kureishi's storytelling that are at issue. He identifies the convolutions and overlap of his dreamers' needs in his stories of Anglo-Asians in London. In so doing, he struggles with racial, cultural, and national quagmires from Delhi to Piccadilly Circus.

Kureishi investigated this paradox of immigration in his early short story "With Your Tongue down My Throat," another narrative characterizing this new immigrant. In this story, the exchanged visits of sisters Nina and Nadia to Pakistan and London, respectively, expose today's inherent contradictions in the dreaming of Anglo-Asians and the prejudices toward them. When the sisters are Pakistanis living in London, like Cherry and Zulma elsewhere in Kureishi's fiction, they suggest the Asian immigrants' illusions regarding their homeland. When, however, they are living in Pakistan, they suggest the Pakistani prejudices toward the west today. As dreamers, the Pakistani sisters have become dual residents of both places. In reality, they are also outcasts in both places. Each is hybrid.

This story is further distinguished by its point of view. The first-person narrator appears throughout to be Nina, but as the story concludes, the reader finds that Howard, a white Englishman, is telling the story using Nina as a narrator. Thus, it turns out to have been not the story of Nadia as her sister Nina sees her, but Howard's story of how he assumes Nina sees herself and her sister. Kureishi's stylistic device strongly brings into focus the overlap between reality and illusion in race, gender, and generation as they are experienced by today's immigrants.

The author's hybrid perspective of the prejudice and contradictory bigotry among and experienced by mixed races today in London is reflected in this story. With the same Pakistani father but different mothers, one of whom is a white Englishwoman, while the other is an Indian "wifey," Nadia and Nina exemplify today's hybrid generation that crosses—and is crossed by—two cultures. Like Kureishi himself, Nina is a hyphenated Briton. Like his later character Changez (*The Buddha of Suburbia*), her sister Nadia has expectations of a London she has only imagined in her homeland. Like Omar in *My Beautiful Laundrette*, the sisters are "in-betweens": Nina is the young Asian born into the contemporary overlapping races/cultures of Anglo-Asian society in lower-class London; Nadia is the upper-class Asian born in an eastern society with ties to east and west.

Kureishi's portrayal of the new immigrants continues in his longer fiction. In *The Buddha of Suburbia*, his first novel, Changez, who lives on the dole after coming from Bombay, and Karim Amir, who, although born in Bromley, remains an exotic, an "almost Englishman," join such traditional immigrants as the shopkeeper Anwar. In his fiction, Kureishi portrays the mutability of immigrant motives, from the dreaming in her father's council house of Anglo-Asian Nina in "With Your Tongue down My Throat" to the militant reactions of Ali in "My Son the Fanatic" as he defends his ancient religious traditions while cruising the violent streets in his father's cab with a whore. It is in these ways that Kureishi expands his redefinition of the immigrant quest beyond last century's dreaming of a geographical Elsewhere. Author Michael Ondaatje labels these dreamers "international bastards—born in one place and choosing to live elsewhere. Fighting to get back to or get away from our homelands all our lives."[1] Kureishi further characterizes their dreams of leaving their homelands and making new homes not in terms of national boundaries, but rather in terms of changing, individual lifestyles. When Kureishi charts his characters' flights to and away from homelands, he is redefining their dreams in terms of today's immigration to Elsewhere.

The real purpose of immigration for his characters is most often not a change in geography, but the realization of a dream. Through his dynamic characters' races, genders, sexual preferences, and generations, Kureishi uses immigration to illuminate the fact that to find Elsewhere today is to attain a desired lifestyle, to fulfill an ironic quest to live out one's dream. The geographical distance between India and London is great, but there may be a greater distance between wherever Kureishi's immigrants live and that Elsewhere they dream about. Consequently, immigrants in Kureishi often do more than travel from overlapping reality to overlapping reality across an ocean; they dream of finding their Elsewhere by inserting their dreams into their real world.

Kureishi's dreamers have already come to England—most, indeed, are born Londoners. Often racially hyphenated, these hybrid immigrants are usually culturally hyphenated as well. *The Black Album*'s Chili, debonair from his Paul Smith shirt down to his Calvin Klein underwear, seeks the right to dream his own dream amid the book-burning London riots sparked off by the Rushdie *fatwa*. He is English, and he demands that the state of being English be redefined to include his dreams. In "My Son the Fanatic," at the other extreme, Ali on his prayer mat demands that his religious tradition be recognized, too. He is English and he demands that his redefinition of himself be accepted as his dream. All of Kureishi's immigrants, as diverse as they are, dream of recognition.

Kureishi's England is a racist society. Race is the tension underlying the journey; and it is most often skin color, that most visible distinction, that frustrates his characters in their bid to attain their dreams. Increasingly, however, his storytelling exposes the conflicting hybridity of contemporary ethnic identities and cultural traditions as the disco seventies and Thatcher's isolationist eighties evolved into the global society of the nineties. All his characters, Asians, Anglos, and Anglo-Asians alike, dream of traveling the distance between being an outsider and becoming an insider.

The dreaming of all of Kureishi's characters has in common the separation between the conventional and the marginal. Some characters dream of emigrating to opportunity; others dream because they can't—or don't want to—conform to the conventional western dream. Because Kureishi remains ambiguous about cultural assimilation, contradictions are a given in his street world—a world that he is aware is made up of many distinct worlds, each with its own codes, languages, classes, and conventions.

His street people are the new immigrants because they have not crossed over the rainbow into contemporary materialism. They illustrate the enormous divide between the marginal society that works the London streets and the conventional mainstream society that is a thin layer of glass away inside the shops, flats, and offices of workaday London. Characters can see through the glass from either side, but the partitioning of their shared environment is a real division. And whether his characters reject or accept consumerism, cosmopolitanism, and capitalism, all of them yearn to belong. This is really the Elsewhere of the urban immigrant: Acceptance.

Immigration stories are no longer as uncomplicated as the quest to find someplace to call home. Now individuals dream of finding a place not only where each is accepted, but where everyone keeps an identity. Identity and assimilation comprise today's immigrants' paradoxical dream. And in Kureishi's work, there is a further rejection of dogmatism. Thus, he shows in his storytelling that even the dream cannot be seen as involving a specific lifestyle for everyone, and as the price of following this dream is recognized, the validity of the dream itself is called into question.

London Kills Me is a story of the quest for the immigrant dream in London. Here, disenfranchised Londoners are the immigrants who dream of traveling up from the squalor of their class to the prosperity of another class—that of white English society. It is also the story of the street society they do not choose to forfeit in pursuit of their dream. Drugs play a part in the quest, as do limousine liberals, Asians, and Elvis Presley. Music is integral to the story, which is also cinema-conscious; in it, eastern and western philosophies collide. The story is hilarious, satiric, and often raw. At its center, the white protagonist by the name of Clint Eastwood searches for a better Elsewhere, in a cosmopolitan odyssey with both stylistic and thematic ties to its author.

As it is a story of our times, the film employs a multiracial cast. Issues of racial prejudice are evident, even though *London Kills Me*'s main character is a white street punk. Other Kureishi characters have been white street punks too, but because the story of "Clint Eastwood" is not a racial one, Kureishi's theme of quest in this case breaks completely from previous immigrant stereotypes and embraces a hybrid perspective. Kureishi focuses here not on immigrant groups defined by race, but directly on the ambiguity that shapes the quest of the urban immigrant.

Pimps, whores, drug addicts, rent boys, and transvestites work Clint's Portobello Road. The sprawling multiracial neighborhood of his story is peopled by, among others, an Elvis impersonator, a dominant bleeding-heart TV reporter, sucker German tourists, yuppie transcendentalists, and a crime boss and his henchman—played by Gordon Warnecke, who also played Omar in *My Beautiful Laundrette*. Everyone pursues his or her own dream, and Clint's dream is to make the move from living off the street to earning a living on the street. The ambiguity of his desperate journey to get that job dominates Kureishi's rock-and-roll look at London.

The unresolved ending, essential to Kureishi's *London Kills Me*, grows out of Kureishi's characterization of Clint and his depiction of the hybrid London street world that this character inhabits. Kureishi is aware of the inherent ambiguity of Clint's dream—a dream of assimilation by a white Englishman living outside his own society and hoping that his savvy best friend, together with the heroin-addicted woman they both want, will accept him.

Incidents as they are reflected and seen through windows are again prominent in this film. The frame of windows reveals and mirrors the kinetic nature of *London Kills Me*'s dreaming. Sylvie is shown riding away from Muffdiver through a moving taxi window; Muffdiver is later seen framed in the window of a moving train as he loses Sylvie. From the street, Muffdiver watches Clint through the restaurant window as he fights for his dream to be a waiter inside the restaurant. Clint dreams that this job will be his escape from Muffdiver and the streets into a whole new world, a world away just on the other side of the restaurant glass.

When Clint climbs a drain pipe to claim the flat he and Muffdiver have dreamed about, he hopes to make it through the liquid windows that separate his class from success. In one of the film's two expressionistic, dreamlike turns of the camera, Clint is shown framed in the window of Dr. Bubba's studio as he ascends to the flat; in this scene, he appears to be a glorious winged archangel ascending from the London street scene into the rarified kingdom.

As Clint continues to climb, in the transparency of glass, a meditator sees not Clint but his own dream of rising above banal, earthbound concerns. Reaching the squat's window above, Clint crashes through the glass to gain entry into the flat—so much for the liquidity of the windows. Clint is no longer an angel gracefully flying to his dream; he is instead a street thug breaking and entering to acquire property.

Windows are real barriers between the goal of the quest and Kureishi's dreamer, who is trying to attain it. People see what they dream of seeing, not what actually is. In Kureishi's stories, partitions divide classes, regardless of how fragile or translucent the barrier appears to be; society has divided the dreamers. No matter how close their dreams appear to be—whether they are just through a window or up on a movie screen— they are, in reality, another world.

Clint Eastwood's story is fundamentally the story of a quest. Clint, an unsuccessful drug pusher, is an experienced street hustler. Constantly itching from his skin rash while working the road, he dreams of a better life as he checks out his reflection in passing store windows. Now mentored by his ambitious lifetime buddy, entrepreneur Muffdiver, a sort of Horatio Alger on speed, throughout his life Clint has been used by everyone from his abusive father to Notting Hill pushers. Clint meets up with his old friend Sylvie, and announces to her that he is "looking for a job."

Early in the film, Clint has an interview to be a waiter and, although it is obvious that he is from the class of those perpetually on the streets or on the dole and has no job experience whatsoever, he nonetheless lands his first job. The only condition is that he must have acceptable footwear. The manager, Hemingway, spells it out: "So, no new shoes—no job. No job—back on the street. Back on the street—shit." An elated Clint rejoins Muffdiver as they walk along a store-lined street, musing, "Look. Hush Puppies, DMs, sandals, brogues, loafers, high-tops. Give me a single reason why I shouldn't get some."

As the story unfolds around him, Clint searches for the shoes he must have to start work. From Clint's first moments in the squat, he tries to find, and then to fashion, a pair of acceptable working shoes. Critics recognized that this footwear device gave the narrative cohesion, one of them writing: "As a motor for the narrative in *London Kills Me*, [the shoe search] also solves one of Kureishi's weaknesses as a scriptwriter: the fact that one scene doesn't always initiate another."[2] Kureishi also clearly makes the shoes emblematic of Clint's quest to escape from life on the streets and assimilate a conventional lifestyle. Throughout Clint's escapades, the displays in the windows of Notting Hill shoe stores are ironically ever-present. While Clint's changing footwear is ridiculed and his situation becomes more desperate, the solution remains merely a purchase away.

Clint is forced out of his old shoes, finds new pairs of shoes, rejects some, and abandons others. The morning he must report to work, he refuses the last, most appropriate pair as he realizes that a condition of this gift from Muffdiver and Sylvie is that he must stay in street life. When Clint reports for his job at the conclusion of the film, he has the shoes required—ironically stolen from the restaurant manager, Hemingway.

Clint has the shoes; Clint gets the job. But it was never just a pair of shoes that Clint sought; he wanted the passport to a better life that the shoes provided. A paying job is Clint's Elsewhere. But the viewer is left asking, Are the shoes really a move to a better life for Clint? Is he really any closer to achieving his quest for a better life? Clint's immigration over the rainbow is not only a quest to acquire new shoes on his feet—it is also a geographical immigration, as he then walks on a journey made by the new shoes on his feet. Thus the changing shoes throughout the film not only represent successive episodes in Kureishi's story, each pair determines a phase in Clint's odyssey. The shoes fit his changing roles, if not his feet.

Clint turns twenty years old as the story opens. He is determined now to take his place in the world, to be recognized, to assert an identity. "You've got to know. It's my birthday," he announces to Muff and Sylvie. "Now, at this moment in the whole history of the world, I'm twenty years old."

When he is stripped by thugs at a rave, Clint hands over his shoes,

Fig. 24. Clint (Justin Chadwick, right) tries on the boots Muffdiver (Steven Mackintosh) and Sylvie (Emer McCourt) have given him, in *London Kills Me*. This solution to his footwear problem, however, quickly proves a ruse, and Clint must continue his quest. (Still photo courtesy of Jacques Prayer.)

along with the drug money he has hidden in them. Although the writer Kureishi had described Clint as leaving the encounter stripped naked, in the film itself he leaves in long underwear, bare only to the waist, due to the weather and director Kureishi's compassion—according to Kureishi, "it was fucking cold shooting in London at midnight in February." Thus the symbolism of Clint being born into a new life at point zero, naked, on his birthday is clearer in the script than it is in the film. Clint thus begins his odyssey: the urban dream. Walking the street naked (or semi-naked), he vows, "I'm going to live an ordinary life from now on. I know it's possible." But a pair of transvestites whom he knows respond to this statement, "Hi Clint. Good start." The men, dressed as women, are costumed to live a life they want and had to make for themselves.

Having forfeited his own shoes, along with their hidden cache, Clint dons a new costume, including a large pair of boots that he salvages from the trash. At the restaurant interview, manager Hemingway informs him the new shoes are unacceptable—they defy health laws and offend the trendy diners—mainly movie people—who frequent Hemingway's. Clint easily tosses them and his street life aside—after all, this costume is only some refuse he was able to scrounge to cover his bare body the night before, while walking London's cold streets; that clothing, including the shoes, doesn't represent the real Clint, who was forced at the rave to hand over his own clothing. Neither does this new costume represent the life he seeks.

A third pair of shoes, bright red cowboy boots, next capture Clint's eye. These shoes have the longest run, and the most dramatic place in the narrative. He finds them as part of a footwear trove that he comes across while experimenting in the remains of the electronic luxury of automatic closet doors, TV stands, and bedside telephones in his room. Trying on a most garish display of footwear accumulated in a closet, he settles on the red cowboy boots. As the boots are too small, with the help of a razor blade, talcum powder, plastic bags, and his buddy, Burns, Clint creates an open-toed cowboy look.

Cowboy boots equip Clint to walk in the footsteps of the strong, silent men he admires who left civilization behind and carved out a new life. And that is the way in which this marginal, main character views them: as marking his path to a new frontier on the gentrified sidewalks of Notting Hill. The red boots strongly evoke movie cowboys: the heroes of celluloid morality plays glorifying American cowboy actors in pursuit of a fictional new life in the fictional untamed west. Cowboy boots—especially the garish Technicolor boots of a larger-than-life spaghetti western star—are appropriate for a macho cowboy such as the appropriately named Clint Eastwood.

The boots are ruby red. The most famous cinematic footwear, Dorothy's ruby red slippers from *Wizard of Oz*, come to mind in Clint's trip down the winding Portobello Road, and a case could be made—though it is not made by Kureishi himself—for comparing the two films closely. Clint's journey down Portobello Road, for example, immediately triggers an Oz-London connection: urban, gritty London streets yellowed by urinating street people are suggested. Hemingway becomes the wizard with the simple solution, telling the protagonist: "But you've always been a waiter, Clint. Wait-persons just like to wear shoes that show them to be service personnel." Bike and Burns are the scarecrow and cowardly lion, while Mr. G and crew are the winged gargoyle monkeys who haunt generations of children's nightmares; sadistic Headley is the wicked bitch/witch, and Tom Tom is Toto.

The point here is not how interpretations should be made, or whether these interpretations should be made, or even which interpretations could be made. The point is that interpretations cry out to be made. That is, the cinematic references flood the story with images. Kureishi taps a global vein—that of the movies. He acknowledges the obvious reference to Dorothy's shoes, but admits that there is "no fucking theory behind it." Thus he window-dresses his street story of a young grifter's episodic search for a pair of shoes with Victor Fleming's evocative ruby red movie slippers.

Clint is a dreamer years later than the Depression era's Dorothy. Kureishi shows us there's no Emerald City to which Clint can get away, and no wizard's palace, only his stepfather's derelict house in Reading. And when Clint and his band of freaks and outcasts realize they just don't fit in there either, there is no clicking of heels to get away. Clint must relinquish the red boots, his magic slippers—and steal his stepfather's shoes. Leaving with Stone's shoes, Clint last sees his stepfather standing with his leashed vicious beast threateningly guarding any return route to Oz. Of course, in this story Stone is dressed not as the wizard, but as Elvis Presley in a sequined jumpsuit with his faded Cadillac behind him.

Kureishi continues his comic and graphic undercutting. *London Kills Me* is a film story, not a remake. Clint's Notting Hill reality would give anyone from Kansas pause: World-weary male hookers discuss the rigors of oral sex. Drug-dealing hucksters practice magic tricks. Street hustlers speak in rhyme. Heroin addicts shoot up in their squat. LSD is taped to a doorman's scrotum. There is, indeed, the story ironically proclaims, no place like home.

Kureishi simultaneously employs and satirizes other music and film references also, throughout Clint's journey to someplace better. This is not a contradiction of imagery, nor is it an inconsistency. It is a methodology. Twentieth-century immigrants—like this twentieth-century artist—realize the corollary existence of contrary images, as well as the contrary needs, desires, and demands of the new quest.

Kureishi does not structure his images to create symbols of a new immigration dream; he uses the images of that dream. Unexplained and unexcused, but selected to be evocative, the red "slippers"—the cowboy boots—are a pop-culture image. Importantly here, Kureishi uses this movie image not to retell Dorothy's story, but to illustrate the fact that Clint dreams a movie dream, revealing with painful clarity the melancholy in today's immigrant dream of never finding happiness Elsewhere—anywhere, except in media, and media fantasy at that.

Clint wears other shoes as well. For a time, he wears a pair of sandals, simple footgear given to him by Dr. Bubba with genuine regard. When Headley ridicules them, Clint leaves them for the showering Hemingway, whose shoes he in turn steals. But Clint turns down the appropriate footwear offered by Muffdiver and Sylvie because their acceptance means that Clint will abandon his job offer and accept his friends' lifestyle. Apparently Sylvie and Muffdiver want the three of them to emigrate from the streets of London together. But Clint knows that wherever he moves with Muffdiver will be merely the same life in a new setting. Instead, he wants to move up, to travel inside the windows on Portobello Road, not merely to move on to pandering on some other street.

The film opens with a documentary feel—still black-and-white shots of Portobello Road are underscored with rock music. The pictures under the opening credits evolve into colorized moving pictures tracking Clint's walk through the neighborhood, and, consequently, his quest for employment and assimilation springs from the artful creation. Thus, references to *The Wizard of Oz* and other movies are cinematic elements to illustrate the new quest for Elsewhere.

At the conclusion, dialogue is again muted into the music as the accompanying sequence of Clint as a waiter serving his customers in Hemingway's mutes the visuals. Kureishi thus frames his colorful story, blurring the end from the rest of the film's frantic pacing and colorful sequences, in a stylized movie sequence. Clint is again, at the film's conclusion, in a Notting Hill street setting, dressed in the waiter's uniform of black and white, from his black ponytail and tie to his starched white shirt and proper black shoes. It is more obvious in the freeze-frame ending of the screenplay that this last shot of Clint ends the story ambiguously: Clint Eastwood has achieved the cinematic dream; Clint Eastwood's quest terminates with him inside the windows as a waiter.

In this final ironic turn of events, Clint gets the job wearing not cowboy boots, but Hemingway's stolen Native American motif moccasins. This switch of footwear bristles with the revisionist imagery of "cowboy and Indian" games. But as Hemingway recognizes his own shoes, does it also suggest that the restaurateur (aptly named for the macho American icon) recognizes his own spark of entrepreneurism, his own ambitions in Clint? Clint's urge to escape the street life leads him to conformity. Hemingway has literally "walked in Clint's moccasins." Will Clint's dream take him all the way—to becoming a Notting Hill restaurant manager?

Does Clint's journey jibe with previous stories about immigrants gloriously fulfilling their dreams in their new homes on streets of gold in a promised land? Kureishi himself is noncommittal in his answer: "If you think being a waiter is a big deal, then [this ending] is optimistic," he says. "But, on the other hand, Clint's become a nothing, wearing a uniform, which is not him. He's wearing clothes that blank him out." Hemingway has kept his promise. Clint has found his shoes; Clint has his happy ending. But if Hemingway's footwear prerequisite is viewed with Kureishi's characteristic ambiguity, the film's ending may be seen to be not so happy after all—for, as Hemingway declares, "So, new shoes— a job. A job—no back on the street. No back on the street—shit."

Kureishi views Clint's story's ending as having more basis in reality, unlike *The Buddha of Suburbia*'s more upbeat finish, saying, "The boy in the *Buddha* is going somewhere—that's soap opera. But Clint winds up a waiter. That's reality." Clint is a searcher who seeks to gain employment without losing his freedom. This dreamer equates making money with making a living. He feels taking a step off the streets is taking a step up in terms of class. He sees money as being synonymous with a happy life, the stuff that Hollywood is made of. Consequently, to portray—and to define—Clint's contemporary quest in *London Kills Me* as a story, Kureishi borrows from the movies.

Hanif Kureishi's new urban immigrant seeks to maintain individuality and identity while being assimilated. His cosmopolitan characters can no longer be simply defined by race, nationality, or gender. Their journey is always complicated and increasingly circular because their quest is paradoxical. The distance between cultures defines their Elsewhere. Sometimes thousands of miles hamper the journey. Other times the equally arduous journey spans the much smaller geographical distance involved in getting off the streets and inside a plate-glass window. The new immigrant wrestles with the contradictions—the illusions, delusions, and allusions—of this cosmopolitan quest.

ten

POSTCOLONIAL IDENTITIES
Redefined Nationalism

Kureishi explored

the dynamics of national identity in his stageplays and shattered its old definitions in his first screenplay, *My Beautiful Laundrette*. He stresses the economic underpinnings in the racial dichotomy of Margaret Thatcher's London. His white and Asian communities are separated not only by color, but also by wealth, as the haves and the have-nots. The quest for power is the common denominator, however, and it is played out across cultural and color lines, from the unsavory manipulations of Asian small-time businessmen to the fistfights of chronically out-of-work white hooligans; from the sexual manipulations of arranged marriages in the traditional Indian community to the problems of homosexual lovers in the street society of lower-class London.

In *My Son the Fanatic*, as is the case in other recent British films, Kureishi boldly laces the issue of racial segregation with an awareness of intraracial class prejudice. His depiction of the partitions, the glass walls, within communities continues to prompt some critics to find discrimination and others to find reverse discrimination—depending on their orientation—in Kureishi's work. Whatever the charges, however, Hanif Kureishi's purpose as he sees it is not to preach doctrines, morals, or politics, nor is it to depict victimization; rather, it is to tell a story—and to tell it his way. And the fact that often the same story has received support from one political camp while being rejected by the opposing—and in some cases the same—political camp actually further indicates how Kureishi's respect for diversity charges his story.

My Beautiful Laundrette, in which Omar searches for himself in the comic, convoluted turmoil Kureishi sees as the Anglo-Asian community, has been lauded by film critics who have recognized the importance of presenting a multifaceted society that encompasses the screenplay's broad range of characters. "Indeed, of its many strengths, the most exciting line in this film is its character development," wrote one such critic. "The complexities of human nature and of relationships are explored in an extraordinarily impressive and rewarding fashion."[1]

Omar himself exhibits some complicated inclinations: his goals seem idealistic, but his motive is ambition. While his goals are apparently those of a scholar—and, consequently, of an idealistic immigrant and a dutiful son—Omar's hard work is not in fact a moral imperative—he is only ambitious. He works himself up from his starting position as an entry-level car washer for his uncle to a job as a small-time hoodlum, and from there he ascends to a career as a fledgling entrepreneur. Once he is exposed to his uncle's world, it becomes clear to the viewer that Omar has his own agenda of rising to the top regardless of the price.

Omar's determination to succeed in business is really a rejection of eastern passivity and an acceptance of western consumerism. Likewise, when Omar dares to double-cross Salim, his shady mentor, in a drug-running deal, he dismisses Asian values. But when he sexually baits both Nasser's sensuous daughter, Tania, and his white bodyguard, Johnny, he also abandons western middle-class ethics. According to one critic, Kureishi's story "in its different way explicitly re-imagined British identity."[2] In fact, Omar transcends stereotype in Kureishi's newly imagined nationalism, which is neither Asian nor British, neither colonized nor assimilated; rather, it has assumed the global identity of post–World War II, twentieth-century urbanism.

Kureishi's portrayal of Omar's dad and uncle, Papa and Uncle Nasser, Asian brothers who immigrated to London, investigates racial and class distinctions in the redefining of identity. Clearly Kureishi uses the characters to illustrate individualism within the Asian community. Since emigrating from Pakistan, the two brothers have taken divergent routes, Papa refusing to conform to the western work ethic by remaining in his bed philosophizing and drinking vodka, while Nasser has embraced capitalism with gusto by becoming a business entrepreneur. Their differences reflect Omar's cultural dilemma.

While Papa and Nasser have traveled a great geographical distance from the Indian subcontinent to England, here again, the distance from Papa's grey East London flat along the city tracks to Nasser's large home in the green suburbs is seen by Kureishi as being equally large.

Papa is as unable to throw himself into the western consumerism of Thatcher's London as he is to cut his own toenails. Staying in bed and drinking in his flat near the unsightly train tracks where his wife committed suicide, Papa hopes that his son will be an educated man, embodying the most romantic yearnings of the immigrant. Papa values his Asian heritage, and his passivity and wisdom, as well as his plans, are stereotypical of Asian immigrants. As Papa's final confrontation with Johnny suggests, however, his savvy and strength separate him from this stereotype.

Nasser, in contrast, is a man of means. He has an entourage and keeps a white mistress, Rachel. Although Nasser is apparently more westernized than Papa—superficially, he is Thatcher's eighties British entrepreneur—he is shown by Kureishi to live comfortably in the familiarity of his old ways: he holds onto his Asian culture in secret, under his business suit. Nasser engages himself in legal business endeavors, and does not dirty his hands by acknowledging the illegal—albeit profitable—western pursuits that he leaves to Salim. Without a son of his own, he turns to his nephew, Omar, to play the filial role of successor. With traditional old-world authority, Nasser even offers Omar his daughter, Tania, in marriage.

But in the end, has Nasser really been assimilated into London society? More importantly, has Nasser really wanted to be assimilated into that society any more than Papa wanted to be? In his portrayal of Nasser, Kureishi looks beyond the dream of immigration to the paradox of defining—and redefining—national, cultural, and personal identity. We must either achieve cultural assimilation, he challenges, or create a new nationalism.

Nasser defines himself in his illusions of London, Papa in his memories of Pakistan. Both men live—but are not at home—in an integrated London. Both brothers' worlds are isolated and unresolved, worlds that are culturally neither one thing nor the other. Kureishi goes beyond portraying simple, hard-working immigrants trying to become accepted in industrialized nations. He expands beyond a stereotypical tale of dark-skinned innocents battered in a white man's world. He sees the Anglo-

Asian worlds of both Papa and Nasser as dream worlds, while he shows Omar to be using both as stepping stones to the real, integrated world of London that he intends to dominate.

Kureishi had also written with the same individualism about diversity among the Asian characters in London in *Sammy and Rosie Get Laid*. In this screenplay, Rafi, a womanizing Pakistani despot, is involved in a long, interrupted interracial affair. A charming, Oxford-educated prig, Rafi returns from Pakistan to his beloved London far more British than any of the film's native Londoners. Yet he urges his son Sammy, who, having spent his entire life in the London of his birth, has never even seen Pakistan, to leave his white wife and "go back home to who [he is]," to the traditional life in Pakistan that Rafi himself has abandoned.

The Asian community in London disapproved of Kureishi's casting Shashi Kapoor, an eminent Indian screen actor, in the part of Rafi, a despot. According to critic Sandeep Naidoo, this offense was compounded by the community's familiar displeasure with Kureishi for "not properly characterizing [Asians] . . . There was no dramatic focus, too much was thrown in and one couldn't get the feeling that these were believable characters, . . . They were all too rootless, with little emotional warmth to them, too buppie [black upwardly mobile professional] orientated with no real anger or guts."[3] Naidoo concluded that this artificiality on film was somehow generated by Kureishi's narrow-minded demeaning of his Asian characters.

In fact, however, Kureishi's breaking of stereotypes in this second film again illustrates his confrontation with the standard definition of nationalism. He refuses to stereotype minorities by patronizing or over-simplifying them. Rejecting the demeaning racist characterizations of the past, Kureishi refuses to categorize individuals or type characters through trendy "Bambification"—defined by Douglas Coupland in his book *Generation X* as "the mental conversion of flesh and blood creatures into cartoon characters possessing bourgeois Judeo-Christian attitudes and morals."[4]

Extending Coupland's reference, like Disney's animated innocent, today's politically correct movie characters have become cartoons. Even if they are less degrading than earlier depictions of minority characters, these contemporary characterizations are no less limited. On the other hand, Kureishi is, one 1993 newspaper article declared, "politically conscious, not politically correct."[5]

Fifties TV homemaker June Cleaver is today a stereotyped icon; the politically correct June Cleaver–types who followed her, shunning pearls and housework, have become equally well-worn stereotypes. Later TV sitcoms that altered the traditional racial patterns simply transferred an archaic white stereotype: the Cleaver family was merely colorized. Just as it is racist to portray the only married, professional characters in movies or TV shows as whites, so it is equally racist to depict all minority persons as well educated, high income, law abiding, and family oriented. *Any* stereotyping reduces the myriad, diversified individuals which every race, nationality, sexual orientation, religion, and gender comprise. Kureishi notes that crime, greed, and materialism, like honor and intelligence, come in all colors, shapes, and persuasions in a pluralistic society, and that it is this diversity that he is attempting to capture in his work:

I'm not really writing about Asians as a category . . . We are all people. I don't think because [a character] is Asian, I have to be reverential. That would be ridiculous . . . Spike Lee put himself in the position of being sort of representative of black America, didn't he? He picked up that burden and said he took on white America because he wanted to fight for his race and his people. He can't really turn around now and slag them off and show them doing drugs, if they're into that. That's why he won't show drugs in his films. But I don't—I'm not in that position. I won't put myself in that position. If I want to show an Asian junkie, then I'll show an Asian junkie. Or an Asian heroin dealer. But I know that I'm not saying that all Asians are heroin dealers because it is not true. I might write about a heroin dealer because it might be interesting to me. I won't be tied. I can't. You can't. It wouldn't be any fun, would it, for me as a writer? If I want to write about a punkster, a gangster, you know, he turns me on because I think it is a good story, what can I do? Otherwise, it is bollocks. It's censorship. It's just censorship.

Hanif Kureishi has seen and been victim of prejudice from both sides, and just as his stories include naivete and greed among individuals in the Asian community, so they also include hypocrisy and intolerance among some, but not all, white characters. Attempting to give an answer to racism would be to theorize, to write a manifesto, or merely to dream; what Kureishi gives us instead is the story, his truth.

Kureishi, who has clearly chosen to be an artist and has strived to teach more than preach, always makes his characters understandable, if not always likable. They view their world with prejudice and are viewed with prejudice. Their world is a human world that has a ring of truth to it. Kureishi's vibrant London stories bring contemporary British society, albeit faltering, to life. He sees the ambiguities of multicultural London—the future looks both optimistic and pessimistic—and it is ambiguity that shapes the endings to his stories: truth denies them resolution.

My Beautiful Laundrette's script is realistic, then, because the community into which Omar seeks entry is as complicated as the Asian community from which he comes, the community of Nasser, Papa, and Tania. Like Kureishi himself, Omar has darker skin and has grown up in a Pakistani culture, but his experiences are not of the Indian subcontinent—he shares the same British heritage as his white school chum, Johnny. National Front Johnny not only becomes dusky Omar's lover, he also becomes Omar the colonial immigrant's employee as the two of them pursue Thatcher's free-enterprise goals. Kureishi's London, their society, is the nexus of three separate communities—the distinct, similar, simultaneous, mutable, and unyielding white, Asian, and Anglo-Asian communities of London.

Kureishi's screenplay conveys the paradoxes and contradictions of today's multiculturalism. His characters' identities are no longer the simple national identities sketched in earlier stories and held by previous generations. Kureishi's characters must live in the postcolonial, conservative backlash of the self-serving entrepreneurism of Thatcher's 1980s recession. Omar, the object of prejudice, exploits other Pakistanis by impeding their assimilation, while also exploiting white Johnny in an ironic reflection of white oppression of Asians. The white street punks ostracize Johnny not for breaking the rules by entering into a homosexual relationship with an Asian, but for working for a "ginger" (slang for "Asian"). Johnny, under his ginger boss, simply cannot be permitted by his perennially unemployed white cronies to succeed beyond them. This low-class fraternity evokes Huck Finn's white-trash father, who insists that Huck honor his heritage by continuing the Finn family tradition of stupidity.

Johnny, whose parents were of the mods and rockers generation, has been disillusioned by post-Beatles British society. Like the rest of the post-psychedelic, youthful world of the 1980s, he has learned that the fantasy of becoming a rich, world-famous celebrity while remaining a drug-taking, fun-loving, working-class bloke won't come true for him. Kureishi's Johnny is caught in Thatcher's national void, where not only success, but fun—even employment—are beyond his grasp. If he is to rise from the crumbled Empire, he must look to immigrant Omar's dusky London world—he actually must root his white-boy survival in Kureishi's London.

Omar, on the other hand, enters his London world through everyday suburbia. Like the majority of London business people, his Uncle Nasser lives away from the city neighborhoods where he makes his success, in a comfortable, "typically English" suburban house. Omar is invited there, into an Asian inner sanctum—Nasser's bedroom—and into the traditional Asian society of his male elders. Among his cushions, giving orders from his bed, Nasser evokes the splendor of the Delacroix despot, Sardanapalus. It is he, not Papa, who now becomes the patriarch passing his wisdom on to Omar.

While Nasser and his men banter, Nasser's daughter nonchalantly strolls past the window and exposes her breasts. The inability of Nasser and his cronies to see past illusions, fantasies, prejudices, stereotypes, and traditions and to recognize reality is evoked in their failure to notice her display. The men are lost in memories of the past, blind to the scene right before their eyes.

Tania sees herself as more independent of Asian traditions than are any of the men courting Nasser in his chamber. Yet when she later chastises Nasser's aging white mistress, Rachel, for her dependent, dated relationship with her father, her independence is shown as an identity defined not by race, nor even by gender, but by Tania's contemporaneity. It is ironically rooted not in her Asian world but in the emerging new status of women that she, not Rachel, has gained by living in Rachel's London. Thus Tania and Rachel's differences are fundamentally of neither gender nor race; rather, they are of generation. Kureishi again blurs the lines between races and nationalities while identifying other overlapping divisions by gender and age.

The screenplay also uses family roles to highlight other ironic racial elements of Kureishi's new society. Using a third bedroom scene, Kureishi now puts uneducated white boy Johnny in Omar's place on Nasser's bed. Thus native son Johnny now becomes the newer immigrant banging on the door for entry into British prosperity and progress. Nasser, like some small-time Asian Don Corleone, can fulfill the peroxide-haired punker's wish if he promises to do Nasser "the favor [Johnny] can't refuse."

Nasser gives Johnny an order. To carry it out, and by so doing, to escape from the dead-end London world of his birth into Thatcher's private-enterprise world, Johnny must abuse other squatters and toughs from his own community. Nasser has already made it into this thriving private-enterprise world. Omar is already exploiting any "Pakis" standing in his way to success. And now, in order to have his share of the power too, Johnny must become Nasser's other dutiful son.

The irony in this skin-color bartering is most effective. This "racial boxing day" propels Kureishi's script. The gnawing rub of color and culture has now been felt by all of Kureishi's traditional communities. In Johnny and Omar's contemporary world, savagery appears necessary for whites and cannibalism appears necessary for Asians. Can black, gay, opportunist Omar and punk, traitor, victim Johnny, from inside the windows of their beautiful laundrette, make the view of their world outside seem better in one way or another? The romantic glory of social revolution seems to have been bludgeoned by the hopelessness of any genuine resolution.

Here, Kureishi again employs a characteristic device of viewing through glass. This stylistic recurs through the film as shots through windshield, washing machine, flat, garage, laundrette, and bedroom windows; likewise, rearview, apartment, office, and hotel mirrors abound. During the renovation of Powders, the window is soaped, the soaped glass obscuring the white street: thus, the neighborhood enemies of Omar (who hate his success but who are friends of, and support, Johnny), as well as the neighborhood friends of Omar (who support him but who hate Johnny) are all unseen. However, the soapy window not only confines the bigotries, it also shields the boys on the other side from view. In the film's key scene, Johnny and Omar finally reveal their beautiful laundrette and invite the neighborhood inside.

At the grand opening, Kureishi shows the crowd waiting outside on the sidewalk in front of the cleaned plate-glass window of Powders laundrette. The spectators watch and are watched by Nasser and Rachel, a pair of Anglo-Asian lovers in the laundrette. The audience sees not only the crowd and the lovers but also another pair of Anglo-Asian lovers—Omar and Johnny—hidden behind the darkened office window at the back of the laundrette. The glass windows thus divide three segments of the story and allow each segment to be viewed through boundaries by the audience.

The focus shifts from the crowd to the office at the back of the laundrette. Now suddenly in the foreground, Omar is shown to be in command behind the laundrette's darkened office windows. First he excoriates Johnny, listing the racial bigotries and treacheries of the white supremacist's youth. Then he strips Johnny down to his blue boxers, kissing him passionately. During their verbal and sexual intercourse that follows, seen by the viewer as it is reflected in the office windows, Omar and Johnny ironically see their reflection in the glass also. In addition, they can also see their sexual coupling figuratively reflected through that same window in the lovers who are dancing in the laundrette.

In the midground, those lovers, Rachel and Nasser, glide with their arms around each other like a couple at a fifties tea dance. As they spin between the spin-drying windows lining the walls of the laundrette, they are viewed through two walls of glass, one between them and the mixed-neighborhood crowds outside the storefront panes, and the other between them and the gay lovers dribbling champagne into each other's mouths behind their darkened office window. The similarities and duality of all the situations is, therefore, reflected in the gleaming windows—the laundrette window, the office window, and the rows of washing machine windows—and by the techniques of intercutting the pairs and overlapping the musical selections.

It is the dynamics of the situation, with these quicksilver shots, that galvanize the film. The story spin-cycles through working-class crowds, floating interracial ballroom dancers, and the sweaty kissing of Johnny and Omar. The sound rolls through lilting waltz-time music and Nasser's preposterously timed, "I must get Omar married," while bridegroom-to-be Omar silently mounts Johnny. Under Stephen Frears's direction, the movie scene spins, too, from street-dressed hooligans, to overdressed Rachel, to undressed Johnny. The film soars here, Frears spilling Kureishi's themes effortlessly into every frame. Director and screenwriter

Fig. 25. Inside the laundrette windows, Nasser (Saeed Jaffrey) and Rachel (Shirley Anne Field) dance to celebrate the grand opening of Powders in *My Beautiful Laundrette*. Meanwhile, while a crowd is kept waiting on the street outside, Omar and Johnny make love in the laundrette's darkened office. (Photo courtesy of Working Title Films, Ltd.)

turn technical tricks to achieve this scene, in which, as is the case throughout the film, Kureishi's unique perspective was maintained by Frears for the camera. Kureishi's story has been both written and told in cinematic terms.

Both couples are as romantic and as ridiculous as the blended score of lilting dance music and majestic classical chords. Both loving couples see each other and life, and are seen by and are hidden from each other by glass separations. Gender, race, and class, protagonist and antagonist, user and object—these are all roles too, slotted by Kureishi into their proper places among the glass partitions. Identity is seen through—and is protected by—liquid windows.

Nasser clearly sees Rachel as sexual entertainment, perhaps partly in order to feel racially accepted. "Speak my language," he gushes to her in an erotic romp early in the film. Rachel clearly sees being Nasser's mistress as a way to better herself, perhaps in order to persuade herself that she has made more of herself than she really thinks she has. In the same convolution, Omar sees Johnny as a sex object, and maybe sees mounting him as a way to assert himself against racial discrimination, while Johnny offers himself to Omar to fulfill his passion, perhaps also to feel love and be loved. Feminist issues, miscegenation, and gay awareness flash in his scenario, but because Kureishi is not interested in writing a tract on—or against—any of these issues, he creates instead real people in ambiguous, changing identities. Kureishi is interested in telling their story. "The bulk of *Laundrette*'s success goes to its uncompromising characterizations," wrote one film critic. "We come to all the Big Issues through a few charming but not necessarily good people and are thus spared the usual mandates and Messages. We are left alone to sort our laundry."[6] Left on their own as well, both of the movie's symbiotic couples function. It is when the confines of stereotypes are imposed upon them by society—from any perspective, be it color, gender, or class—that the pairings are seen to crumble.

Kureishi's decision to mix the races of partners in both love affairs illuminates his insight as an author and is a source of the film's strength. As a dancing couple, Rachel and Nasser break moral, racial, and economic taboos; they suffer from western and eastern, traditional and contemporary, gender and generational biases. As a rutting couple, Omar and Johnny are more superficially controversial; but as written the gay, dark, ambitious immigrant and the white, Nazi, homosexual hoodlum whom he exploits balance Kureishi's story. Ultimately, the guys and their adulterous elders are seen to have both "entirely new" and the "same old" problems, just as their separate identities and common human nature are conveyed when Johnny sees Omar's face behind the office glass over his own reflection in the glass. In this same shot, as Johnny fixes his bleached blonde hair in his reflection, he also fondles Omar's hair. Western and eastern bias, gender roles, and generational conflicts with tradition make what they are doing taboo. But because Kureishi makes his story not one of types, but rather one of individuals, he leads the audience to identify the shared truth in each of his character's individual circumstances.

"I was really uninhibited writing that film," Kureishi remembers. "It was as if I was starting to find my voice." Without the strong, clear narrative the film might easily falter as message. As it is, however, the movie is made by Kureishi's insistent message—namely, that a new national identity exists and must define and assert itself; it is an identity that lies beyond previous lines of class and culture, and that is in varying shades and tones of color, with no regard to race or sexual preference.

Kureishi's screenplay exhibits his balanced point of view, as do his other works. Kureishi suggests that running toward some monolithic enemy in the form of a multicultural society proves as dangerous today as did yesterday's running toward some stereotype of homogeneous nationalism. In other words, the process of redefinition is sometimes violent and is necessarily devastating, but its reality is inescapable. Kureishi writes of a variety of complicated characters—from a variety of communities—who illustrate that no grouping of people, whether it is by color, age, or any other variable, makes the members of that group anything other than *individuals* in a group. His stories end without finding easy resolution. Therefore, in all his writing, including in *My Beautiful Laundrette*, he does more than provide the stories with a plot, he creates their universe.

According to critic Colette Maud, "*My Beautiful Laundrette* is indeed a complex film, showing considerable economy and cohesion in the way it fuses its ideas. And Hanif Kureishi has certainly succeeded in his intentions . . . to create something different and difficult about contemporary London life."[7]

Kureishi's stylistic ambiguity elevates *My Beautiful Laundrette* from being a mere colorizing of identity-finding films of the past. He is able to write with humor about some painfully real, if tragic, and even pitiful, situations. He writes not what his characters stand for, but who they are. Kureishi creates a world that is true; he does not write to promote a world that is more to his liking.

Ironically, his objective awareness of individuals in his stories leads the filmgoer to appreciate Kureishi's underlying, universal truths: he is able to love the humanity of his characters even when he despises what they do. What he writes is, of course, entertainment with instruction: art. According to Kureishi himself,

A jejune protest or parochial literature, be it black, gay, or feminist, is no more desirable than works which do PR. What we need is imaginative writing that gives us a sense of the shifts within a whole society. If contemporary writing which emerges from oppressed groups ignores the central concerns and major conflicts of the larger society, it will automatically designate itself as minor, as a sub-genre. And it must not allow itself to be rendered invisible and marginalized in this way. In similar fashion, the problem of race in England is in danger of being marginalized when it must be seen as central.[8]

My Beautiful Laundrette is a first film and a new kind of film. The screenplay does not seek to solve society's inequalities. It sometimes muddies contemporary multicultural society. The writer rarely misses a chance for a magnificent line or incident, sometimes at the expense of characterization. But its successes are staggering. The writing avoids the trend of politically correct oversimplification: Bad and good are never exclusively one skin tone or another. Both comic and tragic elements make up the lives of people, real people, with strengths as well as failings. Kureishi thus recognizes a fundamental diversity among every cosmopolitan community.

Providing a view through a window, as novelist Henry James imaged the artistic point of view, the artist compels each of us to look beyond our reflections and see our needs and fears. Kureishi's frames are filled with burlesque Asian Indians, families, corrupt "Pakis," homosexuals, adulterers, punk Eastenders, entrepreneurs, gangs, ascetics, fascists, racist police, love, laughter, and rock 'n' roll. He argues that "you want a movie to be wilder and dirtier and kind of rough and cheap—and defiant as well."[9] Kureishi makes us look through a window and see that society, if clearly changing, is still far from perfect. He does not promise contentment, and he neither gives his apology nor seeks ours. Kureishi gives us truth. He leaves the conclusions to us. Critics of *My Beautiful Laundrette* have applauded the daring of his truths and, as immediately, have praised the excellence of the filmscript. One of them, Vincent Canby, wrote:

My Beautiful Laundrette has the broad scope and the easy pace that one associates with our best theatrical films. It puts its own truth above the fear of possibly offending someone. Without showing off, it has courage as well as artistry. There are moments when key narrative points are obscure, and when characters behave in a way that has been dictated not by plausibility but [by] the effect it will create. Towards the end, it threatens to fall apart. It doesn't. *My Beautiful Laundrette* is a fascinating, eccentric, very personal movie.[10]

Kureishi's critically successful first novel, *The Buddha of Suburbia*, deals with defining national identities as well. This personal novel portrays the differing attitudes that isolate immigrants Anwar and Haroon from each other and from other Asians. Kureishi makes further distinctions between the different attitudes of newer immigrants from India and those who, like Haroon's son, Karim, immigrated to London from no farther away than the suburbs. He also looks at differing attitudes between generations—between, for example, Anwar's daughter, Jamila, and Jamila's mother, the Princess Jeeta—as well as at gender-related differences, as evidenced in Karim and Jamila's commitment to politics. Kureishi further stresses Asian diversity by bringing Changez from Bombay as a husband for Jamila, involving him with a Japanese prostitute, moving him into a commune with his wife, her baby, and her female lover, and, at the story's end, seating him next to Karim's brother, Allie, a hairnet-wearing fop, at a fashionable Soho restaurant where they have gathered to celebrate Karim's casting in a TV soap opera.

White London society is as complicated. Haroon leaves his quiet white wife for white Eva Kay, a veteran of a failed marriage and breast cancer. First a promoter of Haroon's transcendental meditation gatherings in the suburbs, the indomitable Eva becomes a self-ordained decorator, interviewed for the Sunday magazine sections of London newspapers. The novel also follows Eva's son Charlie, a rock 'n' roll idol, from the suburbs through his entry into "glam" and punk music in London and then into sadomasochism in New York. Among other characters followed by the novel are: Helen's bigoted father who despises her black friends; Uncle Ted, a mild-mannered, middle-aged, blue-collar suburbanite with a blue-haired, alcoholic wife; Eleanor, who irons in the nude; assorted neurotic actors, groupies, socialists, and communists; and a wife-swapping au courant stage director.

In fact, the diversity among characters in the novel, which portrays a range of white, Asian, and Anglo-Asian characters and their involvements, proves beyond question the artificiality of old national identities. But it is in its particularly brilliant attempt to distinguish between color and culture and in its send-up of cultural poseurs that the novel dually distinguishes itself among Kureishi's works in redefining a British identity.

Kureishi is never more biting nor more outrageously amusing than he is in *The Buddha of Suburbia*. In the latter part of the novel, Karim is drawn into a theater group's improvisation. The group's shaping of characters is a plot device to treat the redefinition of racial and national identities. Quite brilliantly, Kureishi has already introduced this complicated issue as early as in the novel's opening lines, and has involved his readers wholeheartedly in it through his hilarious description of Karim's sexual exploits.

The young actor has already been sexually involved with Charlie, Helen, Helen's dog, and Jamila, has flirted with card-carrying actor friend Terry, has fantasized with his dad's mistress, Eva, and will shortly bed Eleanor and be involved with her in group sex with Pyke and his wife, Marlene. As Karim expresses it in the novel, "It would be heart-breaking to have to choose between one [sex] and another, like having to decide between the Beatles and the Rolling Stones." When the actors begin their improvisation session by talking about the political implications of the racial identities of their sexual partners, Karim realizes that he would "fuck anything," as Kureishi has already made obvious to his readers.

In all of its comic episodes, an indictment of racism is at the center of this novel. In the words of one reviewer, "The question of how a brown person lives in a racist society dominates the book and may be answered in two words: *Screw You*."[11] Color and culture confusion is the crux of its racial theme.

Kureishi's racial issue takes on life when he portrays actors who invent identities for the theatrical characters they will play on stage and Tracey, a black actress, accuses Karim of a racist portrayal of his Uncle Anwar. She tells Karim that his characterization of Asians demeans his black identity. Tracey defines black politically: Anyone who is not white in a racist society is black. The actress is certainly right. In the London of *The Buddha of Suburbia*, power, values, economics, and art are all part of a white person's world.

Karim insists that he is portraying one specific Asian for his stage character and further clarifies that he has included the hunger strike not because it is a stereotypically black action, but because it is a fact. He insists that it attests to Anwar's selfish machinations to control his daughter. Line by line in the novel, Karim responds to the charge of Tracey's words as signs, not as symbols, and as descriptors, not as political tract. Karim insists that his monologue represents truth. Tracey counters that it is only white man's truth.

Finally, in the television adaptation, Karim's answer comes directly from a line from his novel's earlier exposition: Karim declares that he's not black, he's beige. As a buzzword of political language and in the jargon of racial politics, Karim sees "black" as being an unacceptable term to use on himself. He thus chooses to use the color purely in its skin-tone connotation: as a half-British Caucasian, Karim is merely slightly darker in hue than other Englishmen. And he is right—isn't his color the only thing that separates him from them? Karim is, in his own assessment in the novel's opening paragraph, "a proper Englishman. Almost."

The satire is again unbounded, as the reviewer for the *New York Times* noted: "The writer has skewered practically every target in sight in *Buddha*, including suburban social climbers, artistic poseurs, upper-class intellectual twits, Rolls-Royce liberals, scabrous working class heroes and, once again, England's Asian and black immigrants."[12] Never flinching from facing the oppression of racism in *The Buddha of Suburbia*, Kureishi also tackles with as much gusto the misconceptions and silliness of pompous multicultural awareness on the other side. And scrutiny reveals that his satire of these characters targets their heavy-handed quest for the relevancy of crosscultural issues. Here, instead of writing about the racism he abhors that segregates society, now Kureishi lambastes an assimilation of cultures based merely on patronizing trends that reinforce the stereotypes of nation and race.

He mocks the idea, for instance, that because Karim is Asian, he must de facto practice meditation, in the same way that for his dad, Muslim civil servant Haroon, his race demands that he must be a bona fide Buddhist ascetic. Karim assures Charlie that of course he meditates daily and that he does chant—albeit not every day—while thinking of the actual, far more pedestrian, morning rituals of his family's suburban lifestyle. Likewise, Haroon guides his followers down the path to wisdom, even though "Dad can't even find his way to Beckenham."

Fashion and makeup, too, identify characters. Eva wears kohl and Oriental fragrances; she dances like Isadora Duncan, with a scarf that she sometimes drapes over her lamps to get the necessary Oriental glow. Her actions make her appear either the "most sophisticated . . . or the most pretentious" person Karim has ever seen. In turn, Eva finds Karim's costume, headband and all, so very "exotic." Karim, on the other hand, sees his father, Haroon, dressed in his Indian pajamas, as "certainly exotic, probably the only man in southern England at that moment (apart, possibly, from George Harrison) so attired."

Decor also has individual bite in Kureishi's story. As a self-ordained interior decorator, Eva Kay must meditate to find just the right color paint a space demands. And Kureishi sends up almost every excess transmitted from east to west in his portrayal of the barefoot Carl and Marianne's suburban transcendental gathering. Heavily influenced by incense, they open their minds—and their doors—to Haroon's teachings. The suburban white couple's house is more ornate than the Kapaleeswarar Temple at Mylapore with "its sandalwood Buddhas, brass ashtrays and striped plaster elephants which decorated every available space." It is here that Helen encounters the exotic Karim; seeking knowledge of his foreign origin, she is informed that his fascinating immigrant roots lie in Bromley. Karim overhears Carl sagely identifying "two sorts of people in the world—those who have been to India and those who haven't," before he is forced to move out of earshot.

Under the hilarity of Kureishi's indictment of these cultural stereotypes lies an awareness of the necessity for nations to wake up and see who they now are. His yuppie and buppie characters are from a different age than the characters who populated Kipling's colonial Asia. But more to the point, they are a generation after the Beatles had gone to see the Maharishi in India. At the same time that they are called upon to recognize Kureishi's scathing portraits of yesterday's stereotypes, readers are also asked to realize what is real today. There must be a new definition of today's national identities, just as Kureishi's attitude toward his characters and telling their stories is new.

Throughout his career critics may have disagreed on how to get a handle on Kureishi's attitude, but they have agreed that it is new and different. Film critic Stanley Kauffmann has noted that Kureishi's attitude in creating the downwardly mobile characters in *Sammy and Rosie Get Laid* is blatantly different, right from his choice of the film's title:

The very title of the Frears-Kureishi film marks the difference. That title is right, not because it revels in latter-day permissiveness but because, almost offhandedly, it takes that permissiveness for granted. It seems even better afterward because it signals how much we have won and not won in the last 30 years and because in fact it celebrates obliqueness. A new sidewise sophistication, says the title, is now the best way for art to approach ancient troubles.[13]

Yet most critics of the same film completely misread Kureishi's "new sophistication" when appraising class and race in his stories and Kauffmann's "ancient troubles" of identity—as well as his literary techniques. That they have continued to use yesterday's criteria in their appraisal of this film is clear in one critic's grafting of the last generation's term *radical chic* onto Kureishi's story:

When Seymour Karim first used this term in his 1962 essay in the *Village Voice*, and, later, when Tom Wolfe used it, it had narrow, derisive—moneyed—overtones. It referred to the fashionable people who took up the cause of the oppressed—people who were susceptible to manipulation by those who made them feel guilty. *Sammy and Rosie* is so deeply unfocused that it doesn't do much except demonstrate that by now radical chic, as a set of attitudes, extends almost inevitably to the "oppressed" themselves, when they're hip and educated and angry.[14]

Far from failing to "do much," this film actually benchmarks the hybrid elements of Kureishi's storytelling. Kureishi dismisses previous stipulative definitions as dated. Refusing to define individuals by race, he is sensitive to the manipulations of class, gender, and economics masquerading under yesterday's racial buzzwords. The inclusion of characters' failures and idiosyncracies hampers the creation of stereotypical good guys and bad guys out of Kureishi's characters. Removing the staged conflict between two artificially defined sides clouds a conventional, dramatic resolution.

Resolution would be based on a society that could be divided into *them* and *us* by exclusive divisions in terms of color, culture, or class.

Kureishi's writing treats today's world as it is, rather than as it is defined by yesterday's maps or seen in yesterday's movies. This demands the inclusion of this urban society: the pseudo-intellectuals who haunt urban landscapes from Bombay to New York City, from London to Buenos Aires—anywhere the media reaches.

Kureishi, therefore, portrays not yesterday's "radical chic" of the flower-power age, but the *reverse chic*—members of the powerful new society of the information age. His reverse-chic characters are involved in today's generation's struggle to free itself from middle-class ethics, "getting down" by going down to the streets. Kureishi's urban groups splinter and re-ally themselves no longer by age, gender, or race, but by their common disinterest in money and education—which they already have; that is, they ally themselves by being lower class—by playing lower class, without the tears. These characters in reality have as much interest in moving down to another class as they do in moving out to a new country, and as much real sympathy for "the third world" as for enduring a boring weekend. "We can't let a bit of torture interfere with a party," Sammy determines after hearing that his father, newly arrived from Pakistan and the guest of honor at a forthcoming party, is a murdering despot. The characters are into the art of social revolution—they have Virginia Woolf posters, they photograph riots. Sammy explains to Rafi while he walks London's burning streets that if he lived today, "Leonardo Da Vinci would have lived in the inner city."

Including the genuinely artificial limousine liberals and savvy minorities who gentrify city neighborhoods rounds out this story's transcendence of previous literary conventions. Merely using a new patronizing terminology to continue yesterday's stereotyping must be relinquished: Sammy is aware that "not all pricks are male," that not all the masters are western, and that not all the victims are noble or immigrants. The characters do not permit artificial division by yesterday's morals and geography into roles of class and race. They are the fabric of Kureishi's newly envisioned nationals.

Kureishi's cavalcade of cosmopolites targets Asians, British, Anglo-Asians, transsexuals, homosexuals, heterosexuals, bisexuals, transvestites, womanizers, drug pushers, punks, whores, artists, academics, sexists, racists, feminists, professionals, revisionists and reformers, and even visitors, whether they are tourists or exiled despots. What the characters have in common—indeed, sometimes the only thing they have in common—is their residence—whether permanent or temporary, long-standing or new—in a city.

Kureishi's reliance on urban experiences is well illustrated in his journal entries published with the script of *Sammy and Rosie Get Laid*, and in which he frequently records his impressions of cities. Of course, along with the astute observations of the cities themselves, his perceptions carry some weighty social commentary and a peek into his process of composition.

In Milan he finds that the stained-glass windows of a massive Gothic church "resemble the frames of a film." Leaving the train station on his arrival in Venice, Kureishi is swept up in the frenzy of Carnival. He writes: "They dance all night in St. Mark's Square and fall to the ground where they sleep beneath people's feet until morning. Looking at the bridges, I wonder how they don't collapse under the weight of people." In Florence, he takes in his fellow travelers on a train, and observes "the fast and comfortable Italian trains and the businessmen around me in their sharp clothes. The care they take: everything matches; not a garment is worn or shapeless."[15]

In Manhattan Kureishi records in his diary that he has spotted a laundromat named My Beautiful Laundrette from a taxi window. It is abandoned. When Kureishi bravely continues his urban exploration by riding the New York subway, he observes the other passengers and notes that young people in New York are "far less eccentric, original and fashionable than kids are in Britain . . . Here the kids are sartorial corpses. They all wear sports clothes." He recoils at the utter bad taste of American women in their preposterous uniforms of "business suits and running shoes."

The diary records immediate impressions of sunny Los Angeles as well: "LA is blazingly green and bright; how easy it is to forget . . . that this industry town is also sub-tropical; its serious and conservative business takes place among palm trees, exotic birds and preternaturally singing flowers. Everything is resplendent as if I'd taken LSD." Later Kureishi's brush with tinseltown on his Oscar awards trip would spur him to invent a story's plot as he rode the city's streets with one of "several young producers":

One drives me around the city in his Jag. He asks me if I want to fly to San Francisco for lunch. I ask if there isn't anywhere a little nearer we can go. He swears eternal love and a contract. An idea for a story: of someone who inadvertently writes a successful film and lives off it for years, so afraid of ending the shower of financial seductions and blandishments that he never writes anything again.

As an author, it is Kureishi's custom, if an unusual one, to observe cosmopolitan experience and to write with an awareness of the multiplicity of his interpretations. He does not determine a single political agenda from which to evaluate the urban message; this integrity is at the root of his style. The author not only sees a new society composed of individual characters; he relishes the contradictions of their cosmopolitan milieu.

In fact, in bold strokes throughout his stories, Kureishi writes about the city of London as a favorite and essential figure. His presentation of London elevates it from merely providing a setting to actually being a character. Kureishi's personification of London both demonstrates his techniques and illuminates his aesthetics.

As with his other characterizations, his balanced depiction of London ironically both stresses that city's individuality and underscores the universality of city today. Kureishi relentlessly criticizes London for its failures without forfeiting for a moment his great love for the metropolis. This high regard is conveyed as characters ride the Jubilee tube line, dine at Le Caprice, or wander the Portobello market stalls. He employs his characters' relationships with the city and London's relationship with them. His glittering use of contemporary London was noted in a review of his TV adaptation of *The Buddha of Suburbia*, according to which, "The new London scene with its chaotic international flavor, its suburban crassness, and its frenzied pop culture, has seldom been celebrated with such humor and energy."[16]

A montage in *Sammy and Rosie Get Laid* may most dramatically illustrate both Kureishi's intentions in using London in his redefinition of yesterday's racial and national identities, and his mastery at doing so. Kureishi telegraphs images that capture his city. That is, the montage suggests speed and fluidity as shots quickly pass before the camera, accompanied by Sammy's tributes and asides. Beneath one shot, for instance, Sammy narrates, "Or we trot past the Albert Hall." And the first shot in the montage of Rosie and Sammy, scored with lilting travelogue music under scenes of their romantic London, is accompanied by Sammy's message that "on Saturdays we like to walk along the towpath at Hammersmith and kiss and argue." Using voice-over gives the film montage a personal narrative tone. This film technique seeks to transfer the intimacy and believability that is captured by using the first-person point of view in prose.

Moreover, it conveys feelings about London. It is thus easy to imagine hearing not Sammy but Kureishi behind the images. In fact, while making the film, Kureishi wrote about his attraction to London in the published diary: "My love and fascination for inner London endures. Here there is fluidity and possibilities unlimited. Here it is possible to avoid your enemies; here everything is available . . . Heraclitus said, 'You can't step in the same river twice.' In the inner-city you can barely step in the same street twice, so rapid is human and environmental change." The rapidity and juxtaposition of the montage's shots convey Kureishi's ever-changing metropolis as there wash across the screen scenes in cabarets and classrooms, bursts of spring flowers, and the recognizable facade of the Royal Court Theatre, a London sight that is part of Kureishi's personal history.

After all, London is what the author knows. More importantly, London is the actual source of his stories. "[Being a Londoner has] really to do with the place that provides me with stories," Kureishi explains. "I have more people in London, people I need to meet and need to be with. And I understand them. I understand what they are saying. I understand their class, their place in society, so I can write about them. I need that. I understand London."

From the Ivy to the ICA, London illuminates ambiguity in Kureishi's stories. The montage in *Sammy and Rosie Get Laid*, for example, filled as it is with actual locations and lovingly focused as it is on his city, stylistically also includes sights and sounds with contradictory, negative qualities. Throughout the montage, Kureishi's writing plays on the genuine charm of his images while he satirizes them. This balance of perspective imbues London with the same undeniable truth and falsity that he finds to love and ridicule in his other characters.

Again the montage—

The shot: Lovers walking the towpath toward Hammersmith. The scene is beautiful. Voice-over narration tells they "kiss and argue." London is romantic, enlightened.

The shot: Sammy and Rosie doing bookstores together. They share books— "written by women." How equal, how trendy.

The shot: Albert Hall in the spring. Travelogue. Nature and city. A bough of pink blossoms.

The shot: The Royal Court Theatre. Historical. An insider's reference—this is where Kureishi himself wrote.

The shot: Alternative cabaret in Earl's Court. Political. "If there's nothing on that hasn't been well received by the *Guardian*," qualifies Sammy with that critical stance of people in the know . . . Satiric, affected.

The shot: Seminar at the ICA. Anti-intellectual. A rapt audience gets lost in the buzz words of the gentrified, pseudo intellectual. And loves it.

The montage portrays Kureishi's London. His preeminent and preposterous modern cultural center supports both the simplistic trends and the genuinely progressive inclinations of his Londoners. Sammy and Rosie are cutting-edge aware; they live in London, a world capital. As surely, their London is a laughable, loveable urban trap. Thus when Sammy and Rosie define their identity, it is as today's new cosmopolites. "We love our city and we belong to it," Sammy proclaims. "Neither of us are English, we're Londoners you see."

Irony is further enhanced in the montage. Rafi has suggested to his son that he move to Pakistan, Sammy's "homeland" which he has never seen, to be part of a family and nation which he's never known. Sammy argues that he wants to remain in London, the only home he has ever known, with Rosie, the only family he has ever known. Narrating the montage as his answer to Rafi, his father and the ultimate chauvinist, Sammy discovers his hybrid citizenry.

Like Kureishi, Sammy identifies with London, with cosmopolitanism, not with Pakistani or British nationalism. Kureishi as clearly distinguishes between London and the rest of the country as he does between

Asia and Britain. His story makes it equally clear that Sammy's romantic travelogue city—the historical city of Dr. Johnson—and Rosie's burning cityscape of urban violence are one. Accepting the myriad individual images of today's London paradoxically provides the city with its one cohesive, identifiable definition: It is all contemporary London.

London is an apt metaphor for the new national identity that Kureishi defines. It is both assimilation and separation, genesis and tradition. Resulting from the acceptance of multiple realities, Kureishi is a contemporary author who gives his stories endings that are both happy and sad. He sees that in each ending is a beginning, that success and failure are in constant flux. His characters redefine British national identity, in the context of an evolving world identity.

Living with paradox is necessary to explain race and class in today's culture. Accepting inherent paradox is necessary for an appreciation of Kureishi's aesthetic. His is a hybrid point of view for a time in which yesterday's generalizing—especially about race, gender, and culture—has been exposed as inaccurate and limited, and has become consistently painful.

afterword

KUREISHI'S STORYTELLING
Liquid Windows

Popular response to Kureishi has not yet moved beyond initially reacting to his work with hyphenated cultural descriptors. After more than a decade, however, critical response to Kureishi appears to be moving toward an expanded perspective. He neither accepts nor acknowledges making cultural descriptors into literary criticism. Kureishi has not only survived his Anglo-Asian labeling, he has made use of the reputation it helped create. This is, indeed, one of his achievements—that he has not allowed his work to be confined to the mold that had been defined for it either by popular perception or by critics; instead, he has achieved critical recognition of his perspective as a new English perspective, and thereby he has demanded recognition of today's new national hybrid identities.

Kureishi keeps his distance. He creates a complicated fictional universe in which mutability is inevitable. Incidents are blatantly biased in racial, sexual, cultural, political, and gender-related ways. But they are defined by the way in which they occur, by each character's response to them. As to whether he identifies the cause of the brutal fate of his characters, however, a critic of Kureishi's *Sammy and Rosie Get Laid* bemoaned nearly ten years ago, "You can't tell: the movie-makers seem to think they're just looking at the passing parade."[1] He avoids both old stereotypical and trendy revisionist motivation for his characters. He presents them and their stories with affection and without reverence. Fundamentally, Hanif Kureishi is a storyteller. That is, he is devoted not to promoting politics, propaganda, or popularity, but to "telling my story, writing the truth, to entertainment." He continues, "Obviously, entertainment in art must include instruction."

But he refuses to require manipulation of his characters' reality and thus continues to irritate his detractors. This refusal has remained characteristic of his work, and has been evident in his work, including the screenplay of *London Kills Me*, which he directed himself, and in his plays, screenplays, novels, and short stories; in all of these, the sole responsibility for that ambiguity is his. Pointedly, the absence of plot resolution, which results from his refusal to pass judgment and from his fascination with life's passing parade, continues to be an element of his writing that some critics find infuriating. This approach led to his television adaptation of *The Buddha of Suburbia* being damned by the critics, one of whom wrote, "in keeping with the drama's disparate approach to storytelling, there's no conventional plot resolution."[2]

His comic fiction satirizes politics, culture, art, media, and other contemporary issues. References and allusions thus often demand knowledge of current and historical events or a familiarity with literary classics. Kureishi further expands the range of his comic material by juxtaposing comic events with serious ones; that is, some fictional incidents become funny by their context. Still other material is drawn from humor's lowest level: the sexual reference, the preposterous slapstick antic, the punchline joke.

While maintaining a distance from his narrative, the author nonetheless envisions it from a specific character's eyes. Many of his characters relate their world flamboyantly. In "With Your Tongue down My Throat," for example, the storyteller blatantly plays a trick on his readers to underscore the divisions among realities, stories, and perceptions. He draws attention to the artfulness of his creation. Here he flaunts, through first overtly identifying, and then changing, his first-person narrator, the fact that any story is a fiction framed by its point of view. Irony further separates characters' subjective visions of their worlds from the world Kureishi creates around them. In *The Buddha of Suburbia*, his first-person narrator spends as much time qualifying his remarks, questioning his perceptions, and contradicting himself as he does telling the story. Karim Amir seeks to make a place in the theatrical London that he sees and also takes his place in the novel's London that Kureishi writes.

As they do in his first-person narratives, contradictions also underlie Kureishi's third-person stories. In *The Black Album*, for example, he writes about the violent conflict between religious fundamentalism and western society. The conflict between religion and politics is paramount to the novel, but issues of race, exile, immigration, and generation expand the story of Shahid's search for identity. In "My Son The Fanatic," too, revisionism and assimilation collide. Like his second novel, this short story and its film adaptation portray today's paradoxical demand to maintain individualism yet be integrated into society.

Stories widen to include incidents other than those of simple plot exposition, running several narrative lines. For Kureishi, therefore, ending a story does not conclude it. *My Beautiful Laundrette* ends, for example, with the ambitious Omar gaining a business and bed partner. The Asian entrepreneur playfully splashes his beautiful white lover as the film draws to a close, but Omar never finds a solution to the homophobia or to the cultural or racial prejudice he endures outside the laundrette's window. In the final shots of Kureishi's next film, *Sammy and Rosie Get Laid*, the London riots, racial prejudice, and police brutality, as well as Sammy and Rosie's marriage, are left unresolved. Both Clint Eastwood in *London Kills Me* and Karim Amir in *The Buddha of Suburbia* and its television adaptation are last seen in London restaurants, having been successful in their efforts to gain status. Awash in the Puritan ethic, Clint finds a niche announcing today's sun-dried tomatoes and gorgonzola specials to trendy diners whom Kureishi would later describe as flaunting "more pony tails than at Ascot." But Clint finds no happy ending. Nor does becoming a TV soap-opera star fulfill the needs that, according to Kureishi, underlie Karim's melancholy. Karim is last seen as his youthful innocence, like his decade of raunchy freedom, is submerged in the conservative, racist policies of Margaret Thatcher's England. In "My Son the Fanatic," Parvez avoids Fundamentalist threats as, drink in hand, he listens to music in the house now deserted by his wife and son, and is immersed in his adulterous affair with a white prostitute. As he juggles plot incidents, Kureishi balances elements in his stories, which contain both the comic and the tragic, the appealing and the unappealing, the just and the unfounded, leaving resolution of a story too close to call.

In his novels and his film writing, therefore, he creates an ensemble of characters in overlapping narratives. Because Kureishi rejects the labeling of his characters as heroes or villains, they both propel and frustrate the ambiguous action of his stories. "I don't think that I think in

Fig. 26. Sammy (Ayub Khan Din) is oblivious to the riots outside his window as Schubert's lieder *Erlkonig* blares in his headphones in *Sammy and Rosie Get Laid*. (Photo courtesy of Working Title Films, Ltd.)

that way," he says in reference to this characteristic. "I start off writing characters, . . . and then I play with them. I allow them to move into different directions. So the idea of heroes or antiheroes, I don't see things in that way at all . . . I don't make judgments about my characters." He includes threads in his plots that wind through different patterns of integration as they continue to spin. In his short stories, in which the form limits the number of plot incidents, the characters themselves evidence contradictory weaknesses and strengths. In his longer works, the contradictions in the narratives come not to resolution but to a nexus.

Grafted contradictions are the corollaries of his contemporary culture. Refusing to arrange his stories to prove a point or make a case, Kureishi presents the complications of contemporary social and human paradoxes with honesty—even with relish. Thus, the suburban seventies families of *The Buddha of Suburbia* flounder in the middle-class superficiality of their times; the eighties characters of *Sammy and Rosie Get Laid* deal with establishing an urban society in the gentrified next decade; and in contemporary England of the nineties, the assimilated

Asian taxi driver of "My Son the Fanatic" beats his son for having adopted the radical position of returning to their ancient religious traditions.

Frequent pop-culture references are made: rock tunes blare; fashion and fashion trends are catalogued throughout; and popular restaurants in London's West End color the fiction. Classic Hollywood films such as *The Wizard of Oz* and the cult classic *Performance* are alluded to; lost-generation elite F. Scott Fitzgerald and Ernest Hemingway are mentioned; aristocrats Lord and Lady ("Dickie" and Edwina) Mountbatten appear—though, of course, in Kureishi, the term "majesty" indicates rock 'n' roll, not traditional monarchy. Thus, it is (the formerly named) Prince, member of rock royalty, and not the last viceroy, who comes nearest to being the hyphenated-everything hero in Kureishi's fiction. Elvis, however, remains the king.

Contradictions abound. Community both bonds and segregates. Individualism is sought in our urban society, but the city neighborhood becomes the fin-de-siècle family. The author borrows from actual historical events, such as Bill Grundy's London chat-show interview of the Sex Pistols in the seventies and the *fatwa* on author Salman Rushdie in the eighties, to give his fiction the trappings of the real world. He arranges real street names, names pubs, and identifies public transportation tube lines in London to create his otherwise fictional setting.

Historical reality becomes a device in the fiction. Kureishi understands the importance of incidents not as factual record but as reflections of social, cultural, and historical attitudes. Commenting on this aspect of Kureishi's work, Kevin Loader, who produced the television adaptation of *The Buddha of Suburbia*, says, "You've read [Kureishi's essay 'Eight Arms to Hold You']. That is a brilliant piece of work. Music is very important to understand what is going on. But of course Hanif is not merely writing about music. Kureishi doesn't get enough credit for understanding British culture as shrewdly as he does."[3]

The inclusion of his previous fiction in his later work to enhance setting also becomes important in the storytelling. Fictional characters Karim Amir and Charlie Hero, both from *The Buddha of Suburbia*, turn up as referents in his next novel, *The Black Album*. As London restaurants Le Caprice and Alastair Little are mentioned to support the recognizable urban tone of this novel, so too Charlie Hero, *The Buddha of Suburbia*'s rock star, is incorporated in the fictional universe of the novel in the following passage: "Shops were selling T-shirts, cheap jewelry, belts, bags, wispy Indian-print scarves. Ex-students with pink mohicans and filthy dogs stood at small street-stalls selling bundles of incense and bootlegs of The Dead, Charlie Hero, Sex Pistols." And in another passage, fictional actor Karim Amir is named as one of Zulma and Chili's celebrated London set: "The two of them went to dinner with . . . film producers like Ishmail Merchant and fashionable actors like Karim Amir, with whom [Zulma] was photographed by the Daily Mail."

Historical reality is by no means Kureishi's interest, as Kureishi is not a historian. History is simply used to give credence to his fictional universe, the specificity of such material enhancing his fictional world. This sense of historical reality is a classic comic convention. The storyteller explains his process:

[The Black Album] happens to be based about a real event, so then is The Buddha of Suburbia set in a real time with real clothes and real history as well. That doesn't mean that I was somehow writing a book about the affairs of Satanic Verses. I want to avoid this being seen as a book about the burning of Satanic Verses as much as I want to avoid Buddha being seen as a book about David Bowie. I write fiction, stories about someone somewhere, fiction, not history books.

As our world has expanded into a global society, so, ironically, the search for identity and individualism by every group or member of this society has become more pressing. Complicating this worldwide phenomenon, continuing gentrification has made some members of urban society grasp more tenaciously at their traditions. Progress has gone hand in hand with decay. Poverty, drug use, violence, and crime are rampant in our modern world. It is this urban paradox that Kureishi's audience has assimilated, and Kureishi continues to draw from the events/legends that make up contemporary experience. London has become the fiction's ironic microcosm of a global community, divided and overlapping. Thus Kureishi does not merely set stories in London; he creates stories about his London.

More recently, violence is frequently and graphically portrayed. Thus, the existence of violence is at the foundation of Kureishi's stories. From the racially motivated attack in the play Outskirts to the fundamentalist riots in My Son the Fanatic, violence plays a cardinal role in the urban society that he creates. The message is that violence happens and is assimilated; it is inescapable. Kureishi explains:

I don't find violence interesting or eternal or in any way particular . . . There is so much unemployment . . . there is so much despair. People use racism as their excuse, don't they? They say, "You Pakis are taking our jobs!" "You Pakis are taking our houses!" They are unable to understand where that poverty is really coming from. If you live in London's East End, and there are little skinheads and tough lads around on the street beating up people, racial attacks in the East End wouldn't be surprising. They are inevitable.

In his use of violence, Kureishi employs his ironic sense of humor to stylistically underplay it, and thus more frighteningly to mirror the indifference of today's brutal society. Violence in *Sammy and Rosie Get Laid*, for example, is counterpointed with a sense of the ridiculous inconsistency that daily violence plays as part of our world. This makes violence, consequently, the staged subject of a coffee-table book of photographs. Despot Rafi writes a postcard to his friends in Pakistan in which he flaunts urban violence, and inspects with disgust the homemade weapons Sammy nonchalantly uses to protect his city home from attack. Sammy refuses to cancel a party simply because his guest of honor is a torturer, and curses Rosie's liberal tolerance of city violence as the rightful expression of social unrest when it includes trashing his car. The third-world tyrant quietly hangs himself in his son's London flat as Rosie and a group of enlightened Englishwomen chat about women's rights in an adjoining room.

At root, violence in Kureishi is the province of both sexes, every race, and all ages. It is the subject of treatises and discussions by educators, aging hippies, and limousine liberals, as well as the recourse of Fundamentalists, students, and street gangs. And violence flares up without reason or consistency. It is terroristic, ill-directed, and random. It is often the law of the streets and as often the conduct of families. In *My Beautiful Laundrette*, Uncle Nasser's old-country wife uses her black magic to raise welts on the stomach of her husband's white mistress, Johnny throws an old black artist's possessions after him onto the street to "unscrew" his flat, and white toughs beat up the "Paki-loving" white

Johnny while Salim stands in his posh western flat crushing his bare foot into the face of his Pakistani nephew.

Incongruity intensifies the impact of the violence. It also gives the violence its contemporary context. The violence appears without introduction, exposition, or explanation, Kureishi relying on his audience's cognizance of our violent world just as he relies on its recognition of musical or cinematic references. He simply includes the daily barbarism which is part of our society. His stories relate violence as matter-of-factly as it is treated in the pasteurized, programmed bloodletting on the nightly TV news. Violence is utterly in the open, without any excuse and without any pretense of reason.

He ends his narratives without having rationalized the violence. Characters are spectators to violent events; sometimes they even take part in the violent events, but because of the framing of the stories, as well as their humor, distance is still maintained. The charming Rafi tells us quite matter-of-factly in *Sammy and Rosie Get Laid* that until a man commits murder he is a virgin. *The Black Album*'s Shahid rides the tube during the Victoria station tube bombing, a random act of terrorism that is a media event as the body-bag count of innocent commuters mounts. A bookshop disaster results in the senseless maiming of youthful zealots, who firebomb themselves—"film at eleven."

Kureishi laces his stories with music, sex, and drugs among the yuppies, buppies, immigrants, fundamentalists, feminists, racists, idealists, terrorists, and families who are his characters. Cruelty, integrity, and hilarity commingle in his fictional incidents. An Anglo-Asian author in London, Kureishi has known racial prejudice from both sides and has also distinguished himself in both communities. He is sufficiently well grounded in literary traditions to be able successfully to break from them. His is the perspective of the increasingly vocal new nationalist. And it is his hyphenated perspective, both in its similarities to and its differences from his readers' perspectives, that is essential—and unique—to his storytelling.

He respects stories and understands their place in and importance to culture. He knows storytelling in its literary context, and his fiction continues the literary tradition of England, building on the conventions that have come before it and writing in traditional genres; his humor, too, has a foundation in English storytelling. But to brand him as an English comic writer distorts his aesthetic. His social criticism has a similar foundation, but the incidents that he criticizes are new and, like his sense of humor, more mutable and more flamboyant. In terms of his hybrid stance, however, Hanif Kureishi is unprecedented in English letters, although his style has evolved out of the tradition. He is a postcolonial storyteller—he redefines English national identities. That is, his storytelling remains traditional but is unique. The language is quicksilver; the point of view is objective and observational; the vehicle is humor and tragedy; the images are new and renewed images from film, history, and legend; mass media and rock 'n' roll swirl throughout his global storytelling.

Kureishi's Anglo-Asian point of view is new in its own right. He is at a crossroads of contemporary attitudes that is unique, a place where controversial writing now manages to affront restrictive conservatives and politically correct liberals alike. But he will not be boxed in and he refuses to have his perspective defined by anybody else's changing terms. He tells stories for all people and for all times at a time when fundamentalism, modernism, anticolonialism, and revisionism collide and hamper artistic expression from every side.

His writing criticizes both conservatism and liberalism. In "My Son the Fanatic," Parvez is a hard-working pimp; his son is an idealistic terrorist. Throughout his fiction, Kureishi takes on the intellectual community, the liberal press, restrictive censorship, and contemporary media overkill. Riaz is a book burner with integrity, while Bronlow is a liberal without guts. Rafi, a torturer permitted to walk freely about London, indicts the political right, while Rosie's treatise on kissing, with its pseudo-intellectual, trendy sexual jargon, lambastes the feminist left.

It is its place in the English literary tradition that gives Kureishi's writing resonance. His is artful fiction. It is permeated with satiric, political commentary, reminiscent of earlier English writers who assaulted the hypocrisy of the landed gentry, the affectations of London's middle class, and the brutality of the city's street society. Traditionally, social criticism has been balanced by comedy to temper the realism or to relieve the tragedy of the stories, and this is the case, too, with Kureishi, whose writing also has context in art. When *London Kills Me*'s Clint turns to poetic rhythm and meter to describe his pastoral initiation into

Fig. 27. Muffdiver (Steven Mackintosh, left), Sylvie (Emer McCourt), and Clint (Justin Chadwick) strike a pose outside the window of the upscale restaurant, Hem's Diner, in *London Kills Me*. (Still photo courtesy of Jacques Prayer.)

English society, Kureishi expands the satire. Juxtaposing his character's lyric language with the brutality of the street crime and drug dealing of his homeless life in Notting Hill, Kureishi ridicules social as well as artistic conventions, writing from a distinctly contemporary hybrid awareness of contradictions. Thus Kureishi's writing grafts the disdain and nostalgia of a racial outsider onto his comedies of English manners, to which racism, immigration, exile, dream, and prejudice are inherent.

Suburban-bad-boy-turned-literary-lion, Kureishi is himself a character of our century. Literature, comprising created fictions, is therefore a major element in his stories; for example, a literary track runs throughout *The Black Album*, whose defense of the storyteller is a proclamation about the necessity of storytelling in a society. Kureishi argues for the importance of art in our global society, and art is often a subject of his stories as well. Likewise, the reality of drama and the ridiculous superficiality of the world of theater collide in *The Buddha of Suburbia*.

Consequently, in both his description and his composition, Kureishi, as a man of our times, is film-conscious. Not only do movies figure in his fictional world, he also employs film stylistics to create his prose images. The actions of the pairs of lovers at the grand opening ceremony in *My Beautiful Laundrette* are cross-cut, a cinematic editing device. Whether as action, imagery, stylistic, referent, or subject, cinema is an element of Kureishi's aesthetic. He not only writes for the cinema, he writes of and from the cinema as well.

Pop music is also significant in the stories. Kureishi is a storyteller from the electronic generation—the age of computer and virtual reality, and music of that generation is central to his expression. Rock songs, as well as the biographies and legends of rock stars, are resonant. In his second novel, *The Black Album*, the fictional music of the first novel's Charlie Hero becomes a reality, while acquiring tickets to a Prince concert becomes a coda bringing the book to its thematic (and musical) conclusion. Kureishi is writing from, for, and of a musically conscious generation, and music thus has a place in Kureishi's fictional world, just as music figures in the perspective of the author:

I listen to music while I'm writing. Like this morning I was listening to it. My whole life has been taken up with music in a way. Many of my friends are musicians in bands. In school being in a band was our dream. The previous generation, it was the cinema. It was a great means of escape. Cinema was the dream. For me it was pop music.

In the response to his fiction, there has been almost universal recognition that it is not an accurate depiction of history, but, rather, that it is the fictionalized evocation of pop history—of fashions, trends, cinema, and music. Kureishi embraces the almost-telegraphic power of pop conventions and stylistics—cinema and rock music—to create vivid contemporary images in his fiction. This fictionalizing has prompted the universal audience identification. As is clear from the response of its critics and the production team, for example, veterans of London in the seventies have found *The Buddha of Suburbia* to be an accurate evocation of that listless decade. Critics who had grown up neither in that decade nor in London, on the other hand, have viewed this story as a nostalgic return to an interesting time in history. Actor Steven Mackintosh, who played Charlie Hero, described its international attraction as follows:

The seventies return has become quite serious. There's a wildness to the seventies; the seventies were so crazy over here. The music's going backwards to disco. Also to David Bowie. That's why it was such a good move to get [Bowie] interested in doing *Buddha*'s music. I think *Buddha* is funny and that would work in America as it did here. On the other hand, this whole aspect of racism involved in *Buddha* is national—but white people and Asian people would be very interesting to watch in America because that's not really what's going on [there].

[*Buddha*'s] just taken bits from the seventies, only the parts we like the best. Really it's new colors; all those things are mixed in a new way. But Bowie and the music—everyone knows that.[4]

Music intensified the decade's appeal, for both those who knew the era firsthand and those who didn't recognize its music. The music is part of seventies experience today, regardless of the experience of the listeners at the chronological time of the music's release. Thus the music evokes not historic recognition, but rather a strong romantic response from all ages to *The Buddha of Suburbia*, as Mackintosh acknowledges:

It wasn't my childhood, and yet somehow I feel like it was mine. I think I would have been very happy being a teenager in the seventies. It's a whole era of music and stuff that I'm still very much into it. I'm too young to have enjoyed that period and that time. But to me it's still the era in music that I can very much relate to—the Stones and Pink Floyd and David Bowie. It's just such an amazing period. I feel very comfortable with it. I feel very at home with it . . . Also there's so much around. There's so much television footage and so many books to be read about that whole period.[5]

Today, as has been the case ever since the postwar era, music is the art form that most easily transfers across national and economic borders. Even more than cinema, music has become the most accessible cultural entity, and has provided the most important divisions—not by country, culture, or philosophy, but by generation.

This, according to *The New Yorker* critic James Wolcott, is the draw of stories such as *The Buddha of Suburbia*: "To those who lived through the seventies, . . . *Buddha* [is] saying: 'Remember how great it was when you could get stoned and laid without a lot of hassle?' To younger folk in the audience . . . [it is] saying: 'look at what you've missed—this is the fun you'll never have.' Feel bad, everybody!"[6]

In our century, the dreams, expectations, fantasies, and fears of our global society appear to be increasingly expressed in the world of pop art: print, film, and music. Kureishi recognizes that the collective illusions from pop art contradict the individual delusions of twentieth-century urban life. It is this realization of the contradictions in the two worlds that provides the nexus for Kureishi's stories and his place in the storytelling tradition.

He further recognizes the power of today's mass communication in dreammaking. He ridicules the culture scene. Sometimes his artistic observations provoke harmless laughter, as with the nude performance art at the gallery opening in *London Kills Me*, a trendy show that Muff-diver and Clint disrupt in their quest for champagne. Sometimes Kureishi employs pop-art references for outlandish satire, as in the search by *The Black Album*'s aging hippie Bronlow for a recording of the Beatles' *Hey Jude*, as the soundtrack to accompany his depression.

Other times the questioning about art as a pop placebo is more biting and provocative. Bronlow's ex-wife Deedee is satirized for teaching a reading, or more accurately, nonreading, college syllabus in *The Black Album*. Kureishi questions here the racial, class, and educational implications of today's college faculties' lemming-like rush to throw aside traditional study for the new, multicultural, nontraditional "found" art. In other darker pop-culture references, an innocent black woman's murder becomes merely a news event, an urban incident, while urban rioting is reduced to a suitable subject for a black-and-white photo collection in *Sammy and Rosie Get Laid*.

Contemporary pop hysteria is perhaps most broadly satirized in *The Black Album*'s eggplant upon which life's answers may be found, as the vegetable travels from today's human-interest story to tomorrow's refuse. Certainly, pop art is most stingingly sent up in the theatrical escapades of Karim Amir: The group rehearsals, mini-encounters, strangling political correctness, and artiness of it all are preposterously climaxed when Karim finds himself to be not an actor of color, but merely the object of several colleagues' basest sexual desires—simultaneously.

My Son the Fanatic's Parvez is enterprising and degenerate and his son is insurrectionist and zealous because offhanded nihilism and fundamentalist fervor fuel their disposable society. Yet unlike previous artists who were determined to organize experience under the guidelines of religious or political dogma, Hanif Kureishi's hybridity prompts him, as a storyteller, to accept societal contradictions as his aesthetic dogma. Thus fanatic, infidel, and holy man are friends, lovers, and family in his fiction.

His storytelling suggests the dilemma of the disillusioned sons and daughters of immigrants who have pursued Hollywood's cinematic quest for Elsewhere. Whereas hundreds of years of dreaming spawned storytelling traditions, it has only taken one hundred years of motion-picture technology to unleash this electronic aesthetic.

As a storyteller, Kureishi builds on traditions of pictorial art. Techniques were developed in the last century to separate simple replication from the composition and stylistics of pictorial art. The invention of the camera propelled this new visual consciousness. Kureishi further portrays these possibilities in his storytelling. His storytelling becomes most understandable, therefore, in the context of the artistic overlap between literal and pictorial storytelling—that is, in the context of the movie image, comprising moving pictures with sound. This century's artistic invention—the movies—has become its most powerful medium.

Audience reaction to the classics of cinematic history boldly illuminates the quintessential paradox found in Kureishi's cinematic perspective. Viewing Billy Wilder's *Sunset Boulevard* (1950) or *Double Indemnity* (1944), audiences have relished the over-the-top portrayals, the quotable dialogue, and the outrageousness of the artwork as much as—and because—they have revered the story's abiding truths. Thus, Kureishi's stories evidence a contemporary mixing of cultures and a blending of aesthetics that is our reality.

The storytelling is inherently artful—that is, like the movies, it is aware of its pacing, rhythm, and movement. Kureishi's stories don't stop for the audience to catch up. Trivia and reverence commingle. Reporting ugly racism and flaunting graphic physicality, the storytelling is, in turn, uninvolving, mesmerizing, static, brilliant, repulsive, and sophomoric. Weaned on the excesses of our media culture, the storyteller simultaneously respects and ridicules the icons of pop. The audience is expected to be in the know and to get these inside references. Artificiality becomes a real element of the storytelling.

As a storyteller of our times, Kureishi is often engaged in several different forums of expression. Essentially involved with contemporary technology both as subject and method, this amused, terrified, and unimpressed storyteller of today notes—artistically and artfully—the inevitable. This storyteller is not inclined to fashion a reality for his purposes; rather, he offers a hybrid storytelling of today's myriad realities.

The inclusion, not merely the acceptance, of contradictory elements defines a dynamic storytelling that incorporates the gross and the beautiful, the arcane and the vulgar. Mixing without blending the tragic, pathetic, and comic, Kureishi's stories catalog the pop-culture images of television, film, music, literature, news, and hype. They are conscious of art, and redefine the elements of storytelling.

Thus, whether they are prose, drama, TV scripts, or film plays, Kureishi's postcolonial stories exhibit the following discernible traits:

- Objectivity is essential to the heroless narratives; the inevitability of disillusionment marks today's disposable society; moral and cultural opposites commingle; and the gross and the beautiful are in tandem.

- The marginal characters are off-center; the stories present the displaced, and, more particularly, the racially, economically, and sexually disenfranchised; humor—bold, sad, relentless, and merciless—often pervades the fictional world.

- Art games abound; art and the artist are often the subject; a consciousness of storytelling as a process and as a tradition underlies the narratives; while pop culture is a constant term of reference, the stories are elitist in their irreverence and demand recognition of the historical, literary, cinematic, and musical references.

- Audience, character, and narrator are spectators; the stories remain unresolved and are brought to an artistic conclusion without an attempt to bring them to a philosophical resolution; contradictions are integral in subject and presentation.

The storyteller is often in it, it seems, for the fun of the unexpected or the thrill of the unacceptable. So is Kureishi serious? Is he sincere? Or is he tongue in cheek? He is all of these. He flaunts his dry humor in staccato delivery. He laces his deviant, competitive, calculating, marginal heroes with hilarious and endearing qualities. The off-center world of the disenfranchised often looks more appealing in his unresolved endings than the conventional success his characters have so bravely sought.

Although racism, revisionism, liberalism, political paranoia, and fundamentalism share Kureishi's fictional universe with cross-dressing, gritty language, homoeroticism, urban crime, moral decay, and regionally distinct blow jobs, he roots today's sensitivity to multicultural traditions in a recognition of the contradictions of pluralism. His honesty separates his stories from mere nostalgia and camp: He respects the humanity of his characters as he accurately presents their qualities and shortcomings. Kureishi also uses historical periods strategically in his comic storytelling; in fact, he expands his use of history and fashion into biting social commentary. In his artistic universe the collision between history and art results in a merger and Kureishi never loses sight of the fiction of his creation — in fact, he stresses its artfulness. This is both how Hanif Kureishi sees his world and how he tells his stories.

His stories glorify urban street culture and vilify yesterday's rationales. His is a worldwide immigrant audience whose members — like many of the characters in Kureishi's stories — have had the luxury of being able to reject their parents' dreams and life's work. The stories portray a dream born of disillusionment and make social commentary as immediate, inconstant, and disposable as today's mass communications.

Kureishi is English — both traditionally English and newly English. He is a hybrid Englishman, a Pakistani-Briton. As such, he belongs to a group comprising the new citizens of England who, in many ways, cling more tenaciously to nationalism, even while condemning it. These second- and third-generation immigrants are aware that while the identity they seek to protect may be no more than an unfamiliar memory, the identity they seek to reject is an unpalatable illusion.

Kureishi's fiction is darkly comic. It laughs bitterly at situations shown simply as the brutal status quo, but, at the same time, it laughs defensively at the idealistic yearnings to make them otherwise. His fictional world is a post–politically correct world, an intellectual universe where no group, gender, color, or belief is either despicable or praiseworthy, but where all of them are laughable. He confronts the prejudice, cruelty, and failures of his time without emotional solace.

As a contemporary storyteller—one who willingly, and perhaps necessarily, writes as a cinematic new-world dreammaker—Kureishi has evolved from the Hollywood writers of the thirties who lived in monetary exile, like Fitzgerald, Faulkner, and Waugh. In Kureishi, fiction and film have become mutually generative—dream is now tied to the grand illusion of the movies, as evidence of the powerful reality that the movies have achieved in art. Kureishi has evolved into a multimedia raconteur of the dreams of today's global community. His perspective is born of cinema, the international language that has promised the impossible to most of the world. It is trendy and cosmopolitan, aware of the differences between cultures, yet desperately seeking the security of community.

Kureishi's evolution of perspective includes risks, but he has also taken some faltering steps toward polishing his innovative, fancy footwork. A reviewer of *London Kills Me* acknowledged the new perspective from which Kureishi tells his stories while criticizing director Kureishi for losing his author's perspective, commenting that he "might even have ended up with something that film has every possibility of being—fiction you can dance to."[7]

Hanif Kureishi tells richly textured stories. His style is melodic. His subject matter is the blatantly irreconcilable. His vocabulary rings with four-letter words, poetry, doo-da patter, and literary allusions. Even if he is militant about an issue, he knows as well that his militancy is preposterous. Ribald anecdotes metamorphose from hilarity into philosophical musing.

He writes without hesitation in a global culture of coexisting contradictions. His window onto the world gives him insight and space for reflection. He understands immigration and exile. He knows prejudice and celebrity. He writes from a rich context of literary, cinematic, and theatrical traditions. Kureishi's strong sense of his own hybrid perspective is his identity. He uses art neither as a therapeutic means of finding his identity nor as a means of asserting his identity by politicizing. It is because he is so definitely a storyteller that he is able to write so defiantly about the world he sees.

As he continues to create, his craft continues to evolve. Literary tradition gives him resonance. Honesty in storytelling gives him his vocation. His hybrid aesthetic gives him his goal. Hanif Kureishi sees his world in jump cuts and rapid tracking shots, writes with poetic rhythm, and composes life in language.

NOTES

INTRODUCTION

1. Hanif Kureishi first opened the door of his Baron's Court flat to me on New Year's Day, 1993. From that day he has given me ingress to his creative process without reservation. Throughout the research, writing, and publishing of this book, I spoke with Kureishi in the United States and in England about his creative process, his stories, his life, and his career. We conferred by phone and letter as well as in more than twenty face-to-face audiotaped interviews and as many untaped personal visits and conversations. Kureishi's comments are blunt, insightful, humorous, perceptive, bold, and warm. He answered every question, if sometimes in a characteristically tongue-in-cheek manner. A prolific reader and writer, he is an unparalleled raconteur and a biting social critic.

Kureishi introduced me to colleagues and collaborators and welcomed me into his home. He also made all of his journals, personal notes, clippings, family papers, and diaries available to me, providing me carte blanche to his London office. He shared manuscripts, revisions, and drafts of his published and unpublished stories, including all of his manuscripts and the drafts of his earlier fiction. Among these were the early prose working of *My Beautiful Laundrette*; the two differently titled earlier versions of *The Buddha of Suburbia* and his introduction to the Italian-language translation, entitled "The Boy in the Bedroom"; his unpublished play, *The Mother Country*; his version of Brecht's *Mother Courage*; the screenplay of *My Son the Fanatic*; drafts and copies of an unpublished screenplay; and his unpublished short stories. He also shared with me as openly the three electronic working drafts of *The Black Album* as well as the creation of his provocative short fiction-in-progress, some of which were published in early 1997 as *Love in a Blue Time*. Unless otherwise noted, all quoted materials and unpublished drafts included in this text are from these sources.

2. Kureishi, *My Beautiful Laundrette and The Rainbow Sign*.

3. "The Radical Guru of Leafy Suburbs," *Observer* (London), 14 November 1993.

4. Ibid.

5. Kureishi, *Laundrette and Rainbow Sign*, 29.

6. Ibid., 27.

7. Ibid., 15.
8. Nicholson, "My Beautiful Britain," 10.
9. Adair, "The Skin Game," 34.
10. Rushdie, *The Wizard of Oz*, 23.
11. Finler, *The Movie Directors Story*, 141.
12. Pally, "Kureishi like a Fox," 53.
13. Kureishi, *The Buddha of Suburbia*, London: Faber & Faber, 1990, 3.

ONE

1. Dougary, "Interview."
2. "The Radical Guru of Leafy Suburbs," *Observer* (London), 14 November 1993.
3. Wardle, *The King and Me* review.
4. Wardle, "Collision of Cultures."
5. Ibid.
6. Ibid.
7. Kemp, "Piling It On," 527b.
8. Billington, *Outskirts* review.
9. Fenton, "What Did You Sell in the War, Daddy."
10. *Borderline* review, *Times Literary Supplement*.
11. Nokes, "Anthem for Doomed Youth?"
12. Wardle, *Borderline* review.
13. Waugh, "The Sun King."
14. Wardle, "Us, Them . . . and Those."
15. Fenton, "Okay, as a Favour, Tell You What I'll Do."
16. Wardle, "Us, Them . . . and Those."
17. Kureishi, *My Beautiful Laundrette and The Rainbow Sign*.
18. Nokes, "Anthem for Doomed Youth?"
19. Kureishi, *Outskirts and Other Plays*.
20. Kureishi, *Sammy and Rosie Get Laid: The Script and the Diary*.
21. Kureishi, "Erotic Politicians and Mullahs."
22. Kureishi, "Bradford."
23. Kureishi, "Wild Women, Wild Men."
24. Kureishi, "London's Killing Off Its Filmmakers."
25. Kureishi, "Finishing the Job."
26. Mortimer, *Brideshead Revisited* (screenplay).
27. Billington, *Outskirts* review.
28. Adair, "The Skin Game."
29. Buruma, "The English Novel Gets Laid."
30. "No. 276: Hanif Kureishi," *Guardian* (London), 3 November 1993.

TWO

1. Kureishi, "London's Killing Off Its Filmmakers."
2. Newport, "*Laundrette* Takes Writer Kureishi from West End to Los Angeles," 17.

3. Cook, "Edinburgh Festival."

4. Bevan, personal interview, 8 July 1994. Bevan and his office's resources have remained available to me by fax; his insights into Hanif Kureishi's film career have been invaluable.

5. Ibid.

6. Kroll, "A Castle of Dreams and Detergents."

7. Canby, *My Beautiful Laundrette* review.

8. Kael, "Yes, Yes," 118.

9. Lloyd, *My Beautiful Laundrette* review.

10. Bevan, interview.

11. Cook, *My Beautiful Laundrette* review.

12. Kroll, "Castle of Dreams."

13. Kael, "Yes, Yes," 119.

14. Bevan, interview.

15. Root, "Scenes from a Marriage."

16. Pally, "Kureishi like a Fox."

17. Kevin Loader, interview. Loader, who produced the television adaptation of *The Buddha of Suburbia* provided me with the program's production information. He acted as a liaison to actors and technicians involved in the BBC project and provided me with press clippings, filming schedules, log, and scripts. He also provided some interesting background on Kureishi's career and English pop culture elements during the seventies and eighties. His BBC office has been supportive of me throughout my research.

18. Pally, "Kureishi like a Fox," 50.

19. Ibid., 52.

20. Ibid., 53.

21. Kureishi, *Sammy and Rosie Get Laid: The Script and the Diary.*

22. Corliss, "The Empire Strikes Out."

23. Bevan, interview.

24. Hachem, "Hanif Kureishi—Filmmakers in Focus."

25. Kael, "Mindspeak," 140.

26. Broadstreet,"Casebook: *Sammy and Rosie Get Laid*," 50.

27. "Outside Looking In," *Economist*, 14 July 1990.

28. Kael, "Mindspeak," 144.

29. Quart, "The Politics of Irony," 245.

30. Corliss, "The Empire Strikes Out."

31. Kauffmann, "Made in Britain," 24.

32. Quart, "Politics of Irony," 242.

33. Canby, "Chaotic London."

34. Corliss, "The Empire Strikes Out."

35. Kauffmann, "Made in Britain," 24.

36. Canby, "Chaotic London."

37. Ibid.

38. Bevan, interview.

39. Quart, *Sammy and Rosie* review, 40.

40. Kael, "Mindspeak," 144.

41. Ibid., 140.

42. Corliss, "The Empire Strikes Out."

43. Lindroth, "The Wasteland Revisited," 96.

44. Kauffmann, "Made in Britain," 25.

THREE

1. Kureishi, "The Buddha of Suburbia," *Harper's:* 45–51.

2. Ibid., 46.

3. Adair, "The Skin Game."

4. Collins, "Of Race and Class in London," 28.

5. Ibid.

6. Loader, personal interview.

7. Hower, "Life in Britain, through the Eyes of Immigrant's Son."

8. Kureishi, *Sammy and Rosie Get Laid: The Script and the Diary.*

9. Blaise, "A Guru by Night."

10. Jimenez, "Grand Illusion."

11. Saynor, "Rites of Passage in My Beautiful Decade."

12. Kakutani, "Coming of Age in England When India Was In."

13. Buruma, "The English Novel Gets Laid."

14. Fitzgerald, *The Great Gatsby*, 133.

15. Linklater,"Reel News."

16. Kureishi, *London Kills Me.*

17. Loader, personal interview.

18. Jimenez, "Grand Illusion."

19. Sutcliffe, "Spiders from Mars."

20. "Pick of the Day," BBC, *The Buddha of Suburbia* press file.

21. Peter Paterson, "Magical Mysticism Tour."

22. Paton, "Sound of the Culture Clash."

23. Jimenez, "Grand Illusion."

FOUR

1. Flatley, *London Kills Me* review.

2. Considine, *London Kills Me* review.

3. Romney, "The Sound of Silence," 30.

4. Parante, *London Kills Me* review.

5. "United Kingdom 1991/Director: Hanif Kureishi," *Times* (London), 12 December 1991.

6. "No. 276: Hanif Kureishi," *Guardian* (London), 3 November 1993.

7. Hower, "Life in Britain."

8. Bevan, personal interview.

9. Matthews, *London Kills Me* review, 13.

10. "Outside Looking In," *Economist*, 14 July 1990.

11. Malcolm, "Capital Punishment."

12. Matthews, *London Kills Me* review.

13. "Ten Favorite Films," *Sight and Sound*, 20.

14. Quart, "The Politics of Irony."

15. Yates, "London Necropolis of Fretful Ghosts," 13.

16. Steven Mackintosh shared his insights into acting and on working with Kureishi with me over lunch. As well as playing Muffdiver in *London Kills Me*, Mackintosh brought Charlie Hero, Kureishi's literary character from his novel *The Buddha of Suburbia*, to screen life in the BBC's televised version.

17. Kureishi, *London Kills Me*.

18. Bevan, personal interview.

19. Ibid.

20. French, "The Dangers of Going Carol Singing."

21. Bevan, personal interview.

22. Malcolm, "Capital Punishment."

23. Bevan, personal interview.

24. Mackintosh, personal interview.

FIVE

1. Loader, personal interview.

2. Michell, personal interview. (Roger Michell discussed the *Buddha of Suburbia* project with me at the BBC after the broadcast.)

3. "Buddha Buddy," *Daily Mirror* (London), 3 November 1993.

4. Paton, "Sound of the Culture Clash."

5. "Good, Though Not Necessarily Clean, Fun," *Times* (London), 30 October 1993.

6. Thomas, "Bowie: The Man Who Fell Back to Suburbia."

7. Pearson, *The Buddha of Suburbia* review.

8. Saynor, "Rites of Passage in My Beautiful Decade."

9. Elaine Paterson, "Teenage Kicks."

10. Loader, personal interview.

11. Mackintosh, personal interview.

12. Pearson, *The Buddha of Suburbia* review.

13. Elaine Paterson, "Teenage Kicks."

14. Mackintosh, personal interview.

15. Loader, personal interview.

16. Taylor, *The Buddha of Suburbia* review.

17. Peter Paterson, "Magical Mysticism Tour."

18. Elaine Paterson, "Teenage Kicks."

19. "Reviews and Previews," *Time Out*, 163.

20. Michell, personal interview.

21. Ibid.
22. Paton, "Sound of the Culture Clash."
23. Sutcliffe, "Spiders from Mars and Suburban Gurus."
24. Elaine Paterson,"Now and Zen."
25. Wilson, "Bawdy on the Ironing Board."
26. Ibid.
27. Loader, personal interview.
28. Davidson, "It's Time for the Armchair Censors to Grow Up."
29. Dunkley, "Up with Sex, Down with Violence."
30. Mackintosh, personal interview.
31. Dunkley, "Up with Sex, Down with Violence."

SIX

1. Kureishi, "Finishing the Job."
2. Pincus, "Nothing Sacred."
3. Eberstadt, "Rebel, Rebel."
4. Pincus, "Nothing Sacred."
5. Galehouse, "One Man's Very Western Revolt against His Pakistani Parents."
6. Pincus, "Nothing Sacred."
7. Fields, "Literature vs. Piety on the Streets of London."

SEVEN

1. Kureishi and Savage (eds.), *The Faber Book of Pop.*
2. Pally, "Kureishi like a Fox," 55.
3. Nicholson, "My Beautiful Britain."
4. Kureishi, "Dirty Washing," 26.
5. Root, "Scenes from a Marriage."

EIGHT

1. Pally, "Kureishi like a Fox."
2. Jimenez, "Grand Illusion."

NINE

1. Ondaatje, *The English Patient.*
2. Matthews, *London Kills Me* review.

TEN

1. Lloyd, *My Beautiful Laundrette* review.
2. Dodd, "Two Cheers."
3. Naidoo, *Sammy and Rosie Get Laid* review.
4. Coupland, *Generation X.*
5. "The Radical Guru of Leafy Suburbs," *Observer* (London), 14 November 1993.
6. Pally, "Kureishi like a Fox."

7. Maude, "Colette Maude Talks to the Writer and Stars of *My Beautiful Laundrette*."
8. Kureishi, "Dirty Washing."
9. Dudar, interview.
10. Canby, *My Beautiful Laundrette* review.
11. "Outside Looking In," *Economist*, 14 July 1990.
12. Collins, "Of Race and Class in London."
13. Kauffmann, "Made in Britain."
14. Kael, "Mindspeak."
15. Kureishi, *Sammy and Rosie Get Laid: The Script and the Diary*.
16. Hower, "Life in Britain."

AFTERWORD
1. Kael, "Mindspeak."
2. "Number Crunching," *Time Out*, 24 November–5 December 1993.
3. Loader, personal interview.
4. Mackintosh, personal interview.
5. Ibid.
6. Wolcott, "A Time to Boogie."
7. Romney, "The Sound of Silence."

APPENDIX

Below is a content analysis of the first 1,000 words of *The Buddha of Suburbia* (final draft with author's handwritten notes). The analysis considers both structure and meaning and is based on the methodology of Mitchell A. Leaska. I abbreviated his system in this way, initially under his supervision at New York University, for literary content analysis in doctoral research.

CONTENT ANALYSIS

Sentence structure
Total: 67 sentences
Mean: 16 words
Length: Longest (#56): 44 words
Length: Shortest (#51): 2 words

Language
755 monosyllables
133 verbs
135 total concrete words—117 nouns—18 descriptors
189 total abstract words—63 nouns—126 descriptors

Identity and tradition (denoted by underlining)
Eighty-five words, 21 specific to British history or geography like "Englishmen," the most repeated term. Twenty-four terms name family members (e.g., "mum," "dad," and "brother"), while 40 confirm identity (e.g., first-person pronouns and proper names).

Foreign references (denoted by italics)
Twenty-six words, particularly Asian words (e.g., "yoga"), the most repeated.

Mood, judgment, or attitude (denoted by boldface)
Thirty-seven words, extremely diverse category. Note that words are almost equally divided between those conveying melancholy and those conveying excitement.

Conditional statements (denoted by uppercase)
Fifty-five words; ironic or comparative qualifiers often alter, and even negate, words so modified. Words are often ironic.

CONTENT ANALYSIS SAMPLE

1. My name is *Karim Amir* and I am an Englishman born and bred, ALMOST.
2. I am OFTEN considered to be a **FUNNY** KIND of Englishman, a NEW breed as it were, having emerged from two old histories.
3. But I don't **care**—Englishman I am (THOUGH not **proud** of it), from the South London suburbs and going somewhere.
4. PERHAPS it was the **odd** mixture of continents and blood, of here and there, of belonging and not, that made me **restless** and easily **bored**.
5. Or PERHAPS it was being brought up in the suburbs that did it.
6. ANYWAY why search the inner room when it's ENOUGH to say that I was looking for **trouble**, ANY kind of movement, action and sexual interest I could find, because things were so **gloomy**, so **slow** and **heavy**, in our family.
7. I don't know why.
8. QUITE frankly, it was all getting me **down** and I was **ready** for anything.
9. Then one day everything changed, in the morning they were ONE WAY and by bedtime ANOTHER.
10. I was seventeen.
11. On this day my father hurried home from work NOT in a **gloomy mood**.
12. His **mood** was **high**, FOR HIM.
13. I could smell the train on him as he put the briefcase away behind the front door and took off his raincoat, chucking it over the bottom of the banisters.
14. He grabbed my fleeing little brother, *Allie,* and kissed him: he kissed my mother and I with **enthusiasm**, as if we'd recently been rescued from an earthquake.
15. MORE **normally**, he handed Mum his supper: a packet of *kebabs* and *chapatis* so greasy their paper wrapper had disintegrated.
16. Next, instead of flopping into a chair to watch the television news and wait for Mum to put the warmed-up food on the table, he went into their bedroom, which was downstairs next to the living room.
17. He **quickly** stripped to his vest and underpants.
18. "Fetch the pink towel," he said to me.

19. <u>I</u> did so.

20. <u>Dad</u> spread it on the bedroom floor and fell onto his knees.

21. <u>I</u> wondered if he'd **suddenly** taken up religion.

22. BUT NO, he placed his arms beside his head and kicked himself into the air.

23. "<u>I</u> must practise," he said in a stifled voice.

24. "Practise for what?" <u>I</u> said **reasonably**, watching him with SOME **interest**.

25. "They've called me for the **damn** *yoga* <u>Olympics,</u>" he said.

26. He **easily** became **sarcastic**, <u>Dad.</u>

27. He was standing on his head now, balanced perfectly.

28. His stomach sagged down.

29. His balls and prick fell forward in his pants.

30. The considerable muscles in his arms swelled up and he breathed **energetically**.

31. Like many <u>*Indians*</u> he was small but <u>Dad</u> was always SO **elegant** and handsome, with delicate hands and **manners**; BESIDE HIM most <u>Englishmen</u> looked like **clumsy** *giraffes*.

32. He was broad and strong: When young he'd been a boxer and a **fanatical** chest expander.

33. He was as **proud** of his chest as our next-door neighbours were of their kitchen range.

34. At the sun's first smile he would pull off his shirt and stride into the garden with a deckchair and a copy of the <u>New Statesman.</u>

35. He told <u>me</u> that in <u>*India*</u> he shaved his chest regularly so its hair would sprout more luxuriantly in years to come.

36. <u>I</u> reckon that his chest was THE ONE AREA in which he'd been **forward-thinking**.

37. Soon <u>my</u> <u>mother,</u> who was in the kitchen AS USUAL, came into the room and saw <u>Dad</u> practising for the *yoga* <u>Olympics</u>: He hadn't done this for months so she knew something was up.

38. She wore an apron with flowers on it and wiped her hands repeatedly on a tea towel, a souvenir from <u>Woburn Abbey.</u>

39. <u>Mum</u> was a plump and unphysical woman with a pale round face and **kind** brown eyes.

40. <u>I</u> imagine that she considered her body to be an inconvenient object surrounding her, as if she were STRANDED ON AN *UNEXPLORED DESERT ISLAND*.

41. MOSTLY <u>Mum</u> was a **timid** and **compliant** person, but when **exasperated** she could go **nervily aggressive**, like now.

42. "<u>*Allie,*</u> go to bed," she said **sharply** to <u>my</u> <u>brother</u> as he poked his head around the door.

43. He was wearing a net to stop his hair going crazy when he slept.

44. She said to Dad, 'Oh God, *Haroon,* all the front of you's sticking out like that and everyone can see!'

45. She turned to me.

46. "You encourage him to be like this.

47. At least pull the curtains!"

48. "It's not necessary, Mum.

49. There isn't another house that can see us for a hundred yards—UNLESS THEY'RE WATCHING THROUGH BINOCULARS."

50. "That's exactly what they are doing," she said.

51. I pulled the curtains on the back garden.

52. The room immediately seemed to contract.

53. **Tension** rose.

54. I couldn't wait to get out of the house NOW.

55. I always wanted to be SOMEWHERE ELSE, I don't know why.

56. When Dad spoke his voice came out squashed and thin.

57. "*Karim,* read to me in a very clear voice from the *yoga* book."

58. I ran and fetched Dad's preferred *yoga* book—*Yoga* for Women, WITH PICTURES OF WOMEN IN BLACK LEOTARDS—from among his other books on *Buddhism, Sufism, Confucianism* and *Zen* which he had bought at the *Oriental* bookshop in Cecil Court, off Charing Cross Road.

59. I squatted beside him with the book.

60. He breathed in, held the breath, breathed out and once more held the breath.

61. I wasn't a BAD reader, and I imagined myself to be on the stage of the Old Vic as I declaimed **grandly,** "*salamba Sirasana* revives and maintains a **spirit** of **youthfulness,** an asset beyond price.

62. It is wonderful to know that you are ready to face up to life and extract from it all the REAL **joy** it has to offer."

63. He grunted his approval at each sentence and opened his eyes, seeking out my mother, who had closed hers.

64. I read on.

65. "This position also prevents loss of hair and reduces any tendency to greyness."

66. That was the COUP: greyness would be avoided.

67. **Satisfied,** Dad stood up and put his clothes on.

CREDITS

PLAYS

The Mother Country

Opened at the Riverside Studios, London, on 22 July 1980.

Cast

Imran	Lyndham Gregory
Hussein	Saeed Jaffrey
Joe	Peter Sproule

Production credits

Playwright	Hanif Kureishi
Director	Tim Fywell

The King and Me

Opened at the Soho Poly Theatre, London, on 7 January 1980.

Cast

Marie	Elaine Donnelly
Nicola	Jean Trend
Bill	Mike Grady
M.C.	Eric Richard

Production credits

Playwright	Hanif Kureishi
Director	Antonia Bird
Designer	Louise Belson

Outskirts
Opened at the Royal Shakespeare Company's Warehouse, London, on 28 April 1981.

Cast

Del	David Bamber
Bob	Tony Guilfoyle
Maureen	Illona Linthwaite
Mum	Marjorie Yates
Julia	Tilly Vosburgh

Production credits

Playwright	Hanif Kureishi

Borderline
Opened at the Royal Court Theatre, on 2 November 1981.

Cast

Amjad	David Beames
Anwar	David Beames
White neighbor	David Beames
Haroon Anil	Vincent Ebrahim
Farouk	Vincent Ebrahim
Banoo	Vincent Ebrahim
Yasmin	Deborah Findlay
Ravi	Nizwar Karanj
Susan	Lesley Manville
Valerie	Lesley Manville
Amina	Rita Wolf
Bill	Michael Lightfoot

Production credits

Playwright	Hanif Kureishi
Director	Max Stafford-Clark
Designer	Peter Hartwell
Lighting	Hugh Laver

Birds of Passage
Opened at Hampstead Theatre, London, on 15 September 1983.

Cast

Stella	Belinda Sinclair
Paul	Neil Pearson
David	Joe Melia
Audrey	Jean Boht

Eva	Rowena Cooper
Asif	Raad Rawi
Ted	Roger Sloman

Production credits

Playwright	Hanif Kureishi
Director	Howard Davies
Designer	Sue Plummer

Mother Courage and Her Children

Following a UK tour between 9 September and 27 November 1993, the production opened at the Cottesloe Theatre, Royal National Theatre, London, on 6 December 1993.

Cast

Mother Courage	Ellie Haddington
Eilif	Ewen Cummins
Swiss Cheese	Richard Standing
Kattrin	Michelle Joseph
Chaplin	Andy Hockley
Cook	Jeremy Swift
Yvette	Saira Todd
Recruiting officer	Chris Macdonnell
General	Chris Macdonnell
Poldi	Chris Macdonnell

Other parts played by members of the company

Production credits

Playwright	Bertolt Brecht
Adapter	Hanif Kureishi
Lyrics	Sue Davies
Director	Anthony Clark
Designer	Kate Burnett
Music Director	Mark Vibrans
Lighting Director	Paul McLeish
Movement Director	Pat Garrett
Production Coordinator	Sonia Friedman
Assistant Director	Roanna Benn
Production Manager	Miles King
Stage Managers	Adam Gascoine, David Sinclair, and Judith Thorp
Sound Technician	Sue Patrick
Tour Lighting Technician	Julian McCready
Costume Supervisor	Heather Leat

FILMS

My Beautiful Laundrette
First shown at the Edinburgh Film Festival, opened the London Film Festival, and subsequently released in 1985.

Cast

Johnny	Daniel Day-Lewis
Genghis	Richard Graham
Salim	Derrick Branche
Omar	Gordon Warnecke
Papa	Roshan Seth
Nasser	Saeed Jaffrey
Rachel	Shirley Anne Field
Bilquis	Charu Bala Choksi
Cherry	Souad Faress
Tania	Rita Wolf
Zaki	Gurdial Sira
Moose	Stephen Marcus
Gang Member #1	Dawn Archibald
Gang Member #2	Jonathan Moore

Production credits

Producers	Sarah Radclyffe and Tim Bevan
Director	Stephen Frears
Screenwriter	Hanif Kureishi
Photographer	Oliver Stapleton
Film Editor	Mick Audsley
Designer	Hugo Luczyc Wyhowski
Sound Recordist	Albert Bailey
Music Director	Ludus Tonalis
Casting Director	Debbie McWilliams
Costume Designer	Lindy Hemming
Makeup Designer	Elaine Carew

Sammy and Rosie Get Laid
Opened in London in 1988.

Cast

Rafi	Shashi Kapoor
Alice	Claire Bloom
Sammy	Ayub Khan Din
Rosie	Frances Barber
Danny	Roland Gift

Anna	Wendy Gazelle
Vivia	Suzette Llewellyn
Rani	Meera Syal
Cabbie/Ghost	Badl Uzzaman

Production credits

Producers	Tim Bevan and Sarah Radclyffe
Director	Stephen Frears
Screenwriter	Hanif Kureishi
Lighting Cameraman	Oliver Stapleton
Production Designer	Hugo Luczyc Wyhowski
Editor	Mick Audsley
Music Director	Stanley Myers

London Kills Me

Opened in London in 1991.

Cast

Clint	Justin Chadwick
Muffdiver	Steven Mackintosh
Sylvie	Emer McCourt
Dr. Bub	Baroshan Seth
Headley	Fiona Shaw
Hemingway	Brad Dourif
Burns	Tony Haygarth
Tom Tom	Stevan Rimkus
Lily	Eleanor David
Stone	Alun Armstrong
Faulkner	Nick Dunning
Bike	Naveen Andrews
Mr. G	Garry Cooper
Mr. G's Assistant	Gordon Warnecke
Mr. G's Girl #1	Evelyn Doggart
Mr. G's Girl #2	Chale Charles
Plainsclothes Policeman #1	Joseph Alessi
Plainsclothes Policeman #2	David Hounslow
DJ at party	Ben Peel
Black man at party	Danny John-Jules
Black thug at party	Oliver Kester
White thug at party	Paudge Behan
Tramp	Yemi Ajibade
Busy Bee	Anthony Cairns
Melanie	Rowena King
Woman diner #1	Veronica Smart

Woman diner #2	Sandy McDade
Interviewer	Tracey MacLeod
Mr. Runcipher	George Miller
Suited man	Philip Glenister
Kid in loft #1	Charlie Creed-Miles
Kid in loft #2	Delroy Nunes
Barman	Karl Collins
German tourist #1	Sean Pertwee
German tourist #2	Pippa Hinchley
Drug dealer	Steven Lawrence
Rent boy	Greg Saunders
Nanny	Marianne Jean-Baptiste
Mother	Sally Whitman
Baby	Leila Whitman
Boy in Country	James Caplan
Girl in Country	Sarah Worth
Young Clint	Joe England
Heavy	Dave Atkins

Production credits

Producer	Tim Bevan
Director	Hanif Kureishi
Screenwriter	Hanif Kureishi
Cinematographer	Edward Lachman
Editor	Jon Gregory
Composers	Mark Springer, Sarah Sarhandi, and Bruce Smith
Production Designer	Stuart Walker
Art Directors	Diane Dancklefsen and Colin Blaymires
Costume Designer	Amy Roberts

SCHEDULED FILMS

My Son the Fanatic

Kureishi's film adaptation of his short story, a Zephyr Films production, was scheduled to begin showing in London in the fall of 1997.

Cast (as of March 6, 1997)

Parvez	Om Puri
Bettina	Rachel Griffiths
Schitz	Stellan Skarsgard
Fard	Akbar Kurtha
Minoo	Gopi Desai
Fizzy	Harish Patel

Maulvi	Bhasker Patel
Acolyte 1	Parvez Qadir
Acolyte 2	Shakher Bassi
Margot	Rowena King
Rashid	Omar Salimi
Waiter	Shiv Grewal
Drug Addict Prostitute	Moya Brady
Prostitute 1	Olwen May
Prostitute 2	Alison Burrows
Driver	Balraj Singh Somal
Driver	Asher Kaleen
Driver	Rez Kempton
Madelaine	Sarah Jane Potts
Controller	Dev Sagoo
Chief Inspector Fingerhut	Geoffrey Bateman
Drunk Man	Bernard Wrigley
Mrs. Fingerhut	Judi Jones
Comedian	Andy Devine
Driver	Arif Javed
Post Office Man	Paul Simpson

Production credits

Director	Udayan Prasad
Writer/Screenwriter	Hanif Kureishi
Executive Producer	George Faber
Producer	Chris Curling
Director of Photography	Alan Almond
Editor	David Gamble
Production Designer	Grenville Horner
Composer	TBA
Music Consultant	Charlie Gillett
Line Producer	Anita Overland
Costume Designer	Mary-Jane Reyner
Chief Makeup & Hair Designer	Penny Smith
1st Assistant Director	Nick Laws
Sound Recordist	Albert Bailey
Production Manager	Philip Robertson
Casting Directors	Simone Ireland & Vanessa Pereira
Script Supervisor	Emma Thomas
Art Director	Colin Blaymires
Art Director	Sarah Kane
Costume Supervisor	Sandra Milman
Wardrobe Assistant	Graham Meethoo
Sound Editor	Nick Adams

TELEVISION

The Buddha of Suburbia
First shown as a four-part series in 1993.

Cast

Karim Amir	Naveen Andrews
Haroon Amir	Roshan Seth
Eva Kay	Susan Fleetwood
Charlie Kay	Steven Mackintosh
Anwar	Badi Uzzaman
Jeeta	Surendra Kochar
Jamila	Nisha Nayar
Changez	Harish Patel
Eleanor	Jemma Redgrave
Pyke	Donald Sumpter
Terry	Jason Watkins
Shadwell	David Bamber
Margaret Amir	Brenda Blethyn
Allie Amir	Assam Mamodeally
Uncle Ted	John McEnery
Auntie Jean	Janet Dale
Helen	Vicky Murdock
Carol	Henrietta Bess
Tracey	Maureen Hibbert
Richard	William Chubb
First Man	Ian Barritt
Second Man	Michael Lumsden
TV Interviewer	Bob Wellings
Shona	Shona Morris
London Cabbie	Mark Sproston
Producer One	Amanda Root
Producer Two	Mark Strong
"The Condemned"	Garage Love
"Punk Band"	Lip
Shinko	Noriko Aida
Marlene	Sarah Neville
Hairy Back	Keith Osborn
Boyd	Keith Osborn
Jane	Cathy White
Frank	Max Boyd
Carl	Geoffrey Beevers

Marianne	Shirley King
Teacher	Richard Bremmer
Charlie's Girl	Kate Byers
The Fish	Tom Gregory
Heathrow Man	Ashok Scrivastava
Heathrow Woman	Georgiana Dacomb
Amanda	Candida Gubbins
Mark	Mark Hadfield
Designer	Julia Tarnoky
Script Editor	Susie Fairfax
Stage Manager	Jo Duttine
Louise	Dariel Pertwee
John	Kim Fenton
Tiler	Bill McGuirk
Muslim Indian	Moti Makan
Simon	Daniel Flynn
Asian Girl	Syreeta Kumar
Sean Brisby	Michael Gardiner
Frankie	George Anton
Journalist	George Anton
Photographer	Jane Galloway
New York Cab Driver	Caroline Harding
New York Interpreter	Caroline Harding
Tony Bell	Sally George
Joanna	Sally George
Leila	Omar Gonga
Ken	John Rogan
Model	Jaye Griffiths
Pyke's Maid	Jaye Griffiths

Production credits

Producer	Kevin Loader
Director	Roger Michell
Adapters	Hanif Kureishi and Roger Michell
Designer	Roger Cann
Costume Designer	Alex Byrne
Makeup Designer	Marilyn MacDonald
Lighting Cameraman	John McGlashan
Film Editor	Kate Evans
Film Recordist	Stuart Moser

BOOKS

My Beautiful Laundrette and the Rainbow Sign. Faber & Faber: London, 1986.
Sammy and Rosie Get Laid: The Script and the Diary. Faber & Faber: London, 1988.
London Kills Me. Faber & Faber: London, 1991.
The Buddha of Suburbia. Faber & Faber: London, 1991.
Outskirts and Other Plays. Faber & Faber: London, 1992.
The Black Album. Faber & Faber: London, 1995.
The Faber Book of Pop. (Co-edited with Jon Savage.) Faber & Faber: London, 1995.
Love in a Blue Time. Faber & Faber: London, 1997.
My Son the Fanatic. Faber & Faber: London, 1997.

BIBLIOGRAPHY

[*Borderline* review.] *Times Literary Supplement* (London), 4 December 1981, 527B.

"Buddha Buddy." *Daily Mirror* (London), 3 November 1993.

Buddha of Suburbia. BBC Production Office Log, 18 November 1993, 009.

[*Buddha of Suburbia* review.] *Sunday Telegraph* (London), 31 October 1993.

"Distant Relations." *Times* (London), 30 October 1993.

"Good, Though Not Necessarily Clean, Fun." *Times* (London), 30 October 1993.

"Hanif Kureishi." *Current Biography* 53, no. 5 (February 1992): 29–32.

[*London Kills Me* review.] *Times* (London), 12 December 1991, 201.

"No. 276: Hanif Kureishi." *Guardian* (London), 3 November 1993.

"Number Crunching." *Time Out*, 24 November–5 December 1993.

"Outside Looking In." *Economist* 316 (14 July 1990): 92.

"Pick of the Day." BBC: *The Buddha of Suburbia* press file, 30 October 1993.

"The Radical Guru of Leafy Suburbs." *Observer* (London), 14 November 1993.

"Reviews and Previews." *Time Out*, 24 November–1 Dec 1993, 163.

"Spirited Romp That Floats through an Era." *Daily Express* (London), 3 November 1993.

"Ten Favorite Films." *Sight and Sound* 2, no. 8 (December 1992): 18–30.

Adair, Gilbert. "The Skin Game." *New Statesman* 3 (30 March 1990): 34.

Bevan, Tim. Personal interview (at Working Title Films, London), 8 July 1994.

Bhegani, Belkis. "On the Crest of a Wave of Black British Writers." *Broadcast*, 26 July 1985, 21.

Billington, Michael. [*Outskirts* Review.] *Guardian* (London), 29 April 1981, Arts section, 10.

Blaise, C. "A Guru by Night." *New York Times Book Review*, 6 May 1990, 23.

Broadstreet, Graham. "Casebook: *Sammy and Rosie Get Laid.*" *Screen International* 652, no. 3 (14 May 1988): 50–55.

Buruma, Ian. "The English Novel Gets Laid." *New Republic* 203 (20 August 1990): 34.

Canby, Vincent. "Chaotic London." *New York Times*, 30 October 1987, C5:1.

———. [*My Beautiful Laundrette* review.] *New York Times*, 7 March 1986, C8: 5.

Collins, Glenn. "Of Race and Class in London." *New York Times*, 24 May 1990.

Considine, J. D. [*London Kills Me* review.] *Rolling Stone*, 6 August 1992, 66.

Cook, Pam. "Edinburgh Festival." *Sight and Sound* (Winter 1985): 6.

———. [*My Beautiful Laundrette* review.] *Monthly Film Bulletin* 52, no. 622 (November 1985): 332–333.

Corliss, Richard. "The Empire Strikes Out." *Time* 30 (9 November 1987): 91.

Coupland, Douglas. *Generation X, Tales for an Accelerated Culture*. St. Martin's Press: New York, 1991.

Davidson, A. "Working Class Act." *Observer* (London), magazine supplement, 20 March 1994.

Davidson, Max. "It's Time for the Armchair Censors to Grow Up." *Daily Telegraph* (London), 25 November 1993.

Dodd, Philip. "Two Cheers." *Sight and Sound* (November 1992): 30.

Dougary, Ginny. [Interview.] *Observer* (London), 1 April 1990.

Dudar, Helen. [Interview.] *New York Times*, 1 November 1987.

Dunkley, Christopher. "Up with Sex, Down with Violence." *Financial Times* (London), 24 November 1993.

Eberstadt, Fernanda. "Rebel, Rebel; For Allah and England." *The New Yorker* 21/28 August 1995, 117–120.

Fenton, James. "Okay, as a Favour, Tell You What I'll Do." *Sunday Times* (London), 25 September 1983, 39E.

———. "What Did You Sell in the War, Daddy?" *Sunday Times* (London), 8 November 1981.

Fields, Beverly. "Literature vs. Piety on the Streets of London." *Chicago Tribune*, 22 October 1995.

Finler, Joel W. *The Movie Directors Story*. Crescent Books: New York, 1985.

Fitzgerald, F. Scott. *The Great Gatsby*. Scribner's: New York, 1925.

Flatley, Guy. [*London Kills Me* review.] *Cosmopolitan* 213 (August 1992): 18.

French, Philip. "The Dangers of Going Carol Singing." *Observer* (London), 15 December 1991.

Galehouse, Maggie. "One Man's Very Western Revolt against His Pakistani Parents." *Philadelphia Sunday Inquirer*, 15 October 1995.

Hachem, Samir. "Hanif Kureishi—Filmmakers in Focus." *Hollywood Reporter* 301, no 32.21 (21 March 1988).

Herbert, Hugh. "On the Spiritual Trail to Peckham." BBC: *The Buddha of Suburbia*, press file.

Hower, Edward. "Life in Britain through the Eyes of Immigrant's Son." *Philadelphia Inquirer*, 25 November 1993.

Jimenez, Felix. "Grand Illusion." *The Nation* 251, no. 9 (July 1990): 63.

Kael, Pauline. "Mindspeak." *The New Yorker* 63, no. 4 (16 Nov 1987): 140–144.

———. "Yes, Yes." *The New Yorker* 62, no. 8 (10 March 1986): 117–119.

Kakutani, M. "Coming of Age in England When India Was In." *New York Times*, 15 May 1990.

Kauffmann, Stanley. "Made in Britain." *The New Republic* 197 (30 November 1987): 24–26.

Kemp, Peter. "Piling it on." *Times Literary Supplement* (London), 8 May 1981, 527B.

Kroll, Jack. "A Castle of Dreams and Detergents." *Newsweek* 107 (24 February 1986): 82.

Kureishi, Hanif. *The Black Album.* Faber & Faber: London, 1995.

———. "Bradford." *Granta* 20 (Winter 1986): 149–170.

———. *Buddha of Suburbia.* Faber & Faber: London, 1991.

———. "The Buddha of Suburbia." *Harper's* 274, no. 16 (June 1987): 45–51.

———. "D'accord Baby." *Atlantic Monthly* 278, no. 3 (September 1996): 68–73.

———. "Dirty Washing." *Time Out* 795 (14–20 November 1985): 25–26.

———. "Erotic Politicians and Mullahs." *Granta* 17 (Autumn 1985): 139–151.

———. "Esther." *Atlantic Monthly* 263, no. 5 (May 1989): 56–62.

———. "Finishing the Job." *New Statesman and Society* 1, no. 21 (28 October 1988): 19–24.

———. "In a Blue Time." *Granta* 56 (Winter 1996) 209–243.

———. *London Kills Me.* Faber & Faber: London, 1991.

———. *Love in a Blue Time.* Faber & Faber: London, 1997.

———. *My Beautiful Laundrette and The Rainbow Sign.* Faber & Faber: London, 1986.

———. "My Son the Fanatic." *The New Yorker* 70, no. 6 (1994): 92–96.

———. *Outskirts and Other Plays.* Faber & Faber: London, 1992.

———. *Sammy and Rosie Get Laid: The Script and the Diary.* Faber & Faber: London, 1988.

———. "The Tale of the Turd." *em writing & music* and *The Word* (Winter 1996).

———. "We're Not Jews." *London Review of Books* 17, no. 6 (23 March 1995): 34–36.

———. "Wild Women, Wild Men." *Granta* 39 (Spring 1992): 171–179.

———. "With Your Tongue down My Throat." *Granta* 12 (Winter 1984): 19–60.

Kureishi, Hanif, and Roger Michell. *The Buddha of Suburbia, Script Re-Issue,* part 1. BBC Publications: London.

Kureishi, Hanif, and Jon Savage, eds. *Faber Book of Pop.* Faber and Faber: London, 1995.

Leaska, Mitchell. *Virginia Woolf's Lighthouse: A Study In Critical Method.* Hogarth Press: London, 1960.

Lindroth, Collette. "The Wasteland Revisited, Sammy and Rosie Get Laid." *Literature/Film Quarterly* 17, no. 2: 95–98.

Linklater, Richard. "Reel News." *Rewind* 2, no. 3 (1995): 8.

Lloyd, Ann. [*My Beautiful Laundrette* review.] *Film and Filming* 374 (November 1985): 43.

Loader, Kevin. Personal interviews (at BBC Television Centre, London), 4 January and 26 August 1994.

Mackintosh, Steven. Personal interview, the Dome Cafe, Islington, London, 29 August 1994.

Malcolm, Derek. "Capital Punishment." *Guardian* (London), 12 December 1991, 29.

Matthews, Tom Dewe. [*London Kills Me* review.] *Sight and Sound* 1, no. 5 (December 1991): 8–13.

Maude, Colette. "Colette Maude Talks to the Writer and Stars of *My Beautiful Laundrette*, a Serious Comedy by Stephen Frears, Director of The Hit." *Photoplay* 36, no. 12 (December 1985): 10–11.

Michell, Roger. Personal interview, BBC Television Centre, London, 4 January 1994.

Mortimer, John. *Brideshead Revisited.* Granada Television, 1982.

Naidoo, Sandeep. [*Sammy and Rosie Get Laid* review.] *Bazaar* (Spring 1988): 4–6.

Naughton, John. "The Buddha of Suburbia." *Observer* (London), 7 November 1993.

Newport, D. "Laundrette Takes Writer Kureishi from West End to Los Angeles." *Screen International* 600 (16 May 1987): 16–17.

Nicholson, David. "My Beautiful Britain." *Films and Filming* 400 (January 1988): 9–10.

Nokes, David. "Anthem for Doomed Youth?" *Times Literary Supplement* (London), 4 December 1981, 1427A.

Ondaatje, Michael. *The English Patient.* Knopf: New York, 1992.

Pally, Marcia. "Kureishi like a Fox." *Film Comment* 22, no. 5 (September/October 1986): 50+.

Parante, William. [*London Kills Me* review.] *Scotsman*, 28 December 1991.

Paterson, Elaine. "Now and Zen." *Time Out*, 27 October–3 November 1993, 18–19.

———. "Teenage Kicks." *Time Out*, 3–10 November 1993.

Paterson, Peter. "Magical Mysticism Tour." *Daily Mail* (London), 4 November 1993.

Paton, Maureen. "Sound of the Culture Clash." *Daily Express* (London), 4 November 1993.

Pearson, Allison. [*The Buddha of Suburbia* review.] *Independent on Sunday* (London), 7 November 1993.

Pincus, Elizabeth. "Nothing Sacred." *LA Weekly*, 15 September 1995.

Quart, Leonard. "The Politics of Irony." In *Re-viewing British Cinema, 1900–1992*, ed. Wheeler Winston Dixon, pp. 241–248. State University of New York Press: Albany, 1994.

———. [*Sammy and Rosie Get Laid* review.] *Cineaste* 16, no. 3 (1988): 40–41.

Romney, Jonathan. "The Sound of Silence." *New Statesman & Society* 4 (13 December 1991): 30–32.

Ronson, Jon. "Looks Back in Languor." *Time Out*, 29 December 1994–5 January 1995, 8.

Root, Jane. "Scenes from a Marriage." *Monthly Film Bulletin* 52, no. 622 (November 1985): 333.

Rushdie, Salman. *The Wizard of Oz.* BFI Publishing: London, 1992.

Saynor, James. "Rites of Passage in My Beautiful Decade." *Observer* (London), 31 October 1993.

Sutcliffe, Thomas. "Spiders from Mars and Suburban Gurus." BBC: *The Buddha of Suburbia* press file, 4 November 1993.

Taylor, D. J. [*The Buddha of Suburbia* review.] *Mail on Sunday* (London), 14 November 1993.

Thomas, David. "Bowie: The Man Who Fell Back to Suburbia." *International Express* (U.S. edition), 27 October–2 November 1993.

Wardle, Irving. [*Borderline* review.] *Times* (London), 6 November 1981, 18E.

———. "Collision of Cultures: *The Mother Country* Review." *Times* (London), 23 July 1980, 13B.

———. [*The King and Me* review.] *Times* (London), 9 January 1980, 11H.

———. [*Outskirts* review.] *Times* (London), 29 April 1981.

———. "Us, Them . . . and Those: *Birds of Passage* Review." *Times* (London), 17 September 1983, 9C.

Waugh, Auberon. "The Sun King." *Daily Telegraph* (London), 20 November 1993.

Wellen, Nicholas. "BBC Sex Romp in Suburbs Is Too Hot for US." *Evening Standard* (London), 17 September 1993.

Wilson, A. N. "Bawdy on the Ironing Board." *Sunday Telegraph* (London), 21 November 1993.

———. [*The Buddha of Suburbia* review.] *Sunday Telegraph* (London), 14 November 1993.

Wolcott, James. "A Time to Boogie." *The New Yorker* 69 (10 January 1994): 74–75.

Yates, Robert. "London Necropolis of Fretful Ghosts." *Sight and Sound* 6 (June 1994): 12–16.

INDEX

190, 195–196. *See also The Buddha of Suburbia*

sixties, the, 83

Smith, Paul, 141, 205

Soaking the Heat (play), 20

social comedy. *See* comedy

social criticism, 152–156, 227–228, 248

"Some Time with Stephen: A Diary" (essay), 32

sons. *See* family dynamics; father-son stories

Stafford-Clarke, Max, 25

stereotypes, 55–56, 131, 219–220, 230–231

storytelling, need for, 138, 162, 253–254

street people, 98–100, 206, 221

style. *See* fashion/costuming

Sun Also Rises, The (Ernest Hemingway), 133

Swift, Jonathan, 33

Sylvie (character), 15, 93–94, 210, 249

"Tale of the Turd, The" (short story), 164, 165, 172

Tania (character), 222

tense, use of, 64, 65–66, 68

terrorism, 133, 137

Thatcherism, 33, 138, 221

theater, in English tradition, 21, 22

themes, 55, 157; class as, 164–165; family as, 181–194; general, 32–33, 48, 51–52, 135, 160, 162, 169, 247; Islam as, 138–139, 145–146; love as, 123–124; race as, 155. *See also names of individual works*

third-person narrative, 241–242

time, as literary device, 80–81

Tom Jones (Henry Fielding), 34

transvestism, 128, 210–211

Twain, Mark, 77

uncles, 191, 195. *See also* family dynamics; sibling relationships

urban experience, 234–235. *See also* themes

violence: in *The Black Album*, 132; Kureishi on, 245–247; as literary device, 22–23; in *London Kills Me*, 95; in "My Son the Fanatic," 157–159, 199–200; in *Sammy and Rosie Get Laid*, 246–247

Warnecke, Gordon, 43, 43, 197, 207

"Wasteland, The" (T. S. Eliot), 60

Waugh, Evelyn, 34

"We're Not Jews" (short story), 162–164

whiteness, 149, 230. *See also* racism and race

"Wild Women, Wild Men" (short story), 32

windows, as literary device, 4, 9, 17, 102, 207–208, 223–224, 228

"With Your Tongue down My Throat" (short story), 148–152, 189–190, 203–204

Wizard of Oz, The (film), 10, 11, 97, 101, 211–212, 213

Wolcott, James, 252

women characters, 148–152, 189–190, 200–204, 222. *See also names of individual characters and stories*

Working with Stephen (journal), 75

Zulma (character), 135–136, 200–202